AN IMAGINED AMERICA: LANGUAGE, LITERACY, IDENTITY, AND COLONIALITY AT SYRIAN PROTESTANT COLLEGE, 1866–1920

INTERNATIONAL EXCHANGES ON THE STUDY OF WRITING

Series Editors: Steven Fraiberg, Joan Mullin, Magnus Gustafsson, and Anna S. Habib

Series Associate Editor: Eliza Kotzeva and Esther R. Namubiru

Founding and Consulting Editor: Terry Myers Zawacki

The International Exchanges on the Study of Writing Series publishes books that address worldwide perspectives on writing, writers, teaching with writing, and scholarly writing practices, specifically those that draw on scholarship across national and disciplinary borders to challenge parochial understandings of all of the above. The Latin America Section of the International Exchanges on the Study of Writing book series publishes peer-reviewed books about writing, writers, teaching with writing, and scholarly writing practices from Latin American perspectives. It also offers re-editions of recognized peer-reviewed books originally published in the region.

The WAC Clearinghouse and University Press of Colorado are collaborating so that these books will be widely available through free digital distribution and low-cost print editions. The publishers and the series editors are committed to the principle that knowledge should freely circulate and have embraced the use of technology to support open access to scholarly work.

RECENT BOOKS IN THE SERIES

Tiane Donahue and Cinthia Gannett (Eds.), *Supporting International Writing Studies Research: Cultivating Capacity through International Exchanges* (2025)

Mariya Tseptsura and Todd Ruecker (Eds.), *Nonnative English-Speaking Teachers of U.S. College Composition: Exploring Identities and Negotiating Difference* (2024)

Estela Inés Moyano and Margarita *Vidal Lizama (Eds.), Centros y Programas de Escritura en América Latina: Opciones Teóricas y Pedagógicas para la Enseñanza de la Escritura Disciplinar* (2023)

Jay Jordan, *Grounded Literacies in a Transnational WAC/WID Ecology: A Korean-U.S. Study* (2022)

Magnus Gustafsson and Andreas Eriksson (Eds.), *Negotiating the Intersections of Writing and Writing Instruction* (2022)

L. Ashley Squires (Ed.), *Emerging Wrioting Research from the Russian Federation* (2021)

Natalia Ávila Reyes (Ed.), *Multilingual Contributions to Writing Research: Toward an Equal Academic Exchange* (2021)

AN IMAGINED AMERICA: LANGUAGE, LITERACY, IDENTITY, AND COLONIALITY AT SYRIAN PROTESTANT COLLEGE, 1866–1920

By Lisa R. Arnold

The WAC Clearinghouse
wac.colostate.edu
Fort Collins, Colorado

University Press of Colorado
upcolorado.com
Denver, Colorado

The WAC Clearinghouse, Fort Collins, Colorado 80524

University Press of Colorado, Denver, Colorado 80203

ISBN 978-1-64215-267-8 (PDF) | 978-1-64215-268-5 (ePub) | 978-1-64642-821-2 (pbk.)

DOI 10.37514/INT-B.2025.2678

Library of Congress Cataloging-in-Publication Data

Names: Arnold, Lisa R. author

Title: An imagined America : language, literacy, identity, and coloniality at Syrian Protestant College, 1866–1920 / Lisa R. Arnold.

Description: Fort Collins, Colorado : The WAC Clearinghouse; University Press of Colorado, [2025] | Series: International exchanges on the study of writing | Includes bibliographical references.

Identifiers: LCCN 2025041963 (print) | LCCN 2025041964 (ebook) | ISBN 9781646428212 paperback | ISBN 9781642152678 adobe pdf | ISBN 9781642152685 epub

Subjects: LCSH: Syrian Protestant College—History | Literacy—Lebanon—Beirut | Transnational education—Lebanon—Beirut | Postcolonialism—Lebanon—Beirut | Universities and colleges—Social aspects—Lebanon—Beirut | American University of Beirut—History

Classification: LCC LG351.A72 A76 2026 (print) | LCC LG351.A72 (ebook)

LC record available at https://lccn.loc.gov/2025041963

LC ebook record available at https://lccn.loc.gov/2025041964

Copyeditor: Karen P. Peirce

Design and Production: Mike Palmquist

Cover Photo: النجاح وكيف حصل أهل الغرب عليه [Success and How Westerners Achieved It]. [Article in المبدأ الصحيح (*al-Mubda al-Saheeh* or *The Right Principle*)]. Used courtesy of American University of Beirut Libraries.

Series Editors: Steven Fraiberg, Joan Mullin, Magnus Gustafsson, and Anna S. Habib

Associate Editor: Elitza Kotzeva, American University of Armenia

Founding and Consulting Editor: Terry Myers Zawacki

The WAC Clearinghouse supports teachers of writing across the disciplines. A 501(c)(3) nonprofit organization, it is supported by Colorado State University and provides open access to scholarly journals and book series as well as resources for teachers who use writing in their courses. This book is available in digital formats for free download at wacclearinghouse.org.

Founded in 1965, the University Press of Colorado is a nonprofit cooperative publishing enterprise supported, in part, by Adams State University, Colorado School of Mines, Colorado State University, Fort Lewis College, Metropolitan State University of Denver, University of Alaska Fairbanks, University of Colorado, University of Denver, University of Northern Colorado, University of Wyoming, Utah State University, and Western Colorado University. For more information, visit upcolorado.com.

Citation Information: Arnold, Lisa R. (2025). *An Imagined America: Language, Literacy, Identity, and Coloniality at Syrian Protestant College, 1866–1920.* The WAC Clearinghouse; University Press of Colorado. https://doi.org/10.37514/INT-B.2025.2678

Land Acknowledgment. The WAC Clearinghouse Land Acknowledgment can be found at https://wacclearinghouse.org/about/land-acknowledgment/.

Contents

§ Acknowledgments

This book represents two decades of learning and teaching in the field of rhetoric and writing studies, and although it is impossible to name everyone who has contributed to the production of this book, I will mention a few here. My first mentors, Terry Myers Zawacki and Chris Thaiss, introduced me to the field of rhetoric and writing studies when I was a graduate student in the MFA program at George Mason University. I was lucky to be a student in the doctoral program at the University of Louisville, where I experienced remarkable mentorship from many professors, including Bruce Horner, Karen Kopelson, Min-Zhan Lu, Carol Mattingly, Bronwyn Williams, and Joanna Wolfe. I am grateful to my best friends from graduate school who are also today incredible scholars: Carrie Kilfoil, Vanessa Kraemer Sohan, and Samantha NeCamp keep me from feeling lonely even though we are far apart.

At the American University of Beirut, Amy Zenger started me on this journey, in that she accompanied me during my first trips into the archives in 2011. The archives librarians at the AUB Jafet University Libraries supported me a great deal between 2011 and 2014, and I thank them for their assistance, particularly Samar Mikati. I will never forget the support and enthusiasm that faculty in the Communication Skills program and the English department provided to me. I am grateful for the friendship and kindness of so many—in particular, David Currell, Dorota Fleszar, Sirene Harb, Rima Iskandarani, Malakeh Khoury, Jennifer Nish, Rima Rantisi, and Zane Sinno.

I am in awe of the many scholars who came before me and made this work possible. At conferences, Xiaoye You always pushed me, never failing to ask about my book and offering invaluable professional support. Tarez Samra Graban has always exhibited a level of enthusiasm for the value of my work that is much higher than I deserve. I am thankful for the friendships of Liz Kimball and Ligia Mihut, whose work has influenced my own and who are excellent conference companions. I am also grateful to members of the CCCC Globalization Committee— Chris Anson, Christiane Donahue, Bruce Horner, Jay Jordan, LuMing Mao, Vivette Milson-Whyte, Xiaoye You, Terry Myers Zawacki—who modeled for me how scholars can use their expertise to collaboratively push for meaningful organizational change. Jay Peters has been a careful reader of my historical work over the last decade and, at different times, offered crucial insights that are central to the arguments I make in this book.

Acknowledgments

I am indebted to those who supported the publication of this book: WAC Clearinghouse founding editor and publisher Mike Palmquist; International Exchanges series editors Terry Myers Zawacki, Joan Mullin, and Anna Habib; associate editor Elitza Kotzeva; and copyeditor Karen P. Peirce. Two anonymous reviewers, as well as Terry and Elitza, offered vital suggestions to improve what you are reading today. Esther Namubiru produced an episode about this book on the *Beyond Conventions: Global Dialogues on Writing Studies* podcast.

My students enliven me and make the work that I do as a scholar worthwhile—I learn so much from them. Former AUB students Ghada Seifeddine and Yasmine Abou Taha, now scholars in their own right, made enormous contributions to this book by transcribing (Yasmine) and translating (Ghada) the Arabic-language student writing that I discuss in Chapter 5. The graduate students enrolled in my "Decolonization and Writing Studies" course in Spring 2025 read an earlier draft of Chapter 1 and offered important perspectives on decolonial theory and the discipline of rhetoric and writing studies as I finished revising this book.

I received institutional support from the American University of Beirut and North Dakota State University for various parts of this project, including funding for presentations at conferences, translation, and language training. The U.S. National Endowment for the Humanities provided a Summer Stipend grant in support of this book. Analysis of some of the materials discussed in this book was previously published in *College Composition and Communication* (Arnold, 2014) and *College English* (Arnold, 2016).

I have received about a decade's worth of Arabic language training from many official and unofficial teachers, including Arabic-speaking friends and family. In particular, I thank my Cairo-based teacher of the last three years, Ayah Shafei. شكرا على صبرك

Finally, I am grateful to my family and friends around the world for their unconditional support of the work that I do. Thank you especially to my parents and my brothers, Mark and Andrew, who never leave my thoughts. And to Altayib Haroon Ahmed Ibrahim: أنت غيرت عالمي.

§ Preface

I write this preface only a few months after the 2024 U.S. presidential election, under the shadow of devastating assaults on nearly every component of American society, including higher education. It is clear that the rights that most Americans—and many around the world—hold to be foundational to democracy can no longer be assumed. When viewed through the lens of decolonialism, it is easy to see that the new administration is tightening its grip on the colonial matrix of power that Walter Mignolo (2007) and others have described. Take for example the following recent developments:

- Claiming that English is the official language of the United States (The White House, 2025a).
- Scrutinizing and punishing all kinds of institutions, including universities, for their support of diversity, equity, and inclusion (The White House, 2025b).
- Removing websites and withholding federal monies from centers of knowledge production, such as universities and governmental agencies (Bhatia et al., 2025; Hwang et al., 2025; Singer, 2025).
- Disappearing Black and Brown people—including legal permanent residents, international students, and U.S. citizens—in or outside of U.S. boundaries (Meyer, 2025; Uranga et al., 2025).

All of these developments, and many more, underline the colonial epistemology that is, and has always been, deeply embedded in American life. Many Americans are rightly shocked by these developments, but these actions spring out of a long tradition of colonial thinking. They could not occur without a fundamental belief in the superiority of White, Western ways of knowing. Colonial epistemology is what allowed Europeans to conceive of North America as empty and to settle land that was already occupied by Indigenous people. Colonial epistemology is responsible for a rich Western economy built upon slavery and the systemic exploitation of workers. I could go on. My point is that these developments are indeed shocking, inhuman, and immoral, but they are not new. They constitute the American dream. We arrived at this point in history due to the long tendrils of coloniality that are rooted in America as a nation and in American identity itself.

These long tendrils, I argue in this book, have shaped English-language literacy education, which in turn implicates the discipline of rhetoric and writing studies, a discipline based primarily in the United States and focused on postsecondary contexts of writing practices and pedagogy. I investigate and expose these ties by looking outward, beyond U.S. boundaries, to Syrian Protestant College (SPC), an institution founded in 1866 by American Protestant missionaries in Beirut (SPC is today known as the American University of Beirut). This book provides a historical perspective on how American colonial epistemology—and resistance to such epistemology—emerges in English-language literacy education and language policy. I show through this historical account how literacy education and language policy traffic in discourses of coloniality to produce an imagined America that SPC students, faculty, and administrators negotiated rhetorically. Transnational and translingual discourses provide the backdrop and motive for the assertion of coloniality in contexts of literacy education such as SPC.

The geopolitical context of SPC, which I explicate in Chapters 1 and 2, makes the transnational and translingual elements of literacy education and language policy explicit, but uncovering such histories is only one part of the decolonial project. Another part—a part that this book hints at but does not explore at length—is exposing how transnational and translingual discourse circulated in and around seemingly monolingual and monocultural contexts, such as late-19th-century Harvard, where so much of the discipline's historical understanding is rooted. New ways of knowing emerge when the history of the discipline is retold as a transnational and translingual one, and the account presented in this book provides one example of such a retelling. As I indicate throughout this book, retellings such as this one carry important implications for contemporary contexts of literacy education. While I primarily contextualize this book within the scholarship of my field, U.S.-based rhetoric and writing studies, many of these implications can be applied to related disciplines such as education, linguistics, literacy studies, communication, and even literature.

A Few Key Terms

Before continuing, I want to clarify a few terms that I use repeatedly throughout this book. When I refer to the discipline of *rhetoric and writing studies*, I refer to an academic field born in the United States in the 1960s and 1970s (Nystrand et al., 1993). The discipline is characterized by the study of adult writing practices and writing pedagogy, including the study of public rhetoric and rhetorical education, as well as postsecondary writing programs. It is related to but distinct from fields such as communication, linguistics, literature, and education, and it is also referred to as "rhetoric and composition," "writing studies," "composition studies," or some variation thereof.

The discipline of rhetoric and writing studies is partly constituted by numerous historical accounts that tie it to the emergence of first-year writing at Harvard in the mid- to late-19th century, as well as to the Western rhetorical tradition. I describe these historical narratives and how they have helped create a foundation for the contemporary discipline in Chapter 1. When I refer to the *history of rhetoric and writing studies*, I am specifically referring to the U.S.-based historical narratives that have tied the discipline to these earlier histories. As I elaborate in Chapter 1, the connections between the contemporary discipline and earlier histories have been established through the historiography of scholars such as James Berlin, Robert Conners, Sharon Crowley, and others. This book seeks to destabilize such narratives and thus alter scholars' conceptions of what constitutes the history of the discipline.

Rhetoric and writing studies refers to the name of a contemporary academic discipline. In contrast, when I refer to *literacy education*, I mean education related to literacy that may be broader in scope than what American rhetoric and writing scholars think of as writing instruction. In the context of contemporary U.S. institutions of higher education, first-year writing courses are a near-universal general education requirement. Literacy education is a better term to use for contexts outside of the US, in which English is often treated as both a language and an area of study, and also for historical accounts in which "writing instruction," as American rhetoric and writing scholars think of it today, does or did not exist in the same form. It is important, too, to make it clear that I am not referring to the field of literacy studies when I refer to literacy education, although much scholarship in that area is relevant to the history I have presented here.

Throughout this book, I use the terms epistemology and ideology repeatedly. When referring to *epistemology*, I mean a way of knowing or a theory of knowledge. *Ideology* is narrower in scope than epistemology, referring to a set of beliefs that are often political in nature and constitute epistemology. In this book, colonialism is epistemological, whereas nationalism and monolingualism can be understood as ideologies that constitute colonialism. Additionally, religious ideologies are not the same as religion itself. When religious belief is used for political purposes—such as contemporary Christian nationalism— we can call it ideological.

Additionally, as implied in the title of this book, I often use the words *America* and *American* metaphorically to refer to a place or identity that is constructed and therefore representative of colonial epistemology. I highlight the symbolic nature of these words by using phrases such as *an imagined America* or the *idea of America*. Of course, I also use America and American in ways we might expect, such as in reference to the country known as the

United States and to individuals who hold American nationality. In general, the distinction should be clear in context.

Since I frame this project in part through the lens of translingual theory, I want to clarify what I mean by the terms *monolingual, multilingual,* and *translingual,* and how they differ from *monolingualism* and *translingualism.* On the one hand, I agree with scholars such as Bruce Horner, Min-Zhan Lu, et al. (2011) and Suresh Canagarajah (2013) who argued that all communication is inherently translingual—that is, we are always already making meaning across linguistic and communicative boundaries. At the same time, I agree with those such as Scott Richard Lyons (2009) and Keith Gilyard (2016) who have argued that language difference exists and is consequential at a material level, particularly for historically marginalized groups. For this reason, I use monolingual to refer to those people who would self-identify as speaking only one language, and I use multilingual to refer to those who would self-identify as speaking multiple languages. Monolingual, multilingual, and translingual are used as descriptors for people, practices, institutions, or contexts, whereas monolingualism and translingualism are ideologies describing orientations toward language.

Positioning Myself: Languages and Limitations

It has taken me more than ten years to write this book, in part because I needed time to work out exactly what I could ethically and responsibly say about a place and population where I am an outsider. Part of the reason my focus throughout the book is on an imagined America and the discourses that comprise this imagining is because a large part of my identity and thinking is inextricably tied to White American (colonial) epistemology. At the same time, I can speak about a seemingly distant place and population because another part of my identity and thinking is now tied to that distant place and population through lived experience, personal relationships, and language. The relatively recent emergence of conversations about decolonial theory in the field of rhetoric and writing studies has also been important, in that these conversations have allowed me to articulate what I had previously only been able to gesture toward in previous publications about the same history (Arnold, 2014, 2016, 2018).

Given the decolonial approach I have taken in this book, it would be hypocritical to pretend that I am a detached observer of the material, people, or place that I analyze. This book represents a recursive and ongoing process of learning and unlearning that has forced me to come to terms with the limits and benefits of my positionality in relation to this history. I write today as an associate professor of rhetoric and writing at North Dakota State

University, an institution built on the traditional lands of the Oceti Sakowin (Dakota, Lakota, Nakoda) and Anishinaabe Peoples. I am a White American woman who grew up in the midwestern United States immersed in a culture and epistemology similar to that of the evangelical American Protestant missionaries who founded Syrian Protestant College. When I accepted my first academic position at the American University of Beirut (AUB) in Fall 2011 as an assistant professor of English, I was like many Americans in that I had very limited experience with languages other than English and a very limited perspective on the world, even though I had traveled internationally.

It is an understatement to say that during the four years I spent in Beirut, my perspective changed. It is more appropriate to say that the experience fundamentally altered my thinking about the world and my work. I formed deep and lasting relationships with people whose differences challenged and enlivened me. I was exposed to critiques of America and American nationalism previously unavailable to me. I heard stories and learned histories (particularly about Palestine) that I had never encountered in the US, which greatly impacted my own understanding of global geopolitics. I learned that effective teaching and research meant complicating the knowledge that I previously took for granted, knowledge that had always been rewarded in America. There was plenty about the place, the politics, and the culture that I did (and still do) not understand, and I made many mistakes as an outsider—some of which I am aware of and others I am sure that I never knew about.

In addition to my experience of life in Beirut, my change in perspective can also be attributed to learning Arabic over many years. While at AUB, I took a few classes in Modern Standard Arabic (الفصحى or *al-fusha*), giving me a basic understanding of grammar as well as the ability to read and write Arabic script, and I also took classes in Lebanese Arabic at a local Berlitz language school.[1] When I left Beirut in 2015, I was at best superficially conversant in

---

1   Arabic is considered by linguists to be a diglossic language, meaning the formal and informal dialects of the language can be considered two distinct languages used by the same group of people. The different forms are used for very different purposes: Modern Standard Arabic (MSA) is used in formal situations such as in newspapers or on TV news broadcasts throughout the region. The vernacular form, or عامية *amiyeh*, is used on the street. Different regions and countries use different vernaculars, and some of these are mutually intelligible (such as Lebanese and Jordanian Arabic), but others are not (such as Moroccan and Egyptian Arabic). The different vernaculars are all called "Arabic," but it would be more realistic to call them each by a different name—a comparable example is that we call Italian, Spanish, and Portuguese by different names but they are all closely related through Latin (akin to MSA). A speaker of one is likely to be able to understand the others—to find some common linguistic ground—to some degree. In this sense, it might be said that I have actually learned four different languages (Modern Standard, Lebanese, Egyptian, and Sudanese Arabic) over the last 13 years—which makes me feel far better about my language journey!

the Lebanese dialect and could sound out words written in Arabic but was unlikely to understand most of them. There was little opportunity to study Arabic in Fargo, North Dakota, once I started living there because my new institutional home of North Dakota State University stopped offering courses in the language as soon as I arrived and because many of the immigrants with whom I interacted were from other parts of the world. However, the COVID-19 pandemic brought with it the "silver lining" of online synchronous Arabic classes offered by the Middle East Institute in Washington, DC, the University of Illinois-Urbana Champaign, and a private tutor. I pursued the study of Modern Standard Arabic (MSA) for two years, advancing to beginner intermediate proficiency. After an extended trip to Sudan in the summer of 2022 during which I was unable to communicate well with most people in the artificial dialect that is MSA (no one speaks it in everyday conversation; see footnote 1), I decided to switch my focus upon return to vernacular Egyptian Arabic, which is almost universally understood by Arabic speakers because of the popularity and wide dissemination of Egyptian television and film. Since 2022 until the present, I have studied online with a private tutor based in Cairo for approximately four hours per week and am proud to say that I can now converse for a prolonged period of time and with relative depth in Egyptian Arabic at an intermediate or high intermediate level. Achieving this level of language proficiency has taken an almost embarrassingly long time (see footnote 1), but the experience has given me a great deal of humility and empathy for all language learners, including those who are at the heart of this study. The experience of developing functional multilingual literacy has also led me to form rewarding relationships with immigrants, children of immigrants, and international students here in the United States.[2] This development has enriched my teaching, research, and very being in the world. Ultimately, my multilingual proficiency and transnational experience has deeply informed the decolonial, transnational, and translingual approach I take in this book.

---

2   Since returning to the United States in 2015, I have facilitated English language classes as a volunteer (and voluntary volunteer coordinator) every weekend for adult immigrants in my community of Fargo, North Dakota, and Moorhead, Minnesota. Many of the immigrants are Somali and Congolese, and although actual progress in English is often slow, we regularly discover exciting commonalities among Arabic, Swahili, and Somali—reminding me over and over again that all languages, and all people, are related. Every weekend (and in many everyday encounters beyond the weekend), the abstract idea of "language difference is a resource" becomes reality. My multilingual and transnational experience has also impacted my professional life, in that I am able to understand the profound experience of arriving in a new country as an outsider. This has allowed me to connect more deeply with and provide more meaningful mentorship to international graduate students enrolled in my department's graduate programs and also to emphasize transnational and multilingual perspectives in course content.

There are undoubtedly many shortcomings that will be evident to readers of this book. Most obviously, my attention throughout this book focuses on a college founded by Americans, and much of the archival material I rely on was written in English. It could be argued that this focus merely maintains the centrality of Western epistemology, which decolonial theory seeks to undo. But decolonial work does not seek to recenter knowledge; rather, decolonial work requires an acknowledgment of the many centers of knowledge that exist simultaneously—this is the difference between universal and pluriversal ways of knowing. Rethinking and rearticulating history through a decolonial lens means we need to study how colonial structures of oppression work. In order to understand how processes of exclusion have historically and continue to occur in the context of English-language literacy education, we must study the discourses of the American missionary founders of SPC alongside and in interaction with the discourses of SPC students and the surrounding community. This book conducts such an analysis.

Another shortcoming of this book, which I readily acknowledge, is that I am not a scholar of Arab or Islamic rhetoric, nor am I fluent in Arabic. I have tried to do my due diligence in contextualizing SPC within the history of the Ottoman Empire and the geopolitics of the region where the college was located, and I have developed my Arabic language proficiency over many years. However, I still relied on a translator to produce the translations that are central to this analysis, and I still have much to learn about the Arabic language, rhetorical traditions, and literacy education in the region. These efforts are ongoing but incomplete at the time of this book's publication. I invite others who are better suited to do so to (re)contextualize the history presented here through these lenses. In Chapter 5, I have included original texts written in Arabic alongside their translation in English in order for scholars fluent in Arabic to understand those materials on their own terms.

AN IMAGINED AMERICA: LANGUAGE, LITERACY, IDENTITY, AND COLONIALITY AT SYRIAN PROTESTANT COLLEGE, 1866–1920

1 Imagining America

In this book, I trace the history of postsecondary literacy education and language policy at the turn of the 20th century at Syrian Protestant College (SPC), which today, as the American University of Beirut (AUB), is the longest-running American-style institution of higher education outside of the US.[1] I focus on SPC from its founding in 1866 until 1920, when it changed its name and institutional identity.[2] SPC/AUB was and is not affiliated with any institution of higher education in the United States, although the founders of the college were educated in elite Protestant colleges, including Yale, Harvard, and Amherst, in the Northeast United States.[3] SPC was founded by a group of American Protestant missionaries under the leadership of Daniel Bliss, the school's first president and former missionary in Syria with the American Board of Commissioners for Foreign Missions (ABCFM).[4] The original mission of the college "was to give a thorough literary, scientific, and medical education" and the first language of instruction was Arabic to "fit the needs of [local] citizens and their country" (American University of Beirut Libraries, 2023).

The college opened its doors to a student body of 16 in December 1866, occupying only a few rented rooms near central Beirut. The college initially included two faculties, the Collegiate and Medical Departments, and in 1873 a Preparatory Department was added to serve students whose school backgrounds did not sufficiently prepare them for college-level study. The college's

---

1   By "American-style" higher education, I mean a curriculum that prioritizes the liberal arts (arts, humanities, social sciences, natural sciences, and mathematics) and includes general education as a key part of the curriculum, with specializations provided in the later years of an undergraduate degree. American-style colleges and universities grant bachelor's degrees after four years of study rather than the three typical in European universities.

2   The year 1920 is a logical endpoint for this study for several reasons: In 1920, SPC moved from being a college with an explicitly religious affiliation to the secular institution it is today. The transition also marks the point at which Arab faculty gained equal status (including voting rights) to their foreign counterparts. On a broader scale, 1920 marks the end of World War I, the end of the Ottoman Empire, and the beginning of the French Mandate in Lebanon, which eventually led to the creation of Lebanon as an independent nation in 1943.

3   Syrian Protestant College, and today the American University of Beirut, although unaffiliated with any institution of higher education in the United States, has operated under a charter granted by the New York Education Department. AUB is accredited by the Middle States Commission on Higher Education, and the Lebanese government recognizes degrees from AUB. See American University of Beirut (n.d.).

4   See Chapter 2 for a thorough history of American missions and the connection to SPC.

first two buildings, College Hall and the Medical Building (now called the Old Pharmacy Building), were finished in 1873; today, these buildings remain a central part of AUB's beautiful contemporary campus, which overlooks the Mediterranean on the west side of Beirut. The college grew steadily over the next five decades: Ten years after its founding, 77 students were enrolled at SPC; by 1885, the number had grown to 183; in 1897, the number was 309, and by 1902, the year Daniel Bliss resigned as president, the college boasted a healthy enrollment of 615 students (Annual Report; see also Appendix A).

As Betty Anderson (2011) put it in her history of the institution, "the campus has stood at a vital intersection between a rapidly changing American missionary and educational project to the Middle East and a dynamic quest for Arab national identity and empowerment" (p. 2). The field of rhetoric and writing studies, I argue throughout this book, has much to gain from investigating the "vital intersection" between America and the Ottoman Empire at the turn of the 20th century, as represented in and through the literacy education provided by SPC.

As I elaborate later in this chapter, colonial epistemology—marked by linguistic, religious, and nationalist ideologies—was, and continues to be, deeply intertwined with the global project of imperialism. Scholars including Robert Phillipson (1992) and Alastair Pennycook (1998) have made clear connections between the history of British (and by extension European) colonization and the enterprise of English language teaching worldwide. Similar connections underlie the history of American missionary work and the emergence of American-style, English-language higher education outside of the US. I argue that the colonial epistemology that sustained the spread of English-language teaching globally—the focus of Phillipson's and Pennycook's work—is similarly foundational to the history of rhetoric and writing studies inside the US. SPC, therefore, offers a rich site for analysis of the circulation of colonial epistemology in and through postsecondary literacy education, both outside and inside the US.

This book presents a historical, transnational, translingual, and decolonial perspective on questions of identity, literacy, language, culture, and citizenship. In examining a variety of archival documents from the college's founding in 1866 until the fall of the Ottoman Empire in 1920, I show how transnational and translingual negotiations among SPC faculty, students, and administrators, as well as the local and regional community, produced a tenuous and sometimes unsettling vision of America for foreigners and locals alike. I argue that examining these negotiations at SPC allows scholars and educators in rhetoric and writing studies, education, and related fields to consider how literacy education in English has, and often continues to, construct an imagined

America that is both grounded upon and reproduces colonial epistemology. Such constructions, I argue, work to uphold exclusionary practices that are all too vivid in our world today.

In this study, I consider a corpus of archival documents, many written by students, in light of several key moments in SPC's history. These moments include the decision to change the language of instruction from Arabic to English (Chapter 3); the development of a language-centered, liberal-arts curriculum (Chapter 3); two student-led protests against the administration (Chapter 4); and the proliferation of student-authored magazines and newspapers at the turn of the 20th century (Chapter 5). This set of documents, and these moments, illustrate how students, faculty, administrators, and members of the local and regional community negotiated the role of the American college in Syria over time. I contend that these groups used writing and multiple languages to make sense of, and to shape, the college's place as a bridge between an imagined America and the Arab world. Indeed, these translingual and transnational negotiations illuminate differing epistemologies attached to language(s) in the region, conflicting understandings of the meaning of America, and evolving definitions of Arab identity within a dying Ottoman empire and in response to the increasing influence of the West in the region.

This project provides a specific example of the history of colonial epistemology as it circulated historically within English literacy education in non-Anglophone contexts and explores its continued impact today. The following questions shape this work: What did literacy education at Syrian Protestant College look like between its founding in 1866 and the point in which it became the (secular) American University of Beirut in 1920? How was American identity represented and constructed through literacy education and language policy in Syria at the turn of the 20th century? How did SPC students engage, resist, and adapt this representation for their own purposes? In what ways do representations of America and English-language literacy sustain colonial epistemology in writing classrooms and programs? And finally, what are the implications of this study for contemporary students, writing instructors, and writing program administrators, both in and outside of the US?

My goal in presenting this research is twofold: First, I want to highlight the importance of looking beyond monolingual, Anglocentric contexts of literacy education to better understand how literacy in English and in other languages is shaped by multiple forces across borders. This study, on a practical level, expands understandings of the history of rhetoric and writing studies beyond the Americentric contexts upon which much historical work in this field has been centered. Second, I aim to demonstrate through this research that SPC's geopolitical location outside of the US throws into high relief the American nationalist, English monolingual, and Christian religious ideologies underlying the college's literacy curriculum and language policies. These ideologies, which together are indicative of colonial epistemology, are made especially visible because they are constantly in tension with local religious, national, and linguistic ideologies of the time. I make the case throughout this book that such ideologies have similarly shaped the history of English-language literacy education in seemingly monolingual and Anglocentric contexts such as those in which many literacy educators who read this book find themselves working. As I discuss later in this chapter, histories of rhetoric and writing studies have rarely accounted for the ways in which literacy curriculum and language policies in these contexts are *constituted by and deeply responsive to* translingual and transnational discourse, even and perhaps especially when curriculum and policy has suppressed such discourse.

In this chapter, I first situate my argument theoretically, focusing specifically on nationalism, coloniality, and the idea of America. I argue that SPC complicates Benedict Anderson's (2006) concept of the nation as a historically constituted "imagined community," in that the idea of America at SPC traveled beyond national borders and its *ideal* was imagined and constituted by students and faculty outside of the West. This complication moves me to understand SPC through a decolonial frame, illustrating how language and literacy education at SPC reflects a complex interplay of competing epistemologies. I define several key terms that are used throughout this book, including imperialism, colonialism, and decoloniality, and I explain why I have adopted a decolonial rather than postcolonial framework for my analysis. I then describe the historical relationships that exist among literacy education, colonial epistemology, and monolingual ideology. After explicating the theoretical frame, I review the conversations in rhetoric and writing studies to which I hope this book will contribute, including transnational, translingual, decolonial, and historical scholarship. Then, I elaborate my primary claim by deconstructing two seemingly "commonsense" narratives about the discipline's history through a decolonial lens. Finally, I provide a chapter-by-chapter overview of the remainder of the book.

It is through these theoretical and disciplinary frameworks that I articulate the central claim of this book: The history of rhetoric and writing studies must be understood as fundamentally transnational and translingual. This claim troubles some of the underlying and often implicit principles of the field, particularly its tendency to promote writing pedagogies limited by monolingual and Anglocentric thinking. As such, I argue that decolonial, transnational, and translingual historical analysis provides a path for the discipline to (re)imagine the borders that have traditionally defined it, as well as its contemporary and future work.

Nationalism, Colonialism, and an Imagined America

In *Imagined Communities*, Benedict Anderson (2006) theorized the modern concept of the nation as "an imagined political community—and imagined as both inherently limited and sovereign" (p. 5). The nation is imagined because no single individual can know all its members, and it is limited because it is contained by political and geographic boundaries. The contemporary concept of the nation, according to Anderson, emerges out of Enlightenment-era thinking, in which long-standing, dynastic empires were challenged and ultimately dismantled and replaced by sovereign nations. Nations form a sense of community in which members are bonded together by loyalty to the nation, a sense of nationalism.

Benedict Anderson's (2006) understanding of the modern nation-state and nationalism—or the ideology of the nation—is tied to the rise of print culture (in Anderson's words, "print capitalism") beginning in the sixteenth and seventeenth centuries. This development created "unified fields of exchange and communication" that elevated written language above spoken dialects, and legitimized non-Latin (Western) languages such as Italian, English, French, and Spanish (B. Anderson, 2006, p. 44). In turn, conceptions of language became fixed and bounded, legitimizing the epistemologies of those in power and stigmatizing language use that did not fit the "standard" created in print (B. Anderson, 2006, pp. 44–45).

It is no small coincidence that the stabilization of language that occurred as a result of print capitalism also facilitated the emergence of modern nationalism: First, the printing press allowed for circulation of ideas on a much broader scale—for example, the success of the Protestant Reformation is largely credited to the invention of the Gutenberg press and the ability of Martin Luther to distribute his *Ninety-Five Theses* to a much wider audience than previously possible. Second, the visibility and circulation of "vernacular" (i.e. non-Latin) languages during the Renaissance and beyond—facilitated by the printing press—subverted the hierarchies and systems of exclusion that were otherwise preserved in and through the language of the Roman Catholic Church (and, in turn, the Holy Roman Empire). While the audience for these "vernacular" publications was still small due to limited access to education and therefore literacy, the disruption in power was significant, allowing for the rapid transmission of radical ideas that were then translated into action. The best examples of this process are the American and French

Revolutions at the end of the 18th century. At the same time, single languages became tied to the modern nation-state, tying nationalism to monolingualism in the West (Yildiz, 2012).

Sam Haselby's (2015) *Origins of American Religious Nationalism* added a new dimension to Benedict Anderson's (2006) work, arguing that modern nations—and nationalism—depend not just on the imagination, but also on faith. As I discuss in more detail in Chapter 2, Haselby (2015) argued that American Protestant missions' work created a connection between nationalism and Protestantism. America was seen by its Protestant founders as a nation chosen by God, and this American exceptionalism (a pronounced form of nationalism) was communicated in and through the evangelical mission movement (p. 14). Just as modern nations were formed, according to Anderson (2006), through print capitalism, so too, according to Haselby (2015) did the American Protestant missionary movement grow exponentially through print:

> ... [the evangelical missions had an] impressive array of schools, associations, and publications middle-class and modern. In quantitative terms, their literary output was astonishing, amounting to hundreds of millions of pages. . . . With their expansive bureaucracies, centralized authority, ambitious print media campaigns, and extensive scale of operations, these associations were comparable to modernizing nineteenth-century nation-states. (pp. 15–16)

In addition, the missions movement grew through language and print. While the Bible had been translated into 22 European languages over a 300-year period prior to the 19th century, American Protestants "published Bibles in 160 different languages or dialects, producing, in a single generation, Bibles in sevenfold the number of languages as had the previous 19 centuries of Christians" (Haselby, 2015, p. 260). The missionaries saw themselves as following in the footsteps of the first evangelist, Martin Luther, transmitting the word of God directly to people around the world.

As I elaborate in Chapter 2, SPC was founded by American Protestant missionaries attempting to spread the "good word" of American exceptionalism (nationalism) within the complicated geopolitical context of an empire on the verge of collapse. Benedict Anderson's (2006) theory of the modern "nation" conflates the nation—a bounded, limited political entity—with nationalism, an ideology that Anderson defined by those who "imagine" themselves to be members: citizens. For Anderson, as Bruce Masters (2001) pointed out, the nation is inherently political, "imagined" by elites and pushed to the people from top down (p. 9). However, Anderson's theory of the nation does not map well onto the context of the Middle East[5] (or other regions in the Global South), where "ethnic/national identities" were "primordial," and "tribal or dynastic regimes . . . had served the peoples . . . for centuries" (Masters, 2001, p. 10). SPC operated within a dying empire, bringing with it the unique linguistic, cultural, and colonial epistemologies of its American Protestant founders. As I describe in more detail in Chapter 2, the region of Syria within the Ottoman Empire saw itself as distinct in relation to the empire itself; various communities within the region, such as the Druze and Maronites, negotiated protection and autonomy through violence as well as manipulation of outside parties (including the British and French governments and Jesuit and Protestant missionaries). These demands for autonomy were based on their own ethnic, religious, and familial affiliations. In short, communities within Syria were no strangers to the negotiation of competing epistemologies.

American Protestant missionaries, in opening SPC after many years of failed efforts to convert the local population to Protestantism, instead determined a better approach would be to convert the local population to their imagined America, which could be transmitted through education regardless of geopolitical boundaries. Proselytization—a word derived from the Greek root *proselytos*, which means "one who has come over"—requires an invitation, and SPC invited its students to imagine themselves as part of the community represented by the college's American founders and the American-style education that the college was modeled upon. In this sense, SPC students were invited to become a part of the "imagined community" of America, even as they were never—and rarely became—citizens in a legal sense. There was an underlying tension, in other words, between the epistemologies of the faculty and those of the students, and it is the negotiation of this tension—the struggle to "imagine" America, defined by its very presence and absence at SPC—that I explore throughout this book.

---

5   Ironically, but importantly, the "Middle East" is a colonial descriptor for the region where Syria/present-day Lebanon is located, and it begs the question: East of what? I have limited my use of this term as much as possible throughout the book and recognize its colonial underpinnings, but many scholars who have studied the region, including Edward Said (1979), refer to the region as the Middle East, and the literal Arabic translation, الشرق الأوسط, is used regularly within the region. For this reason, I have used the term occasionally, and some quotes include the term. Possible alternatives include Southwest Asia-North Africa (SWANA) or the "Arab World," but there are limitations to nearly any alternative, including their lack of legibility in popular discourse. In general, I try to remain specific in my descriptors of the geopolitical location that I am studying by calling it Syria or present-day Lebanon. For an interesting discussion of the tensions related to term, see Jennifer Case, 2024.

The case of SPC forces us to consider how Benedict Anderson's (2006) *imagined communities* escape or exceed the boundaries of the geopolitical entity of the modern nation, go beyond traditional conceptions of who can hold national identity, and expose the coloniality of such imaginings. As Anderson explained, the only ones capable of imagining the nation and deciding who belongs within it are those who hold positions of power, such as those within the government or press. At SPC, challenges to such thinking emerged in the form of students and the local community, as they encountered a "nation" constructed through literacy education and the English language but outside of the geopolitical boundaries of the United States. America was offered to students and the local community in and through the college's curriculum and policies. Local stakeholders negotiated the meaning of America, attempting to show that they belonged to this imagined community through their behavior and performance at the college. They learned over time that they could not truly belong, and their attempts—and failures—to negotiate belonging show that nationalism and monolingualism can best be understood as attempts to demarcate difference. In other words, nationalism and monolingualism—embedded in literacy education as much today as in the past—are key ideological markers of colonial epistemology.

Imperialism, Colonialism, and Decoloniality

Before continuing, I want to define some key terms and justify my use of decolonialism as a theoretical frame of analysis. I rely on Barbara Arneil (2023) and Karen Pashby (2012) to define *imperialism* and *colonialism*. Both concepts refer to epistemology and should be understood as related but distinct from each other. Imperialism refers to the use of force by a foreign power to dominate peoples or lands in geographically separate locations. Colonialism refers to the cultural and social occupation of foreign or domestic spaces. Epistemologically, imperialism presumes the superiority of the empire and insists on the people's subservience to it, while colonialism justifies the occupation of lands and peoples on the basis of the presumed "backwardness" of the colonized; colonizers, who live with the colonized, offer "improvement" to the colonized land and peoples based on the colonizers' own values and beliefs (Arneil, 2023, pp. 6–12). Pashby (2012) pointed out that "both concepts involve overt, direct measures as well as less obvious discursive modes of power that work at the level of 'imagination' to govern powerfully both on a level of physical and social institutions and on an epistemological level by enforcing a particular worldview" (p. 12). This book examines how literacy education has used, and in some cases continues to use, discourse and imagination to propel and sustain colonial epistemology.

In relation to the historical account I provide in this book, Walter Mignolo (2007) pointed out that Western perceptions of the Ottoman Empire changed between the 16th and 19th centuries. Prior to the 19th century, Western powers conceived of the Ottomans through the lens of "imperial difference"—Ottomans were seen as mistaken (particularly in their beliefs as Muslims) but, because of the empire's relative power and development, not necessarily unequal. Ottomans began to be viewed through the lens of "colonial difference"—as candidates for colonization—beginning in the 19th century, as the empire became weaker and the West took a more active role in the region (Mignolo, 2007, p. 474). Because the focus of this book is on the late 19th and early 20th centuries, I generally refer to Western, Eurocentric, Anglo-American, and Christian missionary epistemologies as *colonial*. When referring to empires that existed in the 19th and early 20th centuries, such as the Ottoman or British empires, I name the epistemology propelling their work as *imperial*.

Understanding colonialism's power is productive for my account of literacy education because it helps build understanding about how the specific practices and processes at work at SPC were justified. The faculty and administrators of the college were never directly involved in colonization, and Syria was not officially colonized by a Western power during the 19th century, but the policies and education provided by SPC were founded on the logic of coloniality, and they operated through what Mignolo (2007), via Aníbal Quijano, has called the *colonial matrix of power*. The colonial matrix of power produces colonialism, racism, and patriarchy through the assertion of Western centrality and control over the local economy (including land and labor), authority (through military and government), knowledge and subjectivity (prioritizing Christian and Western knowledge and identities), and gender and sexuality (based on Christian understandings of both) (Mignolo, 2007, p. 478). Colonization does not always require force but it is always violent, in that it envisions the world through the "imperial concept of Totality," and it deploys this vision to insist on the inferiority and displacement of other visions, other epistemologies, and other histories (Mignolo, 2007, p. 451).

A decolonial lens requires *delinking* from the centrality of the West in order to *recognize* and *re-place* the visions, epistemologies, and histories that have been subsumed in and/or interpreted through the colonial matrix of power. This means going further than adding to existing knowledge or "recovering" other voices. Delinking also requires the decolonization of knowledge—in other words, a decolonial perspective illuminates how existing knowledge and epistemology is framed within colonial thinking. While postcolonialism and postmodernism present other, perhaps more familiar, lenses of critical analysis, for Mignolo (2007) via Quijano, they do not go far enough because their critique remains Eurocentric and focused on the West (pp. 451–452), a limitation that I discuss more thoroughly later. Decolonial analysis does not seek to replace Western views of the world—Western epistemologies exist and function in the world whether we like them or not—but rather, decolonialism seeks to engage in *border thinking*. Border thinking highlights plural (pluriversal) visions of the world that run equally alongside each other, and it also identifies and values the histories of those who have been subjected to, and negated by, imperial and colonial power (Mignolo, 2007, p. 493; see also Ellen Cushman et al., 2021, for a useful discussion of pluriversality and the discipline of rhetoric and writing studies).

This project analyzes the history of language and literacy education and the production of identity at SPC through a decolonial lens. Specifically, I trace how colonial epistemology worked within the college to produce and justify its linguistic and educational practices and policies. Additionally, I articulate how this epistemology was negotiated by local students and the wider community as they attempted to identify themselves in relation to it. Colonialism within SPC was deeply tied to conceptions of language, literacy, and identity—and the power of this epistemology can help explain why and how SPC survived and eventually thrived (as the contemporary American University of Beirut) in a most unlikely place. Within the Ottoman Empire and Syria in particular, SPC represented a White, Protestant America that was unattainable by students by virtue of their Arab and sometimes Muslim identities, but to which they were nonetheless expected to aspire. As John Willinsky (1998) put it, this "one-way gaze to another form of life . . . left them suspended between worlds . . . [which] they could learn to appreciate, but could never fully achieve" (p. 94). SPC's colonial epistemology repeatedly ran up against local linguistic, ethnonational, and religious ideologies. It is this epistemological conflict, in relation to ideologies of language, literacy, and identity, that this book explores.

This historical account resists simply *adding to* our discipline's existing historical knowledge. Instead, I follow the path of an emergent decolonial tradition in the field of rhetoric and writing studies as it "return[s] the gaze . . . from colonized to the colonizer" (Ruiz, 2021, p. 55). This account sheds light on translingual, transnational discourses that, I argue, are a fundamental part of the history of rhetoric and writing studies; in the process, recognizing such discourses illuminates the colonial premises upon which the discipline has been grounded. Recentering our understanding of the history of rhetoric and writing studies through a decolonial lens requires us to "attend to the mechanisms where distinctions between the historical and the Other of history are maintained, *both* in historical artifacts *and* in the methodological and theoretical tools of academics" (deTar, 2022, p. 197). In other words, we must investigate how colonialism has historically underpinned our discipline's dominant conceptions of language, literacy, and identity, as well as how this epistemology has worked to conceal and devalue alternative conceptions of the same. We must study not only colonialism at work in the discipline's historical discourse but also how those marginalized by it negotiated to be heard.

Because American identity is tied deeply to colonialism (Stuckey & Murphy, 2001), it can be difficult to separate the two in contemporary U.S. contexts of literacy education. It is often easier to identify colonialism in contexts seemingly distant from our own. Therefore, this historical account's focus on a "foreign" site of literacy education outside the US at the turn of the 20th century—and the imagined America produced by it—allows us to see more clearly how American identity and colonialism are intertwined. We can then use this knowledge to (re)turn our gaze to our present context(s), to better understand how colonialism has altered our understanding of the history of rhetoric and writing studies, and how it continues to inflect contemporary approaches to writing instruction and research. Indeed, this decolonial, transnational, and translingual historical account can help us better understand the limitations of many of our disciplinary approaches, which, as Xiaoye You (2016) pointed out, continue to rely on American nationalism and English monolingualism (both a result of coloniality), even as they sometimes seek to disrupt these frames (p. 5).

The decolonial analysis in this historical project has the potential to help move the discipline away from colonial frames by "account[ing] for colonial knowledge practices [that] still limit[] the study of written language," which in turn can lead to "anti-colonial resistance and transformation" (Ruiz & Baca, 2017, p. 226). Understanding how coloniality inflected the production of knowledge, education, and writing pedagogy outside of the United States 150 years ago demonstrates that the disciplinary history of rhetoric and writing studies is complicated not only because it is a transnational and translingual history, but also because it is a colonial history. To fully account for the discipline's entanglement with colonialism, scholars and practitioners need to understand how colonial epistemology has been used to position the "other" in relation to writing and literacy practices, specifically how English and monolingual ideology has been used to suppress transnational and translingual discourses circulating in the same contexts. Additionally, studying how colonialism is and has been negotiated at a local level, and how this negotiation has materialized rhetorically, allows us to recognize pluriversal epistemologies that may otherwise be hidden in colonial contexts (see Jackson, 2021).

Competing epistemologies can be seen at work in literacy education by looking both historically and abroad, in places where Western epistemologies and literacy practices were "foreign" and therefore stand in marked contrast to the non-Western contexts in which they were situated. That is the work of this history. But for decolonization of disciplinary knowledge to occur, specialists in rhetoric and writing studies cannot stop there—we must bring what we learn from this historical account, and the workings of colonialism, back to the contemporary discipline. This work involves both reconsidering and rewriting the historical narratives that tell us who we are and where we come from, which in turn will prompt a rethinking of the assumptions that ground our contemporary pedagogical and programmatic approaches to writing instruction. This book helps substantiate other scholars' efforts to decolonize the discipline's present and future by highlighting the colonial underpinnings of literacy education in the past.

From Postcolonial to Decolonial

Throughout this book, I use a decolonial lens instead of a postcolonial one to conduct my analysis. However, readers may question why I have not used a postcolonial lens, particularly since the focus of my analysis, Syrian Protestant College, is located in Syria, in the same region that postcolonial scholar Edward Said (1979) focused on in his critique of Orientalist discourse. In this section, therefore, I explicate what I see as the shortcomings of postcolonial theory in making sense of literacy education, rhetoric, and identity at SPC, and I show how a decolonial perspective opens up more productive avenues for recognizing and investigating the complexity of this historical account.

From a postcolonial perspective, it is easy to claim that the work of Christian missionaries was inevitably colonial and inevitably Western. Indeed, it is impossible to separate missionary work from the larger colonial, racist framework in which the mission emerged and operated. The 15th-century Doctrine of Discovery, followed by the Age of Enlightenment in the 17th and 18th centuries, articulated the logic supporting the European slave trade and colonialism, including settler colonialism in the Americas.[6] This context helped to produce the discursive logics that defined and justified the work of Christian missionaries. For Said (1979), these logics are inherently Orientalist, "a set of

---

6   The Doctrine of Discovery refers to Pope Nicholas V's 1452 papal bull Dum Diversas, followed by the bull Romanus Pontifex of 1455. These two bulls gave authority to Catholic European powers to seize non-Christian lands and enslave non-Christians in Africa and the Americas. Pope Alexander VI released the Inter Caetera bull in 1493, which created the "Law of Nations," in which Christian nations could not claim the right to other Christian lands (Indigenous Values Initiative, 2018).

constraints upon and limitations of thought" about how "the East" might be understood, as well as "the West's" relation to it (p. 42). Modern conceptions of the nation, too, were supported by self-reinforcing networks of Orientalist discourse, in that national boundaries and languages encouraged distinction, and separation from, the Eastern "other." This, in turn, produced artificial structures of power based on nationality, which were also tied to race, ethnicity, religion, and language.

However, as I discuss more thoroughly in Chapter 2, we must be careful neither to generalize all Christian missions as the same or necessarily holding nefarious intentions nor to assume that local communities were without agency in relation to the missions that targeted them. The missionaries themselves held different, sometimes incongruous, views of colonialism and slavery as well as the communities they targeted. There were conflicts within American Protestant missionary organizations about both American settler colonialism—the United States government's illegal claim to native land—and slavery during the 19th century, with many arguing that both institutions were unjust and immoral.[7] Although American missionaries largely failed to convert many within the communities they targeted, they were sometimes successful in cross-cultural interaction, and their writing helped bring cross-cultural awareness to Anglo-Americans.[8]

The missionaries' conflicting intentions create important complications that prevent scholars from writing a cohesive narrative about American Protestant missionaries' work in Syria, complications that I elaborate in more detail in Chapter 2. Alastair Bonnett (2004) and Claire Conceison (2004), neither of whom worked from an explicitly decolonial lens in the books I examine here, nonetheless offered important critiques of Said's (1979) theory of Orientalism, suggesting that it is built on problematic generalizations about "the East" (and "the West") that do not account for the rich diversity of the regions to which the term refers. These generalizations prove to be ironically similar to those criticized by Said. For Conceison (2004), who in her

---

7   For example, within the American Board of Commissions for Foreign Missions (ABCFM), there was dissension about the organization's neutrality about the issue of slavery. Another organization, the American Missionary Association, was explicitly abolitionist and some Presbyterian churches affiliated themselves with that organization instead of ABCFM as a result.

8   For example, missionaries of the ABCFM Samuel Allis and John Dunbar "joined the Pawnees during their winter buffalo hunt in the Central Plains. During this five-month journey the missionaries lived beholden to tribal members for linguistic and cultural education, as well as for food and shelter. They developed a better understanding of Pawnee ways during the next few years, but they claimed no conversions. Pawnee leaders showed interest in the missionaries but ignored their appeals to abandon their semi-nomadic lifestyle" (Galler, 2011).

book was interested in the representation of Americans in China in Chinese drama, the West should not be understood as the sole "'possessor' of any given colonial or postcolonial discourse by virtue of its assumed pervasive political and cultural power" because such understanding reduces everyone who is not part of the so-called "West" as "Alien" (p. 52). Conceison argued that perpetuation of such essentialization relies on an inherently Orientalist logic even as it seems be the very logic that Said's argument is grounded upon (p. 58). Bonnett (2004), who explored in his book the origins of the idea of "the West," argued that postcolonialism has questionably maintained the central role of the West in its scholarship, discursively essentializing what is meant by "the West" and, in turn, "the East" (pp. 6–7).

Additionally, both Conceison (2004) and Bonnett (2004) insisted that in focusing on Orientalism, or "the West's" views of "the East," postcolonial specialists have paid little attention to "the East's" views of "the West"—a perspective Conceison (2004) called "Occidentalism" in an effort to recuperate the term from Said's denigration (p. 41). Conceison argued that Occidentalism, according to her definition, allows scholars to understand "the West" as a discursive object, much as Said (1979) argued that Orientalism constructs "the East" through discourse. Conceison's (2004) point was to highlight the constructed nature of both "the West" and "the East" and to challenge assumptions that suggest the structure of power critiqued by Said is unidirectional (p. 53). Bonnett (2004) claimed that it is useful to study "the political and social *uses* and *deployment*" of Occidentalism because of the ways in which it highlights "the mutually constitutive nature" of identity formation (p. 7).

Conceison (2004) defined Occidentalist discourse as: "(1) paradoxical (or contradictory/dialectical) in character and function; (2) existing in both paradoxical relation to and continuous dialogue with Orientalism (and other discourses); and (3) open-ended, changing, active, and self-consciously temporal" (p. 54). She argued that this definition allows scholars to disconnect conceptions of "the West" from "the Occident" and to see Occidentalist representations of "the Other" as far more complicated than Said's (1979) Orientalist "Other." Such representations are "*layered*" rather than hierarchical, within a range of positive and negative representations rather than within a binary (Conceison, 2004, pp. 54–55). Conceison's theorization of Occidentalist discourse helps scholars move away from a postcolonial lens and toward a decolonial one, in that she resisted postcolonialism's tendency toward Eurocentrism and uncovered a range of pluriversal discourses *about* the West, which Western scholars have historically ignored. Additionally, Conceison's study highlights the agency of those who have been positioned as relatively powerless within postcolonial scholarship.

In this book, I am interested in building on the work of Conceison, Bonnett, and recent decolonial scholars because their theorization of colonial discourse and epistemology allows one to better understand the relationships among local stakeholders, including SPC students, and the college's American faculty and administrators as multilayered relationships. As problematic as the colonial epistemology of the college's founders and faculty was, the relationship was not one-sided; rather, a decolonial perspective allows one to see the interactions between the local community and the college administration and faculty as a *negotiated* relationship, where identities were co-constructed against the backdrop of an imagined America, a settler-colonial nation still emerging in the real and abstract distance. Within this relationship, all parties struggled to identify themselves and each other within the liminal space of the American college in the semi-autonomous region of Syria before the fall of the Ottoman Empire. SPC's curriculum, student protests and faculty responses, as well as student writing, all provide examples of how this negotiation played out over time. Understanding SPC—as a representative of the American mission (and the nation itself)—and local stakeholders—representatives of the mission's targets—through the lens of decolonialism allows for an identification of power relations and identities that were far more complex than what is allowed for in an analysis informed only by postcolonial theory.

Literacy (Education), Coloniality, and Monolingualism

In order to fully value SPC's place in the history of rhetoric and writing studies, those of us living and working in monolingual Anglophone contexts must first make connections between our contemporary contexts and a much longer history of English-language literacy and literacy education that emerged out of colonialism and empire. This history, in turn, helps us to denaturalize monolingualism and English as a *lingua franca* as developments over time rather than ahistorical "givens." These contextualizations can then lead us to question some of the fundamental principles of rhetoric and writing studies—questioning that is aligned with the work of decolonization and to which this book aims to contribute.

Let us first step into the history of Western literacy as it emerged in the context of colonialism and empire. As already discussed, the Enlightenment led to print capitalism in Europe, which in turn led to linguistic hierarchies that privileged formal, print-based language over spoken vernaculars throughout the continent. This elevated literacy itself to a higher status, privileging writing over speaking, and in turn privileging Western epistemologies (Canagarajah, 2019, p. 9). But language hierarchization occurred outside of Europe, as well, through colonization. Speaking from the Global South, Finex Ndhlovu and Laketi Makalela (2021) noted that colonizers stabilized non-Western languages by inventing and recognizing "standard" versions of non-Western languages, which resulted in the "invisibilis[ation of] other language practices" (p. 17). So-called "standard 'national languages'—also known as vernacular languages—were invented [by colonizers] and then deployed towards sociocultural and political engineering processes that produced skewed versions of local native/Indigenous identities" (Ndhlovu & Makalela, 2021, p. 17). The process of stabilizing language and making Indigenous language practices invisible is tied, for Ndhlovu and Makalela (2021), to "the project of Christianisation," which created "self-proclaimed colonial linguists" including "native affairs commissioners, missionaries, anthropologists, diarists, hunters and travellers" (p. 28). Such stabilization of language through colonization and religion in and outside of the "West" thus worked in favor of privileging those who did the stabilizing over those who actually used language, in all its messiness, in everyday life.

Additionally, as Benedict Anderson (2006) pointed out, colonization required multilingual workers, "who to be useful had to be . . . capable of mediating linguistically between the metropolitan nation and the colonized peoples" (p. 115). Beyond these practical purposes, multilingualism was also valued as a component of secular and private education for its role in transmitting modern Western culture and knowledge to colonized peoples—a practice justified on the basis of colonizers' sense of a so-called moral imperative. This worked, also, to bring "models of nationalism, nation-ness, and nation-state produced elsewhere" to colonized spaces (B. Anderson, 2006, p. 116).

While multilingualism initially supported colonization for the reasons I have described, modernity—tied inextricably to colonialism (Mignolo, 2007)—required the invention of monolingualism, a language ideology in which "individuals and social formations are imagined to possess one 'true' language only, their 'mother tongue,' and through this possession to be organically linked to an exclusive clearly demarcated ethnicity, culture, and nation" (Yildiz, 2012, p. 2; see also Phillipson's, 1992, discussion of English linguistic imperialism). Even as multilingualism *as practice* was valued by the colonizers for its economic and political uses in advancing empire and colonization, monolingualism *as ideology* reinforced the hierarchies of knowledge, cultures, and peoples that are lasting hallmarks of colonial epistemology.

The modern development of monolingualism is connected to colonial epistemology, which can likewise be connected to the emergence of English as a *lingua franca* and the teaching of English worldwide, as both Phillipson (1992) and Pennycook (1998) have discussed. Phillipson (1992) traced the history behind the global spread of English and the ways in which the language "has been equated with progress and prosperity" worldwide (p. 8). He called English's global dominance *linguistic imperialism*, describing its deeply permeating modes of communication and constructions of culture, occurring at least in part through the teaching of English. For Pennycook (1998), English is deeply interwoven with the history of British empire and colonialism, and for this reason he claimed we must consider English—and English language teaching—as a "product of colonialism not just because it is colonialism that produced the initial conditions for the global spread of English but because it was colonialism that produced many of the ways of thinking and behaving that are still part of Western cultures" (p. 19). Pennycook (1998) argued, and I agree, that "it is not so much that colonialism produces unique behaviours, words and ideas, but rather it makes a set of practices and discursive frames more available, more acceptable" (p. 25). These ways of thinking include persistent hierarchical distinctions between "native" and "non-native" speakers of English and characterizations of "Self" and "Other"; assumptions about the incontrovertible value of English around the world; and broad generalizations about "non-native" students' home cultures, rhetorical practices, and epistemologies. It is important to note that these ways of thinking were, and continue to be, produced and reinscribed not only in Western contexts but also globally through the teaching of English.

While imperialism and colonialism as economic and political forms of control fell out of vogue in the 20th century, colonial epistemology remains particularly sticky even in contemporary life, including in the context of the teaching of English. Although multilingualism continues to characterize the everyday lives of the vast majority of people worldwide, English's status as a *lingua franca* exists as a reminder of colonization's lasting global impact. English language pedagogy outside of Anglophone contexts, according to Phillipson (1992), perpetuates the dominance of English worldwide: Demand for English exists not to support colonization *per se*, but rather to accommodate so-called "market" forces, born out of colonization, which continue to privilege English. In other words, as Suresh Canagarajah (2019) pointed out, "literacy is a contested activity with ramifications for social and geopolitical life" (p. 9).

Rhetoric and Writing Studies as Transnational and Translingual

Throughout this book, I characterize SPC as an inherently *transnational* institution, by which I mean it was an institution comprised of "relationships that transcend the nation-state. . . . There are social ties and relationships that are not constrained by or contained within nation-state boundaries" (Canaga-rajah, 2018, p. 47). Although transnationality is characterized by relationships that go beyond the nation-state, it does not mean that ideas about *nation* and *nationality* are abandoned. The case of SPC shows how nationalism produced an imagined America that came into conflict with the college's students, faculty, and the local community specifically because the relationships among these parties was transnational. The transnational transformed language and pedagogical practices at the college, as well as created conflict due to competing epistemologies. In this section, I provide an overview of transnational and translingual research in rhetoric and writing studies with the aim of showing how this history contributes to this area of research.

Though the vast majority of its scholarship remains centered in the United States, rhetoric and writing studies has explored transnational sites of writing instruction, including transnational literacy practices.[9] Transnational research is important in rhetoric and writing studies because it can allow the discipline to "adapt, resituate, and perhaps decenter" our assumptions about writing programs and pedagogies (C. Donahue, 2009, p. 215). In other words, a transnational lens pushes the field to recognize writing research, pedagogy, and practice in languages other than English and in a variety of geographic locations around the world. The recognition of pluriversal traditions of writing research, pedagogy, and practice, in turn, disrupts the colonial epistemology that has historically limited the discipline and defined our work.

Even as awareness of international and transnational locations of writing grows in the field, transnational histories of literacy education are relatively scarce.[10] As You (2018) pointed out, historically, "writing education," even in

---

9   Scholarship in rhetoric and writing studies that focuses on transnational literacy practices include Charles Bazerman et al., 2012; Suresh Canagarajah, 2002; Conference on College Composition and Communication Statement, 2017; Nancy Bou Ayash, 2016, 2019; Rebecca Dingo, 2012; Christiane Donahue, 2009; Amber Engelson, 2014, 2024; Steve Fraiberg., 2017; Eileen Lagman, 2018; Jerry Won Lee & Christopher Jenks, 2016; Rebecca Lorimer Leonard, 2013, 2017; Mike MacDonald, 2015; David Martins, 2015; Vivette Milson-Whyte et al., 2019; Esther Milu, 2021; Mary Muchiri et al., 1995; Iswari Pandey, 2015; Anne Marie Pederson, 2010; Angela Rounsaville, 2015, 2017; Tricia Serviss, 2013; Rachael Shapiro, 2019; Patrick Sullivan et al., 2012; Chris Thaiss et al, 2012; Kate Vieira 2011, 2017, 2019; and Xiaoye You, 2016, 2023. Additional transnational scholarship has been published in special issues and sections of journals such as *Research in the Teaching of English*, Ellen Cushman & Mary Juzwik, 2014, and Mya Poe, 2014; and *College Composition and Communication*, Kathleen Blake Yancey, 2014, June, and also in the books published in the WAC Clearinghouse International Exchanges on the Study of Writing series.

10   A few of the transnational histories of college-level literacy instruction published in English include Lisa Arnold, 2014, 2016, 2018; Damián Baca, 2009; Joseph Jeyaraj, 2009; Paul Kei Matsuda, 2006; Susan Romano, 2004; Milson-Whyte, 2015; and You, 2010.

seemingly monolingual contexts, "has almost always been transnational" (p. 20). However, most disciplinary histories fail to recognize the ways in which students' literacy practices, even in monolingual or American contexts, represent transnational exchange. You (2010) noted that "for centuries, English . . . has been utilized by both monolingual and multilingual writers for various situated needs and desires" (p. 180). Transnational histories can help contemporary scholars and teachers better understand the different ways in which "English" and "writing" are defined, used, and valued across the globe. This will, in turn, help serve increasingly diverse student populations in the US and abroad. You (2010) critiqued rhetoric and writing scholars for generally lacking "cognizan[ce] of the geopolitical differences and stakes involved in the teaching of English writing" (p. xi). I argue that English at SPC was—and continues to be today—laden with "a whole different constellation of values and practices" than those that we tend to attach to English in the United States (You, 2010, p. xi).

Transnational histories of literacy education contribute to the decolonial project in that they delink the history of the discipline from presumed English monolingualism and highlight that knowledge is not universal but rather pluriversal and geopolitically situated. In other words, transnational histories emphasize the idea that knowledge "emerg[ed] from different historical locations in the world that endured the effects and consequences of Western imperial and capitalist expansion" (Mignolo, 2007, p. 462). Transnational histories of writing instruction such as this one illustrate how colonial epistemology, linked to the teaching of English and conceptions of the nation, was received, rejected, and negotiated—and with what consequences—in different ways by local populations around the world.

Transnational research also promotes new thinking about language, in that most sites of transnational literacy education are also multilingual, even when multilingual people and practices are devalued and oppressed. For this reason, I characterize SPC not only as transnational but also as an inherently *translingual* site of literacy education. Examining SPC as translingual means studying "the ways people come in contact through language and assum[ing] that most of the world's peoples, through much of the world's history, have used language in multiple and varied ways" (Kimball, 2021, p. 7). The translingual approach to writing practices and pedagogies addresses questions of language difference in writing (Horner, Lu, et al., 2011, p. 303) and emerges out of conversations related to the politics of globalization, multilingualism, second-language writing, World Englishes, and the *Students' Right to Their Own Language* statement (Smitherman, 1999). All of these conversations provide important critiques of the monolingualism that haunts our research and pedagogy, despite the fact that "language use in our classrooms, our communities, the nation, and the world has always been multilingual" (Horner, Lu, et al., 2011, p. 303). Literacy scholars including Eileen Lagman (2018), Jerry Won Lee and Christopher Jenks (2016), Rebecca Lorimer Leonard (2013, 2017), Esther Milu (2021), and Kate Vieira (2011, 2017, 2019), among others, have gone beyond the theoretical to trace tangible connections among multi- and translingual practices, mobility, and migration in transnational contexts of literacy.

A number of histories of the field have focused on multilingual populations in North America, even as they treat multilingualism itself with varying levels of emphasis. In *Refiguring Rhetorical Education*, for example, Jessica Enoch (2008) focused two chapters on women educators for Mexican/Mexican American and Native American students around the turn of the 20th century, highlighting especially the racial and gender identities of the pedagogues and students with relatively less attention paid to the multilingualism that also characterized their identities. Hui Wu (2007) examined the writing curriculum and pedagogy of Japanese internment camp schools during World War II, considering particularly the racialized identities of the students in relation to the injustice they suffered at the hands of the U.S. government. Wu mentioned but did not consider deeply how multilingualism may have influenced the educational environment or student-teacher interactions. In her book *Vernacular Insurrections*, Carmen Kynard (2013) considered Black student protest rhetoric in the context of the 1960s civil rights movement in the US She focused particularly on the relations among race, language—including African American Vernacular English—activism, and literacy education. Additionally, Cristina Devereaux Ramírez's (2015) analysis of writing in Spanish and English by Mexican and Mexican American women journalists from the late 19th to mid-20th centuries adds to the field's understanding of how these public-facing writing practices contributed to Mexican politics, culture, and identity. Throughout the book, Ramírez highlighted the multilingualism of her subjects and included Spanish primary texts along with their translations.

Two other scholars specifically uncovered histories of multi- and translingualism in the United States to demonstrate that the emergence of English as the dominant language was not a given. Focusing on the turn of the 19th century, Elizabeth Kimball (2021) analyzed archival materials from three different language communities in post-revolutionary Philadelphia through an explicitly translingual lens in *Translingual Inheritance*. Collectively, the three case studies she presented in the monograph argue that the story of English in the United States cannot be understood as a foregone conclusion but rather the result of "a story of the sedimentation of standard language ideologies in key moments of public deliberation" (Kimball, 2021, p. 38). Kimball's (2021) book presents a productive roadmap for translingual historiography, suggesting that such an approach provides a way to "read in and around [the influences of a particular language], examining both how people entered into conversation with ideas about language and how they used language itself to exercise agency" (p. 37). Jason Peters (2013) provided a historical account of an early-20th-century conflict between French-speaking New Englanders and the English-only educational policy of the Catholic Church. In this article, Peters drew on decolonial and Indigenous scholars to show how language hierarchization and enculturation has historically manifested in the United States. He argued that studying the conflict itself allows for a recognition of the geopolitics of language, including "the linguistic construction of racial and ethnic identity among white monolinguals," which in turn reveals Whiteness itself as a construction that covers up histories of oppression even in seemingly homogenous contexts (p. 578). The historical account that I present takes up a similar translingual historiographic approach in its exploration of the range of responses, and the agency, with which students and the local population approached and negotiated English literacy education at SPC.

A few rhetoric and writing scholars have specifically presented histories of the field that have emphasized both translingual and transnational relations, although they have not always explicitly named them as "translingual." Susan Romano (2004) highlighted translingual and transnational negotiation at the Colegio de Santa Cruz de Tlaltelolco, a 16th-century college in the Valley of Mexico, in order to prove the central role that colonialism has held in the field's history. She argued that the rhetorical negotiations that took place between Spanish colonizers and the Indigenous colonized in "New Spain," as seen at Tlaltelolco, have parallels to the contemporary history of rhetoric and writing studies in that the college was a "site designed for those perceived as needing instruction in the dominant culture's uses of language . . . [and] a site perceived as not properly carrying out this function" (Romano, 2004, p. 258). Paul Kei Matsuda (2006), in "The Myth of Linguistic Homogeneity in U.S. College Composition," presented a useful history of international students in U.S. higher education throughout the 19th and 20th centuries. He argued that rhetoric and writing studies' neglect of second-language writing and writers has problematically grounded the discipline on an assumption that the vast majority of students are English-speaking monolinguals. You's (2010) *Writing in the Devil's Tongue* is notable for its book-length treatment of the status and role of English, and its relationship to Chinese, in college-level writing instruction in China from the second half of the 19th century onward. Throughout the book, You underlined the political and cultural forces at work in and outside of formal educational contexts as China moved from a primarily monolingual educational system to a bilingual one through the introduction of

English. More recently, Florianne Jimenez (2023) described translingual student writing in the colonial context of the Philippines around the turn of the 20th century. Her historical and decolonial analysis focused on "language's role in colonization and resistance" and found that students displayed translingual agency even in English-only educational environments (Jimenez, 2023, p. 110).

For Cushman (2016), a translingual approach has the potential to support the decolonial project in rhetoric and writing studies in that, at the paradigmatic level, it can "hasten the process of revealing and potentially transforming colonial matrices of power" and at the pedagogical level, it "can also work . . . wherein students' languages and categories of understanding can be expressed in the classroom in ways that allow these knowledges and practices to persevere" (p. 235). At the same time, Cushman expressed caution about assuming that translingual theory *is inherently* decolonial—she argued that many liberal movements in the field, possibly including translingualism, have failed to achieve the goals of decoloniality because they do not question the core principles that comprise the foundation of the discipline (pp. 238–239). Translingual scholarship, Cushman (2016) argued, faces similar challenges, in that it "reveal[s] the ideologies established in modernity's colonial matrix of power" but does not necessarily "generate pluriversal understandings, values, and practices" (p. 239). In other words, while translingual theory succeeds in critiquing language ideology, it does not automatically transform the foundations of disciplinary knowledge or writing curriculum and pedagogies which are based upon that knowledge.

The historical account presented here attempts to circumvent the potential shortcomings raised by Cushman (2016) in that it asks questions about some of these principles—specifically, this study exposes the English monolingual and Anglocentric assumptions upon which the discipline's historical narratives, and its subsequent scholarship, are often grounded. I argue that the discipline's history is fundamentally transnational and translingual—a shift in perspective that allows us to rethink the work of the discipline. This perspective calls into question the field's reliance on writing pedagogies and curriculum that continually privilege the monolingualism, graphocentrism, and logocentrism that characterize colonial epistemology.[11] This perspective thus creates an imperative for the field to redefine itself beyond the borders

---

11   See Canagarajah's (2024) critique of dominant conceptualizations of writing pedagogy, which have continually privileged dominant (i.e. White, Western) epistemologies. He articulated well how the majority of these pedagogical approaches over time—including product- and process-oriented, social and cognitive, posthuman and multimodal, and second-language writing—maintain monolingual, graphocentric, and logocentric orientations toward knowledge (pp. 291-295).

it has historically drawn, and it helps paves the way for the field to recognize other, pluriversal ways of knowing and doing writing and rhetoric.

Decolonial Scholarship in Rhetoric and Writing Studies

In the field of rhetoric and writing studies, a discipline historically situated within the settler-colonial context of America, it is difficult to dislodge English from its ties to colonialism and to recognize the ways in which these ties continue to inflect our work as writing scholars and teachers today. Position statements such as Federico Navarro et al.'s (2022) "Rethinking English as a Lingua Franca in Scientific-Academic Contexts" and Bruce Horner, Min-Zhan Lu, et al.'s (2011) "Language Difference in Writing: Toward a Translingual Approach," and journal articles such as Horner, Samantha NeCamp, and Christiane Donahue's (2011) "Toward a Multilingual Composition Scholarship," Matsuda's (2006) "The Myth of Linguistic Homogeneity in U.S. College Composition," and Horner and John Trimbur's (2002) "English Only and U.S. College Composition," to name but a few, contribute to this work by imploring the field to question the standardization and dominance of English in the teaching of writing and publication of academic scholarship.

However, facing a 500-plus-year history of linguistic oppression *vis-à-vis* colonization and its related institutions (i.e., Indigenous boarding schools, slavery, Christian missions, English language teaching), rhetoric and writing studies is likely to be more successful in its efforts to dislodge monolingual ideology if it invests more deeply in adopting a decolonial perspective on its work. This means explicitly recognizing the colonial epistemology that underlies English-language literacy education and pushing for meaningful curricular and pedagogical change that investigates and invites pluriversal ways of thinking and doing rhetoric and literacy. In this section, I provide an overview of decolonial scholarship in rhetoric and writing studies and how my work contributes to this conversation.

A number of scholars in rhetoric and writing studies have recently shown the necessity of decolonial perspectives for the discipline.[12] Decolonial scholars in rhetoric and writing studies collectively ask: "How can teachers and

---

12   Some of the rhetoric and writing studies scholars who have taken up a decolonial lens include Maryam Ahmad, 2023; Kristin L. Arola, 2018; Baca, 2009; Resa Crane Bizzaro & Patrick Bizzaro, 2023; Canagarajah, 2019, 2023, 2024; Ellen Cushman, 2016; Cushman et al., 2021, 2015; Tabitha Espina, 2023; García et al., 2023; Tamara Issak and Lana Oweidat, 2023; Rachel C. Jackson, 2021, 2023; Florianne Jimenez, 2023; Kelsey Dayle John, 2023; Eunjeong Lee, 2022; Cruz Medina, 2019; Mya Poe, 2022; Nora K. Rivera, 2020; Iris Ruiz, 2016, 2021; Ruiz and Baca, 2017; Rachael Shapiro and Missy Watson, 2022; Vieira, 2023; and Qianqian Zhang-Wu, 2021, 2023.

scholars move beyond the presumption that *English* is the *only* language of knowledge making and learning?" (Cushman, 2016, p. 234). Decolonialism moves the discipline from graphocentric to geopolitical orientations: Iris Ruiz and Damián Baca (2017) argued that "decolonizing [writing studies] involves rethinking and revising the field's teleological macro-narratives of human progress, with whitened, Europeanized fourth-century Greeks cemented as the field's intellectual cradle" (p. 226). Ruiz (2021), in her chapter on disciplinary research traditions, argued we must question "current critical methods" because they "are embedded in traditions of Whiteness and Western oriented epistemologies" (p. 39). And Canagarajah (2024) traced "'autonomous' and 'graphocentric'" conceptions of literacy to a Eurocentric ontology that has "had powerful influences on writing pedagogy in educational institutions" (p. 291). Historically, these pedagogies have valued the finished text and approached writing and reading as primarily *mental* processes over which individuals can gain control through a focus on structure, cohesion, and coherence (p. 292). While contemporary approaches to the teaching of writing emphasize its social, contextual, and multimodal components, Canagarajah noted that these approaches "also lack the geopolitical perspective, critical edge, and archival work that inform decolonizing approaches" (p. 293; see also Canagarajah, 2019; Rivera, 2020).

Additionally, rhetoric and writing scholars who have taken up decolonial perspectives highlight language and literacy practices as embodied, relational, and racialized, in contrast to the "deracialized and disembodied politics" of the monolingual ideology that has historically saturated the discipline (Do, 2022, p. 453). Recognizing language practices as both corporeal and networked, Canagarajah (2024) pointed out, disrupts colonialism's—and the discipline's— prioritization of "cognitivism, logocentrism, and individualism" (p. 292). Indeed, Mya Poe (2022) advocated for a writing pedagogy that complicates the development of Western thought as "a series of epistemological developments and exchanges" among a variety of stakeholders rather than a straightforward, linear progression of thought over time. Milu (2021) and Tom Hong Do (2022) both problematized the discipline's tendency to homogenize multilingual and globally connected student populations in the US. Instead, they argued, racial, national, and linguistic differences are tied to colonialism and therefore produce embodied experiences of literacy and literacy education that cannot be universalized (see also Do & Rowan, 2022; Jiang, 2024; E. Lee, 2024). Such embodiment, Cushman et al. (2015) highlighted, should not be reduced to only those who are "marked" in Western culture by the color of their skin or the accent on their tongue: In their critique of the discipline for "reif[ying] the position and imposition of English only," they tied English's position "at the top of the language hierarchy" to Whiteness, an invisible racial presence that produces "a monolithic baseline against which all other [people] are labeled" (p. 333).

All these scholars suggest that a decolonial lens offers more promise than other approaches (such as those informed by Marxism or postcolonialism) in forwarding the discipline's social justice efforts. Other approaches often, according to Cushman (2016), "fall short of their social justice goals because they critique a content or place of practice without revealing and altering their own structuring tenets" (p. 239). In fact, "social justice" is a term used broadly within the field to designate any approach meant to lessen social inequality. However, as a "structuring tenet" of much research and curricular development within rhetoric and writing studies, the idea of "social justice" cannot be understood as universal. In her discussion of "linguistic justice," Ligia Mihut (2020) noted that transnational writing teacher-scholars' definitions of what constitutes "linguistic justice" are dynamic and "largely geographical/socio-politically dependent," informed by individuals' social positioning and their experience(s) with(in) U.S.-based and extra-U.S. contexts of teaching, writing, and research (p. 273). Along similar lines, Keith Gilyard (2016) gently critiqued translingual theory—a strand of writing studies generally assumed to promote social justice—for its tendency to present "language as an abstraction" and to universalize or "flatten[] language differences" (p. 284). I too have called attention to the ways in which power inflects language practices and is particularly heightened in non-Anglo contexts where English carries what I have called a different "weight," or "a power dynamic that affects those using so-called 'non-standard' varieties of English" (Arnold, 2021, p. 189; see also Vieira, 2019). And Milu (2021) called for a pedagogy that highlights rather than reduces Black students' experiences with language ideology as differently *raced* and *colonized* depending on those students' transnational affiliations and backgrounds. Even when students are encouraged to draw from their many linguistic resources in the writing classroom in the interest of promoting social justice, rhetoric and writing studies scholars have shown that many students still conceive of literacy through a monolingual lens and are unwilling or reluctant to take risks that run counter to English monolingualism (see for example Arnold, 2018; Medina, 2019; R. Shapiro & Watson, 2022; Zhang-Wu, 2023). Definitions of "linguistic social justice," then, must be understood as highly contextual, heterogeneous, and historically situated. Chapters 3 and 5 in this book provide concrete examples that resist universal understandings of language and power.

Another "structuring tenet" of rhetoric and writing studies is the concept of "citizenship." The concept of citizenship, and the development of a "critical citizenship," has long been assumed to be an unquestionably positive outcome of writing pedagogy, as well as higher education more generally. Amy Wan (2011) critiqued the rhetorical power of the concept of "citizenship" that pervades scholarship in English studies as well as many of the discipline's professional documents, writing: "At its core, the citizenship we create through literacy is aspirational, a promise" (46). The field's contemporary attraction to the ostensibly "uncontrovertible" stronghold of the "production of the citizen" (Wan, 2011, p. 28) in the writing classroom can be linked to public nationalist rhetoric and official U.S. policy surrounding the "new" wave of immigrant populations around the turn of the 20th century. Both NeCamp (2014) and C. Kendall Theado (2013) suggested that the "army" of immigrants (as cited in NeCamp, 2014, p. 12) who arrived in the United States between 1880 and 1920 prompted legislation linking the concept of Americanness with literacy. Specifically, many of the educational projects developed in response to the wave of immigrants were intended to "creat[e] a literate public that could support democratic government and preserve 'traditional' American values" (NeCamp, 2014, p. 13) and thus "[link]" literacy "with the ideal American identity" (Kendall Theado, 2013, p. 712).

In contrast to its approach toward enculturating new immigrants to American culture and values, the US has also historically allowed for the disenfranchisement of African Americans and other minority populations by using literacy as a weapon with which members of these groups were barred from voting and not provided with equal educational opportunities. A decolonial approach highlights the historical connections between literacy, history, culture, nation, and citizenship—effectively delinking them—and asks in response: When educators promote "citizenship," what kind of citizen do they mean? To which nation, race, ethnicity, religion, or gender do ideal "citizens" belong, and what kind of literate behavior is expected of them? What are the goals of literacy education for those who have historically been excluded from civic or social life, who are denied or cannot obtain citizenship in the nation where they reside, or for whom citizenship has been used as a tool of oppression (see Bloom, 2018; Ribero, 2016)? In the context of SPC, I problematize universal constructions of citizenship in Chapter 4.

A decolonial perspective helps identify and complicate the uncritical deployment of "social justice," "citizenship," and other key concepts in writing studies, which are often understood as universal when they in fact represent one of many ways of thinking about literacy and literacy education. We can approach the seeming inevitability of monolingualism and English as a *lingua franca* similarly and draw from a more nuanced understanding of the history of these developments to productively question the modern history of rhetoric and writing studies. This history traditionally has been conceptualized as a monolingual, monocultural, and Anglocentric history. This key assumption about the field has shaped (and continues to shape) scholarship in rhetoric and writing studies in fundamental ways, resulting in limiting perspectives about the scope of the discipline and approaches to writing instruction and curriculum. In the next section and throughout the rest of this book, I expose the "structuring tenets" (Cushman, 2016, p. 239) of English monolingualism and Anglocentrism as ideologies grounding the discipline's historiography, and I make the case for a decolonial (re)imagining the discipline's history as transnational and translingual.

Toward a Decolonial Historiography in Rhetoric and Writing Studies

As part of the process of its stabilization and legitimation as an academic discipline, rhetoric and writing studies has, over decades, constructed historical narratives about itself that have in many ways determined the field's focus and scope. These narratives, I argue, rely on historiography grounded in colonial epistemology, and they have been used even in contemporary scholarship that seeks to disrupt the same narratives. The first historicization of the discipline is often traced to Albert Kitzhaber's (1953) dissertation, *Rhetoric in American Colleges* (published as a monograph in 1990), which one reviewer characterized as the study that "ushered in the discipline as we know it" (Morris, 1991, p. 472). This trend toward disciplinary historicization grew significantly in the 1980s and 1990s with the publication of histories of the discipline, including those written by James Berlin (1984; 1987), Susan Miller (1991), Robert Connors (1997), Thomas Miller (1997), and Sharon Crowley (1998). These historians, focusing primarily on 19th- and 20th-century elite colleges with textbooks and other written materials as evidence, constructed an Anglocentric disciplinary history. Later histories published over the last 20 years have sought to complicate these initial constructions of the discipline with sharper focuses on non-elite, working class, and sometimes transnational sites of adult writing instruction, as well as on diverse student populations.[13]

---

13   Some of the historians who have complicated these initial historical narratives include Arnold, 2014, 2016, 2018; Baca, 2009; Amy Dayton-Wood, 2012; Patricia Donahue & Gretchen Flesher Moon, 2007; Katherine Fredlund, 2021; Jessica Enoch, 2008; Candace Epps-Robertson, 2018; David Gold, 2008; Jane Greer, 1999, 2015, 2023; Jaclyn Hilberg, 2020; Susan Jarratt, 2009; Jeyaraj, 2009; Emily Legg, 2014; Sue Mendelsohn, 2017; Milson-Whyte, 2015; M. Amanda Moulder, 2011; Samantha NeCamp. 2014; Susan Romano, 2004; Jacqueline Jones Royster & Jean C. Williams, 1999; Ruiz, 2016; Mira Shimabukuro, 2011; Patricia Sullivan, 2012; Hui Wu, 2007; You, 2010; Michelle Zaleski, 2017; Scott Zaluda, 1998.

In spite of more recent historical work, the discipline's first historians and their historiography were highly influential, and the narratives they produced are repeated almost without question today. These narratives are particularly important because they emerged at a time when rhetoric and writing studies was marking itself as a discipline distinct from closely related fields, including literature, linguistics, and communication. Two narratives that have proven especially important to establishing rhetoric and writing studies as a discipline, and which remain familiar today, include what I call the "Harvard narrative" and the "decline and fall narrative." The Harvard narrative ties the foundations of the contemporary discipline to the establishment of first-year writing at Harvard in the late 19th century, when Harvard moved from the classical model of education to the modern liberal arts curriculum that we associate with most American or American-style universities today. The "decline-and-fall" narrative is similar to the Harvard narrative in that it identifies Harvard's shift away from a classical, or rhetorical, curriculum as key to the disciplinary history of rhetoric and writing studies, but it ties the discipline to a much longer and renowned history— the Western rhetorical tradition. For example, Connors (1997) lamented the "decline and fall" of rhetorical instruction in the American university and linked this fall to composition's low status in contemporary higher education; according to Connors, rhetoric courses were "sought by students" prior to the Civil War, but by the turn of the century, such courses were instead "despised and sneered at"; and while professors of rhetoric once occupied the "empyrean of named chairs," they became, over time, "oppressed, ill-used, and secretly despised" (pp. 171–172). Rhetorically speaking, the decline-and-fall narrative enables the field to construct a "narrative of retreat [from] and return [to]" a much longer Western rhetorical tradition (Hawk, 2007, p. 14). Both narratives have worked to help establish rhetoric and writing studies as a stand-alone discipline: Tying the discipline to Harvard is useful because it provides a concrete and recognizable origin point for the establishment of first-year writing in American higher education. Tying the discipline to a longer rhetorical tradition is useful because that tradition holds a high status in academia that is comparable to the status of literature.

At the same time, both the Harvard and decline-and-fall narratives prove problematic when examined through a decolonial lens. The Harvard narrative has been constructed through evidence based on textbooks and other written materials from selective and primarily White institutions of higher education. Such archival materials are limited in scope and representation. The Harvard narrative assumes that rhetorical education ended on a broader scale after Harvard changed its curriculum—a fact that has been persuasively challenged by a number of disciplinary historians over the last 20 years.[14] The decline-and-fall narrative is problematic through a decolonial lens because it assumes there is a logical throughline that can be traced from ancient Greek rhetoric to present-day American literacy education. The narrative assumes a linear historical progression that relies on Western thought as the primary marker of progress—what Mignolo (2007) called the colonial rhetoric of modernity. Further, the narrative seeks to create an ahistorical equivalence between the past and the present that fails to acknowledge important geopolitical, historical, and linguistic differences that make such equivalence deeply problematic. Finally, true to its colonial foundations, the narrative constructs a hierarchy of knowledge that assumes that Western "classical" or "rhetorical" approaches to literacy education are superior to others.

Rhetoric and writing scholars have relied on and repeated these narratives in different forms to substantiate their contributions and add legitimacy to the discipline. This historicization has worked, rhetorically and politically, to highlight and complicate some of the central concerns of the field, such as best practices for the teaching of writing, the role of first-year writing and its legacy as a "service" course in American higher education, and the field's interdisciplinary ties to rhetoric, literature, communications, education, and linguistics. This historicization has also raised questions about, and prompted proposals for, the future of the discipline. Disciplinary historiography and historical understanding, in other words, affect contemporary teaching and research in rhetoric and writing studies. For this reason, scholars must consider not only how these historical narratives have shaped the discipline, but also how to productively question and potentially dislodge the assumptions underlying those narratives.

For an example of what can be gained by rethinking these narratives through a decolonial lens, I would like to show how one historical account of the discipline makes a valuable, potentially decolonial argument about monolingual ideology but falls short of shifting disciplinary knowledge because it relies on both the Harvard and decline-and-fall narratives. Horner and Trimbur's (2002) article, "English Only and U.S. College Composition," won the 2003 Conference on College Composition and Communication (CCCC) Richard Braddock award for the best article published in *College Composition and Communication* (CCCC, n.d.), considered one of the discipline's flagship journals. This article is significant because in it, Horner and Trimbur (2002)

---

14   For example, Enoch, 2008, Gold, 2008, Jarratt, 2009, and Ruiz, 2016, have effectively complicated this assumption, providing evidence from other institutional, geographical, and cultural contexts demonstrating that rhetorical education continued in other institutions around the turn of the 20th century.

questioned how "a tacit, unidirectional monolingual language policy" came to dominate the teaching of writing at Harvard (and ostensibly other American colleges and universities) in the mid- to late-19th century (p. 595). Horner and Trimbur relied upon both the Harvard and decline-and-fall narratives to argue that Harvard's shift from a classical to liberal arts curriculum effectively "territorialized" and sidelined foreign languages in the modern curriculum, leading to the reification of a problematic English-only approach to writing pedagogy and programs that persists today. Following the same logic as the decline-and-fall narrative, they implicitly suggested that the classical curriculum that preceded Harvard's shift in curriculum was superior because it centered the study of multiple languages. At the time of its publication, Horner and Trimbur's article was one of the first to analyze the workings of monolingual ideology in writing pedagogy through a historical lens.

While Horner and Trimbur's (2002) analysis is important when contextualized as a new reading of the discipline's history that exposes how monolingual ideology gained traction in the field, it is problematically grounded on both the Harvard and decline-and-fall narratives. Specifically, Horner and Trimbur did not question the accuracy of the Harvard or the decline-and-fall narratives as representations of actual writing curriculum and pedagogies throughout the United States in the mid- to late-19th century. Additionally, while they acknowledged that students and faculty were dissatisfied with the "translation English" approaches to language instruction at Harvard prior to the shift, Horner and Trimbur did not question the implications of the fact that only Western languages (i.e. Greek, Latin, French, German, and Italian) were taught at Harvard prior to, and after, the shift (p. 596).

Possibly because they relied on previously published historical narratives about the discipline to make their case, Horner and Trimbur (2002) focused on *the fact of the shift* at Harvard, rather than asking *why* the shift at Harvard occurred or even whether the previous historical accounts they relied on are representational. If we scholars in rhetoric and writing studies shift our focus to *why*, we can (re)consider the foundation of modern writing instruction in the US, and thus the roots of our disciplinary knowledge, as colonial. A decolonial lens would suggest that Harvard and other elite colleges changed their curriculum in part as a response to translingual and transnational discourses that existed and circulated in the same historical and geopolitical context of the mid- to late-19th century. Institutional curricular changes and language policies deliberately meant to suppress these discourses.

Transnational and translingual discourses—visible in the US during this time period as a result of waves of new immigrants, the abolition of slavery, and the continued displacement of Indigenous people from their land—posed threats to the settler-colonial structures, ways of life, and established social hierarchies foundational to the new United States and at institutions such as Harvard. These threats pushed Harvard and other institutions to change the curriculum to promote English and Anglophone culture—and with it, American nationalist and monolingual ideologies—while suppressing multilingual practices and transnational perspectives. Transnational and translingual discourses in the context of colonial epistemology constitute an absent presence that much of the discipline's historiography has ignored or has treated as separate and disconnected from primarily White, monolingual contexts of education. As much value as Horner and Trimbur's (2002) analysis has brought to the discipline in raising awareness about how English-only monolingualism gained traction in U.S. writing classrooms, it falls short of questioning the roots of disciplinary knowledge, which is based in part on the discipline's historical narratives.

Institutional curricula and language policies were (and continue to be) responses to extra-institutional realities. The historiography of rhetoric and writing studies has focused more on the *inside* of institutions of higher education than on the discourses circulating *outside*, and it has not gone far enough in analyzing how those (sometimes competing) discourses affected institutional decision-making. An example of such analysis would consider translingual and transnational discourse in the context of Harvard's founding in the early 17th century, as well as broader shifts in American culture and American higher education during the mid- to late-19th century, in relation to the introduction of a general writing requirement. Harvard and other elite colleges and universities were founded in a pre-revolutionary American colonial context. The Anglo-European wealth upon which these early institutions were built was generated in large part through the deeply transnational and translingual enterprise of slavery (Smith & Ellis, 2017).

Moving forward into the 19th century, the United States continued to expand through settler colonial practices that were transnational and translingual; in order to build the nation, the federal government illegally gave away to settlers, including new immigrants, land owned by Indigenous nations across the continent. In tandem with these developments, "land-grant" colleges and universities were established on stolen land (see U.S. National Archives and Records Administration, n.d.). Much of the success of settler colonialism in the United States was dependent on English-language literacy, a rejection of Indigenous sovereignty, the suppression of Native languages and voices, and the maintenance of existing social class structures.

The establishment of Historically Black Colleges and Universities (HBCUs) particularly during the post-Civil War Reconstruction era attests to both the success of former slaves in demanding and acquiring higher education but also the reality of Jim Crow laws in the U.S. south, which maintained racial segregation and prevented many Black people from enrolling in already established colleges and universities. Scholars recognize today that HBCUs played (and continue to play) an important role in supporting the translingual practices of African Americans.

Another example of the largely unacknowledged circulation of transnational and translingual discourse was uncovered in Matsuda's (2006) account of international students in U.S. higher education during the 19th and 20th centuries. The presence of these students, and the transnational and translingual discourses they brought with them, led to the development of policies of what Matsuda called "linguistic containment," or multilingual exclusion, in writing curriculum. Linguistic containment, Matsuda argued, further reified monolingual ideology and the construction of what he terms the "myth of linguistic homogeneity" in rhetoric and writing studies today.

To add another layer to this analysis, as Kimball (2021) made clear, English was not the inevitable language of the United States in the late 18th century, when the republic was new. Other colonial languages, such as French and Spanish, circulated throughout North American colonial territories during the 18th and 19th centuries. Together, these colonial languages contributed to the erasure of other languages, such as those spoken by newer immigrants, African Americans, and Indigenous peoples. What's more, the emergence of the doctrine of individualism (Spack, 2002, p. 29) and nationalism, both of which are linked to colonial epistemology and spread through discourse, contributed to the erasure of languages other than English in the United States. In her study of how English was imposed upon, and then used by, Native peoples in the United States during the 19th and 20h centuries, Ruth Spack (2002) argued that 19th-century individualism led European Americans to understand the communalism characteristic of Native tribes as "barbaric"; English was "the language of individualists," and as such, Anglo Americans "believed" the language was "capable of breaking [the] barrier [to Native peoples' acculturation] and thus of improving students' lives" (Spack, 2002, p. 29). English, therefore, was used as a tool for colonization, in that it became "[tied] . . . to the notion of progress in civilization" and was promoted at the same time as other languages were wiped from the mouths of Indigenous peoples (Spack, 2002, p. 30). As such, we must understand institutional moves to promote English, within and outside of the United States and often at the expense of other languages, not merely as internal curricular decisions but as responses to translingual and transnational realities outside of the institution.

A decolonial lens allows for seeing that institutional shifts such as those that occurred at Harvard in the mid- to late-19th century run parallel to, and in conversation with, larger cultural shifts in which colonial epistemology is both foundational and oppressive. Calling her historiographic approach translingual, though I would also call it decolonial, Kimball (2021) urged researchers to "first recognize an overarching, centripetal power of 'English' over . . . discourses, and . . . then do our best to read across—to transgress—our own familiar ideas of . . . discourses and languages alike, keeping the languaging of the languages always in the foreground, and reading especially for the absences created" (p. 62).

The decolonial historiographic approach that I take in this book builds upon Kimball's (2021) approach in two important ways. First, this approach highlights the value of examining transnational and translingual histories such as SPC's history through a decolonial lens. Second, this approach allows for an understanding of histories such as this one as evidence of the power of English monolingual and American nationalist ideologies in determining literacy curriculum and language policy more generally. Throughout this book, I show that SPC's curriculum and policy were meant to suppress translingual and transnational discourses both internal and external to the college. Indeed, monolingualism and American nationalism *are evidence of* the presence of transnational and translingual voices: Monolingualism and nationalism are direct ideological responses to the threats posed by such discourse. While translingual and transnational discourses were certainly more visible at SPC than they were at Harvard and other American institutions during the same period due to SPC's specific geopolitical location, a decolonial examination of seemingly monolingual literacy curricula and language policies can illuminate extant translingual and transnational discourses and therefore show how these discourses in fact shaped seemingly monolingual literacy curricula and language policies both in and outside of the US.

In this way, I argue, the history of rhetoric and writing studies can be understood as deeply transnational and translingual. The discipline's representation of its history—through a historiography grounded in colonial epistemology—has been limited by primarily focusing on monolingual practices and pedagogies rather than investigating the translingual and transnational contexts in which monolingualism and nationalism operate. A decolonial, translingual, and transnational historiography requires not only an exploration of contexts of literacy education outside of the United States, as I do here, but also an examination of the transnational and translingual contexts in which institutions such as Harvard were motivated to promote monolingual and Anglocentric ideologies. Traces of translingual and transnational discourses in histories of the field that have accounted for the educational experiences of non-White and multilingual populations inside the US can be seen (see my discussion of these histories earlier in this chapter). These traces can be interrogated further. But scholars can also reconceptualize the discipline's history as translingual and transnational by revis(it)ing the foundational accounts of seemingly White monolingual and monocultural contexts of higher education. Even when translingual practices and transnational perspectives are not visible in institutional records, scholars can re-examine language policies, curricular decisions, and other archival materials as *responses to* a larger context that included translingual and transnational discourses, which institutions of higher education have long sought to suppress. This revisioning of the discipline's historical foundations also encourages contemporary writing scholars and teachers to study and learn from non-Anglophone contexts of writing instruction and apply this new knowledge to their own teaching and research going forward.

Chapter Overview

In the next chapter of this book (Chapter 2), I provide deeper context for Syrian Protestant College as an institution that has a specific geopolitical and transnational history. This context helps establish the significance of SPC as a site of colonial literacy education and its relevance to the field of rhetoric and writing studies. Specifically, I outline social and educational developments in the Ottoman Empire and Syria during the 19th century. Additionally, I provide an overview of the modern history of Christian missions in the region and the missionary organization that was tied to SPC: ABCFM. Throughout this discussion, I establish the strong ties that bind colonial epistemology and American nationalism to literacy education at SPC as well as the ways in which the larger geopolitical context fostered the establishment of such ties. Appendix A, which provides enrollment and demographic information for Syrian Protestant College, supplements this chapter and the next three.

The following three chapters analyze specific moments in SPC's history that illustrate well how colonial epistemology is transmitted and sustained through literacy education. In Chapter 3, I show how common, specifically American, understandings and assumptions about literacy move across national, cultural, and linguistic borders through curriculum and policy. Specifically, I analyze archival documents such as SPC's annual reports, course catalogues, and other materials in light of existing histories of writing instruction in the US in order to make connections between SPC and its North American counterparts. This inquiry demonstrates how the idea of America was exported in and through literacy curriculum and language policy at SPC while interacting with the colonial logics of Christian missionary work. The process of exportation was never smooth or complete, however, as it interacted with sociocultural, political, and linguistic realities on the ground in Greater Syria and the Ottoman Empire. For example, in contrast to the shift toward monolingualism that occurred at many U.S.-based institutions of higher education at the turn of the 20th century, SPC's curriculum remained solidly multilingual. At the same time, while SPC's administrators and faculty debated the merits of teaching primarily in the Arabic vernacular or in English (ultimately deciding on English), the terms of the debate upheld the power, paternalism, and coloniality of the college's American founders.

The analysis presented in Chapter 3 illustrates how colonial assumptions about culture, language, and identity become rooted within literacy education and policy, resulting in the racism and xenophobia that underlies much of the history (and to some extent the present) of writing instruction. The example of SPC also points to the limits of scholars' and educators' understandings of what writing and literacy in English (and in other languages) mean outside of Anglophone contexts, where English carries a different "weight"—a different material value—for multilinguals. This analysis, in other words, arms teachers and scholars committed to social justice with a way to recognize the processes by which colonial epistemology becomes attached to literacy education through seemingly mundane features of writing education, such as curriculum and policy.

The focus of Chapter 4 is on two moments of student protest at SPC, during which students drew upon their literacy education and an imagined America to negotiate their educational goals with the college's American administrators and faculty. In the first moment of protest, the 1882 "Lewis Affair," students spoke up in response to the forced resignation of a beloved professor in the medical school. They wrote a series of petitions to the college administrators, using rhetorical appeals that leaned heavily on American values and beliefs. During the academic year 1908–1909, students staged a second, more prolonged protest after a visiting missionary gave an Islamophobic sermon during the college's required chapel service. Muslim and Jewish students of the college refused to attend chapel and attempted to force a change in the college's policy, which required attendance at all chapel services regardless of students' religious identities. This protest, known as the "Muslim Controversy," is notable in that it demonstrates how SPC students drew upon their literacy education to spark debate not only within the college but also among local and regional community members: By the end of the year, more than 60 articles in Beirut- and Cairo-based newspapers and journals had been published about the controversy, largely as a result of the literacy work of the protesting students.

Both student protests failed to enact change, and my examination in Chapter 4 of the petitions and other written documents surrounding the protests identifies this failure as largely epistemological. Specifically, the protests highlight competing understandings about what America represented in the region, what an American education meant, and whom such an education was for. Additionally, students' writing during the protests illustrate their attempts to identify themselves as distinct from, but also a part of, the America signified in and through the college. Students learned through their failed protests that the literacy education that they received at SPC was not neutral and was ultimately meant to serve colonial interests rather than their own. This analysis provides rhetoric and writing scholars a more nuanced picture of the ways in which contradictory definitions of literacy and the desires of stakeholders define writing instruction today. Additionally, scholars and educators can gain a better appreciation for the reasons why students from historically underrepresented groups may resist writing pedagogy or otherwise struggle in the American writing classroom. SPC students' experiences of the tension between the epistemologies attached to literacy education, particularly in English, have parallels to the experiences of many students today.

Similar tensions are explored in Chapter 5, in which the focus is centered on student writing produced in nearly 50 English- and Arabic-language student magazines and newspapers published between 1899 and 1920 at SPC (Appendix B provides a full listing of these publications). On the one hand, the student writing produced during this time period is important to the history of rhetoric and writing studies because it illustrates not only student and teacher engagement with and support for writing at the college but also the college's role in sponsoring literacy even outside the bounds of the classroom. However, more than its significance for the historical record, the student writing analyzed in this chapter reflects students' negotiation of their identities as multilingual Arabs living in a rapidly changing geopolitical context and schooled within a Western colonial frame.

Throughout Chapter 5, I provide specific examples of the relationships among extracurricular student writing, language, nationalism, and identity. Additionally, I show how their publications highlight how students both constructed an imagined America through writing and at the same time also used writing—particularly writing in Arabic—to critique and sometimes resist the dominant colonial epistemology characterized by SPC as an institution and also the literacy education it provided. My analysis in this chapter suggests that the English language served as a constraint for students, as they expressed themselves in markedly different ways when writing in Arabic. Rhetoric and writing scholars and teachers benefit from the examination presented in this chapter in that it drives us to conduct a more thoughtful accounting of the ways in which multilingual learners may encounter and experience the English-language writing classroom. Specifically, our classrooms may unwittingly (pre)determine the rhetorical stances and claims that historically underrepresented students and multilingual students can make due to the historical ties between coloniality and the teaching of English.

I conclude the book with Chapter 6 by synthesizing six ways in which SPC's version of literacy education, as explicated in Chapters 3, 4, and 5, conveyed implicit and often false promises to its students about what might be achieved in and through literacy. Literacy education at SPC, I argue, was deeply tied to ideologies of American nationalism and English monolingualism, clear markers of colonial epistemology. I first trace how the archival evidence presented in the book explicates the relationship among power, language, and literacy education through its nuanced examination of materials in both Arabic and English as well as in the experience of multilingual students. Second, the archival materials examined in this study also reveal that the "weight" of English is highly variable and contextual, dependent upon historical and geographical factors as well as personal identity and even imagined futures. Third, I reiterate how the analysis presented throughout the book affirms Phillipson's (1992) and Pennycook's (1998) claims that English literacy education outside of Anglophone contexts is profoundly entwined with colonial epistemology. As a fourth point, I review the evidence presented in earlier chapters that reveals how language constructs place, identity, nationhood, and belonging through epistemology. Fifth, I highlight how the specifically transnational and translingual context of SPC created the conditions for the high stakes and implicit promises that students experienced in their pursuit of literacy, particularly in English. Sixth, I point to evidence in the historical record that reveals student agency in their literacy education and their deployment of this agency to complicate the imagined America constructed by the college.

Finally, I underline in Chapter 6 the larger implications of this study for the field of rhetoric and writing studies. I argue that scholars, program administrators, and teachers have much to gain from the decolonial historiographic approach that I enact throughout this book. Studies such as this one add to a growing body of evidence that the history of the discipline is, at its foundation, deeply transnational and translingual. This new understanding of the history of rhetoric and writing studies, in turn, calls the discipline's "structuring tenets" (Cushman, 2016, p. 239) into question and enables us to more clearly see the limitations that such tenets have created for the field's scope. A decolonial lens, I argue, brings into view not only the problems of our past but also pluriversal understandings of writing and rhetoric that can enrich our work in the future and ultimately serve *all* our students well.

2 Syrian Protestant College Within Its Historical Context

For those born and educated in the Western world, such as myself, it is incredibly difficult to identify colonial epistemologies as such, because these ways of seeing the world are so deeply intertwined with our identity and our geopolitical location. It is often difficult to understand and respond effectively when our approaches to literacy education are challenged by scholars whose personal histories are marked by colonization and subordination, because we do not see how our own visions of literacy education have been colonized. Part of this conflict occurs because we do not have a full or nuanced understanding of history. Therefore, looking at the historical context surrounding literacy education during the colonial era, particularly in a geographical context that is often referred to as the intersection of the West and the East, can help make visible the ways in which colonialism has shaped the ways we have historically engaged, and in many cases continue to engage, in literacy education and writing research in Western contexts.

In his book, *Learning to Divide the World*, Willinsky (1998) demonstrated how Christianity and Western education worked in tandem to support colonialism and the "moral economy of empire" (p. 91). Colonial schools, Willinsky explained, were both removed from but implicated in empire in that they insisted on the production and spread of a particular kind of knowledge, which created "peculiar and powerful ideas of race, culture, and nation" that continue to exist today (pp. 2–3). While Willinsky's focus was on schools established within colonial outposts, his larger point still applies to the Protestant and Jesuit schools that were established around the world outside of official Western spheres of influence—as was the case of American Protestant mission schools in the Ottoman Empire. The missionaries who established these schools did so not as the result of an official mandate or in the interest of empire, but because they sincerely believed that God had called them to spread the "good word" around the world. But, as this chapter shows, their methods were largely informed by colonial epistemologies, which assumed that Christian and Western ways of knowing were superior to the local population's beliefs, values, and knowledge. In other words, it was a colonial mindset that allowed missionaries to justify their work, to cast judgment on the populations that hosted them, and to insist that others adopt (or pretend to adopt) these epistemologies in order to access the resources offered by the missionaries.

In order to understand the significance of Syrian Protestant College (SPC) as a site of colonial literacy education, it is necessary to recognize the broader context and epistemological currents in which the institution was founded. In this chapter, therefore, I first provide an overview of the geopolitical context, including relevant social and educational developments in 19th-century Ottoman Empire and Syria. Because SPC was founded by American Protestant missionaries, I next provide a history of Christian missions in the region and discuss how the mission context led to the establishment of SPC.

The Larger Geopolitical Context

SPC was located in Syria (present-day Lebanon), in the Beirut *wilaya* (state). At the time of the college's founding in 1866, Syria was part of the Ottoman Empire. In this section, I provide an overview of the political, social, and educational history of the Ottoman Empire in the 19th and early 20th centuries, a time of great change and precarity. The period between 1839 and 1876, known as the Tanzimat period, promoted societal reforms and relatively modern ideas such as the right to life, property, and honor, as well as equality of all men regardless of religion (Faroqhi, 2004/2009; Masters, 2013). Changes in property law led to the privatization of land and creation of large estates. Bureaucracy was modernized during the Tanzimat and throughout the reign of Sultan Abdulhamid between 1876–1909. For example, the Tanzimat ushered in modernizations such as paper money, taxation, post offices, a census, identity cards, telegraphs, modern universities, and ministries of education and healthcare.

The Ottomans were economically and politically tied to Europe throughout the 19th century (Masters, 2013). The Anglo-Ottoman Treaty of 1838 ensured Britain's support in reclaiming Syria during Egypt's occupation of the region. Further, trade tended to privilege Europe, and British traders could settle anywhere in the Empire without paying taxes. France and Britain allied with the Empire against Russia in the mid-century Crimean War. Manufacturers entered the global market and took on debt. The Empire's bankruptcy in 1875 meant an increased reliance on Europe to address the debt; the Ottoman Public Debt Administration was created in 1881 and was managed by several European countries.

Inspired by democratic ideals spreading throughout Europe at the time, a group known as the Young Ottomans briefly worked with Abdulhamid to establish a constitution and Parliament in 1876, but both were dissolved by the Sultan in 1878. Abdulhamid retained his power until 1908, when the Young Turks staged a revolution and took power. World War I brought the dissolution of the empire.

Islam was a major political ideology in the Empire. At the same time, Christians and other non-Muslim religious groups—many of whom lived in the Balkans, Greece, Syria, Armenia, Kurdistan, and Palestine—were officially granted equal protection in 1839 via the Edict of Gülhane and sovereignty in 1856 via the Reform Edict. This commitment was made partly under pressure from Britain and France after their support during the Crimean War and partly to secure the support of the Empire's non-Muslim citizens as the Empire's strength waned—in other words, the Tanzimat reforms were a matter of survival for the Empire. However, the relationship among different Ottoman subjects and the Empire was complex. As Masters (2013) explained it:

> The Ottoman regime equally exploited all of its subjects . . . for the revenues they might produce and considered them to be a largely undifferentiated mass of taxpayers. Exploitation and coercion went hand in hand to establish and maintain the Ottoman Empire, as was the case with other empires. At the same time, however, its survival over time required the cooperation and collaboration of at least some of the subject peoples. In that regard, the invocation of Islam as a political ideology was crucial as far as many Arabs were concerned. (p. 5)

In other words, Islam operated at an ideological level to provoke a sense of unity and support from the Empire's Muslim subjects, even as they were spread across a large geography.

There were major cultural divides between the rich and the poor in the Empire during this period, but a rising middle class in the latter half of the 19th century proved to be important for sociopolitical change. The biggest development within the Ottoman Empire in the late 19th century, according to Benjamin Fortna (2002), was the competition that came from within the Empire and not from outside of its borders; this was an experience that was markedly different from the experiences in Russia, China, and Japan:

> What was once a traditional military confrontation fought along a more or less distinct frontier was emerging in the modern era [within the Ottoman Empire] as a battle being waged internally for the hearts and minds of the population. The massive underlying economic imbalance ensured that this battle favored those who could marshal the various manifestations of technology (steamships, printing presses, etc.) to their own advantage. (p. 84)

In other words, the wealthy of the Ottoman Empire used the tools and technology of modernity to create economic competition domestically and to maintain power. While modernity is often conceived of as a Western construction, Ussama Makdisi (2011) argued that, for better or worse, the emergence of liberalism and modernity in the Arab context was simultaneous to, rather than after, Western constructions of the same (p. 216).

Greater Syria in the 19th-Century Ottoman Empire

Prior to the Tanzimat period, three major metropolitan areas in the Middle East were important for the Ottoman Empire: "Damascus . . . was the city from which was organized the Pilgrimage . . ., Aleppo [was] the centre of international trade, [and from] Baghdad . . . the frontiers with Persia must be defended" (Hourani, 1983, p. 32). Outside of major urban areas such as Beirut and Damascus, a localized form of feudalism prevailed, and the mountains of Lebanon, Palestine, and Kurdistan governed themselves.

During the Tanzimat period, the Empire gained greater control over Arabic-speaking regions, including Greater Syria, a region which included present-day Lebanon, Syria, and occupied Palestine. An ongoing power struggle between Egypt and the Empire led Egypt to occupy Syria between 1832 and 1840. European powers held a stake in the conflict, with France and Spain supporting Egypt in its occupation but Britain, Austria, and Russia supporting the Empire. The 1839–1840 war in Syria led to a resolution of the crisis with Britain promising Egypt its autonomy. After the war, Arabs were conscripted to local armies, which provided a new sense of security in the region but also led to resentment among the local populations.

Under the Ottoman Empire, Syria housed a variety of religious groups (including Maronites, Greek Orthodox, Melkite Greek Catholics, Druze, and Sunni and Shia'a Muslims), and various European powers held a stake in the well-being of groups that they saw as important to their influence within the Near (Middle) East. Between 1840 and 1860, the Ottoman Empire tried to exert direct control over the region through centralization, ending the traditional independence of areas such as Mount Lebanon, which is located in the middle of present-day Lebanon. As a result of these pressures, religious identity increased and became politicized. In Mount Lebanon, where the Druze claimed power, the number of Maronites increased, as did their wealth through the production of silk. Meanwhile, the Druze permitted Protestant Christian missionaries from America and Britain to enter Mount Lebanon, leading to further tension with the Maronites, who viewed the missionaries' presence as a threat. The British supported the Druze with arms, and France and Austria helped protect the Maronites.

The Ottomans' efforts to control the region led to changes in the political and economic conditions, such as competition over land. The Empire split Mount Lebanon into two political units—the northern one governed by a Christian and the southern one governed by a Druze—both responsible to the Beirut governor. The Empire's efforts to intervene in Mount Lebanon resulted in conflict between the Maronites and the Druze, culminating in the 1860 war, which resulted in between 7,000 and 20,000 casualties and the Druze claiming victory ("1860 civil conflict," 2025). The developments between 1840 and 1860 signaled the advent of political sectarianism that persists in the region even today (Makdisi, 2000; Masters, 2013). According to Makdisi (2000), sectarianism "emerged when the old regime of Mount Lebanon, which was dominated by an elite hierarchy in which secular rank rather than religious affiliation defined politics, was discredited in the mid-nineteenth century" (p. 6).

After the 1860 Druze-Maronite war, French troops arrived in Beirut as part of a "humanitarian" expedition under Napoleon III—a move that foreshadowed the creation of the French (colonial) Mandate in Lebanon after the First World War. To prevent the control of Syria by France, other European powers—including Great Britain, Russia, Prussia, and Austria—brokered a peace agreement with the Ottoman Empire, allowing European troops (half of them French) to occupy the district of Mount Lebanon and restore order. The *Règlement Organique*, or Organic Regulation, not only normalized the presence of foreign military powers in the area, but it also gave autonomy to the Mount Lebanon *mutasarrifate,* or district), which was to be, from that point forward, under the control of a Christian governor.[1]

The Beirut *wilaya* or *vilayet* (administrative division similar to a state) was, according to Rashid Khalidi (1991b), much less conservative and more diverse than interior parts of Syria. Between 1865 and 1915, Beirut experienced a rapid rise in population, doubling to 175,000 and becoming the third largest city in the region by 1914. Meanwhile, an 1864 law gave power to Arab Muslim elites, and local government news began to be transmitted in Arabic. There were also networks of communication and influence between Beirut and Cairo in the second half of the 19th century. There was a long history of trade and intellectual influence, as well as Syrian emigration to Cairo from the eighteenth century on.

Ethnic and Religious Identity Within the Ottoman Empire

The question of how Arab subjects in the Ottoman Empire defined themselves in relation to the Empire as well as Europe is challenging, and any

---

1 Mount Lebanon today comprises the central part of the modern state of Lebanon.

answers must be understood as highly nuanced. Some contemporary historians have criticized how Arab identity has been presented previously through an Orientalist lens. For example, Franck Salameh (2010) argued that the idea of the "Arab world" is a "Western caricature of a Western concept of identity that was never extant in the Middle East" (p. xiii). He suggested that such efforts to generalize the people who occupy the region, today or in the past, fundamentally relies on a Western understanding of national identity, where language is often conflated with citizenship and belonging. Instead, "[i]n both the ancient and modern Middle East, assortments of cultural and ethnic groups have always wielded the languages of their times' dominant civilizations, without necessarily merging into those civilizations and integrating the latter's ethnic and cultural parameters" (Salameh, 2010, p. 3). Masters (2001) noted, also, that some historians who have written about religious minorities in the Empire tended to be biased against Muslims and did not recognize the ties among Muslims, Jews, Christians, and other groups, whereas others, while not anti-Muslim, promoted Arab nationalism by insisting that the Empire was inherently imperialist and oppressive (pp. 2–3). Neither view fully captures the complexity of Arab identity in the Ottoman Empire, particularly in the dynamic 19th century.

Masters (2001) argued that religion was at the heart of identity in the Ottoman Empire around the turn of the 19th century, and religion was tied to politics as well. Identity was often literally marked by clothing; for example, Muslim women wore the hijab, while non-Muslims wore blue or black clothing or red shoes, or they were not allowed to wear green clothing or white turbans (pp. 5–6). According to Masters (2013), Muslim Arabs did not view or describe themselves as occupied, but they identified with a cultural heritage distinct from their colonizers. They had already been occupied prior to the Ottomans, so switching to an Ottoman sultan in 1453 was not a significant change locally. Just as empires have always relied on their subjects to support colonization, urban, elite Muslim Arabs can be seen as collaborators in the imperial project. During the early part of the Empire's occupation of the region, this elite group benefited from the occupation and gained wealth; in the 19th and 20th centuries, they supported the status quo for their advantage, and they shared a religious identity with their colonizers (pp. 7–8).

Historians generally agree that Middle Eastern culture was heterogeneous and always changing. It is impossible to generalize, but Muslims tended to be less likely to accept innovations such as Western education or political ideology, and Christians, too, were uneven in their acceptance of change (Masters, 2001, p. 7). Muslim and non-Muslim Arab elites in the region avoided violence by choosing to adopt a secular political identity (p. 9). North African and Egyptian subjects did not always see themselves as Arab; Egyptian culture and citizenship was understood as distinct from the rest of the Near East (Masters, 2013, p. 205). Within the Empire, European influence was the strongest in Syria; it was Syrian Christians and Jews who were primarily responsible for bringing Western knowledge to the region (Masters, 2001, p. 14). John Stuart Mill, Charles Darwin, Herbert Spencer, and Thomas Henry Huxley—representing "scientific knowledge, industry, and constitutional government"—influenced Christian intellectuals in particular (Sharabi, 1970, pp. 60–61, 68–70). While some Jewish people were interested in Arab identity, most preferred separatism (Masters, 2001, p. 174).

Christians began to imagine themselves as Arab around the second half of the 19th century, when they began "to study and learnt to appreciate the classics of Arabic literature.... With that newly acquired appreciation, many in the Arab Christian elite started to define themselves culturally as Arabs with an acquired pride in a brilliant literary past that they acknowledged as shared with, and produced by, the ancestors of their Muslim neighbors" (Masters, 2001, p. 173). This new identification is known as the *al-Nahda* (the renaissance) and led some to support a universal Arab nationalism that would connect them more deeply with their Muslim neighbors. At around the same time, Muslim scholars in the *salafiyya* movement sought to marry Islamic values with modern (Western) culture. These scholars were well aware of European Orientalists who saw Islam as responsible for the region's "backwards" culture. Ultimately, *salafiyya* intellectuals hoped to recast Islam as progressive and meld it with Western technological, scientific, and socio-political advances (Masters, 2013, pp. 202–203). While the *salafiyya* movement generally did not support the idea of a new Arab state, as some Christians did, both movements signified "the emergence of an Arab cultural consciousness among Arabic-speaking elites" (Masters, 2001, p. 175).

By the end of the 19th century, Muslim Arabs expressed less confidence in the security and stability provided by the Empire. They were conscripted into military service in various Ottoman wars (such as the 1877 Russo-Turkish War and World War I), and national and ethnic difference was promoted over religious faith, leading Arab Muslims to feel marginalized in relation to their Turkish counterparts (Masters, 2013, p. 19). At the same time, the majority of Arabs in the Middle East, including Christians, were not eager to see the end of the Ottoman Empire—they saw the British and other European powers as a threat to their culture and identity, and many held out hope that change could occur from within (p. 193).

The turn of the 20th century also saw the rise of a new, elite middle class (Khalidi, 1991b, pp. 63–65; Masters, 2013, p. 195). In Syria, this group was comprised of those newly educated in modern institutions, bringing new skills and expectations to the social sphere. This group—which comprised approximately 10% of the total population—in turn changed politics. Increased press freedom and political activity characterized Syrian culture during the few years prior to the Great War.

Arab Nationalism

Nationalism was on the rise throughout the Ottoman Empire during the post-Tanzimat period, particularly for those residents who were not part of the Muslim *umma* (community of believers), such as the Greeks and Armenians. Even Muslims, however, began to differentiate themselves along Western political categories; references to "Turk" changed from meaning any Muslim to people who specifically spoke Turkish (Masters, 2001, pp. 10–11). Sultan Abdulhamid promoted the Ottomans' traditional references to Islamic solidarity; however, a secular Turkish nationalism—popularized by the Young Ottomans in 1875 and later the Committee of Union and Progress (CUP) and the Young Turk movement—emerged out of opposition to his reign.

Syrian Arabs, such as Butrus al-Bustani and Rashid Rida, were supportive of these nationalist movements and saw Arabic as a language that could unify otherwise disparate groups traditionally defined by religious identity. Masters (2001) attributed Arab nationalism, which brought Muslim and Christian elites together in recognition of a shared identity, for the dissolution of tensions in Syria after 1860 (pp. 172–173). In general, Arabic-language newspapers and books in the second half of the 19th century supported new understandings and constructions of an Arab past (p. 178). Arab nationalism was in many ways unique within the Empire, as other groups who could have unified through a shared ethnic or cultural identity chose instead to emphasize religion or sect (Masters, 2013, p. 206). Indeed, Arab Ottoman subjects took pride in their cultural history, no matter their religious background (Masters, 2013, pp. 204-205). Arab nationalism grew, but so did other senses of nationalism, such as Lebanese and Syrian nationalism (Faroqhi, 2004/2009, pp. 129–130; Hourani, 1983, pp. 100–102, 285, 299). Although Arab nationalism gradually gained in popularity—reaching a peak around the 1930s (Salameh, 2010, p. 8)—writers around the turn of the 20th century advocated, in various ways, for "a transformation of Arab society rather than a major social or political revolution" (Masters, 2001, p. 197).

Several developments during and after World War I heightened Arab peoples' attunement to Arab nationalism, including the 1916 Arab Revolt, in which Arab and British forces defeated the Ottomans (Dawn, 1991, p. 23).

Later, the division of much of the region into "mandates" governed by Britain and France through the Sykes-Picot Agreement complicated the idea of nationality and disrupted Arab peoples' understanding of themselves as Ottoman subjects (Masters, 2001, p. 187). As a result, many in Syria supported Faisal I—a figure who promoted pan-Arab nationalism and who became King of Iraq—as king of the Arab Kingdom, which would have included Syria, Lebanon, Palestine, and Iraq, rather than the French and British occupation of the region (pp. 187–88).

Education in the 19th-Century Ottoman Empire

During the 19th century, elementary education in the Ottoman Empire was mostly private, with Quranic schools (*medreses*) and Christian parochial schools, including missionary schools, available to students. State secondary education emerged slowly: public Muslim elementary and middle schools were formed during Abdulhamid's governance (Faroqhi, 2004/2009). No modern Ottoman-run universities existed until 1900; the first was the Imperial University [*Darülfünûn-u Şahâne*], which today is Istanbul University [*İstanbul Darülfünûnu*] (Faroqhi, 2004/2009; Istanbul University, 2025). Part of the reason for the slower educational development in the Empire during the 19th century is because bureaucrats worried that education would increase the chances of student revolts as nationalist ideology grew throughout the Empire (Faroqhi, 2004/2009).

Fortna (2002) argued that the Ottoman state's decisions regarding education were not wholly influenced by the West nor particularly alien to it. The Empire was influenced by Enlightenment ideals of progress, with the difference in the Empire being the integration of Islamic and Ottoman values. The educational project was not secular (p. 3). The Ottomans recognized the competition brought by missionary and local minority groups' schools, as well as education offered by nearby countries (pp. 8–9). During the Tanzimat period, the French educational model was imported with few alterations into the Empire, but Sultan Abdulhamid II viewed this system with caution and made changes to realign education with Ottoman values and policies while also dramatically expanding public education (pp. 9–12).

The changes in the Empire at this time were part of a much larger global trend. France, Russia, Japan, and the Ottomans all saw educational transformations in the late 19th century, which suggests that the influence of the West within the Empire should be understood but not exaggerated or assumed to be unidirectional. Indeed, education was understood as a source of optimism: "Like their counterparts elsewhere, Ottoman educators believed that public education would solve a host of problems, ranging from those of economic and military competitiveness, to those relating to manpower, social control, cultural identification, and political loyalty" (Fortna, 2002, p. 30).

The Empire moved toward educational reformation partly in order to resist the West—by borrowing from the West (Fortna, 2002, pp. 32–35). However, there was also a belief that traditional Islamic education (the *medrese* system) was not strong enough to remain competitive on a global scale. Because the Ottomans did not have a pre-existing system of public education, they had to create one. Bureaucrats were concerned about the threat to Ottoman identity across the Empire, and education was one way in which to create a sense of shared identity; this was not very different from similar nationalizing efforts occurring in the United States and Russia at the same time. Fortna (2002) noted, "Such simultaneity suggests that there was a common world-time reaction to the perceived speeding up of time" (p. 40). Change was motivated in large part by fear—of modernity, ideological battles, falling behind, and losing culture or identity. In the Ottoman context, the threats were magnified, and some—such as missionaries—seemed stronger than the Ottomans themselves (Fortna, 2002, pp. 43–45).

Education, Literacy, and the Press in 19th-Century Syria

The 19th century was characterized by a rapid rise of access to education and literacy, as well as press activity, in Syria. In the early 19th century, Catholic and Protestant missions established schools and brought European languages and ideas to the region. American missionaries helped to modernize the Arabic language through their translation of the Bible, for which Butrus al-Bustani, an early Protestant convert, is credited. In the 1888 *wilaya* (state) of Beirut, which included Latakia, Tripoli, Mount Lebanon, and Nablus, there were five French and four British schools, with approximately 4,400 students enrolled (Fortna, 2002, pp. 51–53). American missionary schools, as well as Italian and German state schools and Maronite, Greek Catholic, and Greek Orthodox schools, enrolled around 500 students in total, 90% of whom were Ottomans. The Empire was concerned about foreign influence within the schools and began to establish national schools, with the number of state schools rising from 153 in 1886 to 359 in 1914 (Khalidi, 1991b, p. 56). Prior to the Great War, literacy rates outside of cities ranged from 10 to 20 percent (Masters, 2013, p. 196).

Prior to the 1860s, newspapers were published primarily by the government in Ottoman Turkish or French, as well as in minority languages, in Constantinople and Egypt. Little was published in Arabic or in Syria. However, the 1870s saw the publication of two new kinds of periodicals in Arabic:

the independent political newspaper and the literary/scientific periodical, the latter of which translated European and American ideas into Arabic. Published in both Syria and Egypt, many of these periodicals were led by Syrians who had been educated in French and American schools, including Ya'qub Sarruf and Faris Nimr (*al-Muqtataf*), Jurji Zeidan (*al-Hilal*), Farah Antun (*al-Jami'a*), and Bustani (*al-Jinan*) (Hourani, 1983, pp. 245–47, 263; see also Sharabi, 1970, and Khalidi, 1991b). Literary societies and clubs also existed in Syria around the turn of the 20th century (Sharabi, 1970). Books—ranging from reproductions of Arab classics, translations of Western work, or new culturally significant tomes—became widely accessible in the late 19th century and were often summarized in Arabic-language newspapers or taught in schools (Masters, 2001, pp. 204–205). Ultimately, writing in Arabic circulated widely within the region, particularly between Syria and Egypt, from the late 19th century onward.

Historicizing 19th-Century American Protestant Missions

It is in the context of the Ottoman Empire that SPC was established in 1866 by a group of American Protestant missionaries. To fully appreciate the significance of SPC as a site of colonial literacy education, it is necessary to also understand the longer history of Protestant missions during this time period. Therefore, in this section, I provide an overview of the Protestant missionary movement, zeroing in on the American Board of Commissioners for Foreign Missions (ABCFM), as it emerged and grew throughout the 19th century.

Protestant missionary movements emerged in the late 18th and early 19th centuries in both American and British contexts. Multiple missionary organizations were born around the turn of the 20th century, including the Baptist Missionary Society in London in 1792, the Church Missionary Society in Britain in 1799, the London Society for Promoting Christianity among the Jews in 1809, the ABCFM in Boston in 1810, the American Bible Society in 1816, and the American Tract Society in 1825 (Haselby, 2015; Masters, 2001). These movements were connected to the Second Great Awakening, a populist evangelical movement centered primarily in the United States that focused on elevating religious fervor and spreading Christianity beyond the Anglo–Saxon Atlantic region. In the context of growing literacy, ordinary laypeople could join missions if they felt "called" by God to do so, and those who did not could still support these organizations financially.

In the context of the United States, Protestant missionary organizations particularly gained momentum in the New England region, where, post-American Revolution, the people holding much of the nation's wealth also enjoyed a sense of manifest destiny. Many Protestants at the time were Calvinists (represented in denominations such as Presbyterian, Reformed Anglican, and Congregationalist) and socially conservative. At the time, schools were supposed to maintain the social order and propagate religion. The clergy and upper social classes controlled education. Literacy was necessary for religious instruction and to fulfill the demands of social class; education was not associated with social mobility in part because it was not open to all (Lindsay, 1965, pp. 32–33). Schools were believed to be socializing and corrective institutions. American colleges, which in the early 19th century were primarily located in the Northeast, imported Enlightenment ideologies. Mathematics, classics, and languages were all believed to be important for "mental discipline" and civic life; however, the introduction of the scientific method challenged Calvinists because it seemed to threaten the authority of scripture. The most conservative theories of education influenced missionary training in this context.

For Haselby (2015), Northeastern Protestants distorted the history of religion in America, saying that missionary work was a part of that history, even though American Christianity had previously been focused on developing and guiding its communities rather than orienting itself outwards. In other words, around the turn of the 19th century, Protestants in New England began to connect nationality with missionary work (pp. 193–194). This link led to the proliferation of Protestant missionary organizations—between 1787 and 1827, 933 Protestant missionary or "moral improvement" societies were founded by New Englanders (p. 59). The missions movement ultimately helped solidify religious nationalism in early America (p. 58).

Haselby (2015) argued that the post-Revolutionary group the Connecticut (later Hartford) Wits was the group primarily responsible for establishing the connection between American nationalism and evangelicalism. For the Wits, the "national empire became the community through which one sought salvation" (p. 58). These elitist Yale graduates believed they would play a pivotal role in deciding American culture, leading educational institutions and government based on their specific bourgeoisie understanding of manners and taste (p. 52). Indeed, one member of this group, Timothy Dwight, became the president of Yale in 1795. Yale and other elite Northeastern colleges, including Amherst, Princeton, Columbia, and Andover Theological Seminary held a leading role in "contribut[ing] men, ideas, and money to the missions movement" around the turn of the 19th century, as the missions movement grew (p. 199). The largest American missions organizations, established in the early 19th century, were similarly elitist and nationalist. According to Haselby (2015), "they enjoyed an acute sese of posterity, planned for the distant future, and thought of themselves, accurately, in elitist and nationalist terms, as the leading Americans" (pp. 256–257). They understood themselves as distinct from (and higher than) those they sought to reach through their proselytization—an unsurprising attitude in the context of colonial American culture.

Taking advantage of the rise of print culture in the 19th century, American Protestant missionary organizations produced a barrage of religious literature that simultaneously conjured up an image of America as a nation bound together by shared religious principles (Haselby, 2015, pp. 235, 249–251). Organizations such as the American Tract Society and the ABCFM—supported primarily by business and religious leaders in the Northeast—aimed to distribute religious tracts to every American household and across the frontier. Their goal was to create a common religious discourse—"a complete chain of communication"— across the country (pp. 261–62). Such work, religious leaders at the time believed, had the power to dismantle the separation of social classes. Thus, these missionary organizations can be understood as "creat[ing] American mass media. Their pamphlets and periodicals were the first media conceived of and produced for the general American population" (p. 262). They played a clear role in linking the nation with an imagined America.

Missions, Nationalism, and Colonialism

America was still a young country at the beginning of the 19th century, and the idea of American nationalism, according to Haselby (2015), was not set in stone (p. 59). The American missions movement took advantage of this uncertainty, creating strategic—but as mentioned earlier, historically inaccurate—connections between the new nation and Christian obligations to spread Christianity throughout the world. At least among Protestants in the Northeast, there was a shared belief in American exceptionalism—the idea that God had chosen American Christians to play a special role in history— which helped spur the missions movement forward and solidified Christian definitions of American nationalism (pp. 200–201).

While it can be tempting to see 19th century missions as inherently colonial or imperialist, scholarship suggests that there was a great deal of heterogeneity within missions, and many were motivated by a sense of altruism rather than a specific desire to colonize (Harris, 1999; Kieser, 2002; Makdisi, 2011; Porter, 2002; Tejirian & Simon, 2002). The sociohistorical context in which any given mission operated also complexifies any discussion about missions and their effects. However, as Eleanor Tejirian and Reeva Spector Simon (2002) noted, the underlying logic for Protestant missions was colonial: "The . . . goal, for all Christians, was the establishment of a worldwide kingdom and the missionaries were a major force for education about what came to be regarded as the 'developing world'"—with both positive and negative consequences (p. vii). For example, Christian missionaries have been credited with creating the conditions for the emergence of an Arab nationalism, while others have criticized missions, rightly, for their inherently colonial and ethnocentric views (p. vii). Tejirian and Simon (2002) credited missions for raising public awareness about other regions of the world, including the Middle East, in the United States, which in turn has influenced U.S. foreign policy, for better or worse (p. ix).

Similarly, while acknowledging the damaging and destructive consequences that often occurred because of missions, Andrew Porter (2002) resisted an inherently negative view of missions, in which "any instance where awareness of the wider world of the West has influenced cultural change" (p. 9) is understood as problematic. Instead, he argued, those instances of cross-cultural interaction that lie at the heart of missions should be investigated critically for both positive and negative effects. Makdisi (2011) also argued that the history of Protestant missions highlights the ways in which colonialism has historically failed to achieve its goals, noting that while missionaries' views were deeply inflected by colonial epistemology, they viewed their work abroad as "ostensibly free of the entanglements and corruptions of American colonialism and Western empire" (p. 11). In other words, he suggested that it is worth paying attention to the ways in which the colonial epistemology underlying the Protestant missionary movement was challenged and disrupted in overseas contexts.

In reality, no matter what missionaries believed about the separation between their work overseas and the unpleasant realities, American Protestant missionary organizations like the ABCFM were inevitably tied to settler colonialism. Some of the first American Protestant missionary projects were directed toward Native American populations. This "vexed relationship with power at home inevitably framed the perceptions and expectations of foreign fields," particularly in places where "American power was notably absent" such as the Middle East and Africa (Makdisi, 2011, p. 11). In other words, the epistemology that justified settler colonialism in the United States—suggesting that Indigenous populations and their land were inherently subordinate to the ways of life and desires of Anglo-Europeans—also shaped American missionaries' worldviews as they moved abroad. Missionaries to the American frontier undoubtedly held mixed feelings about the U.S. government's violent efforts to relocate Native Americans, and some supported Indigenous peoples as they resisted these efforts. In the Ottoman Empire, a region where America had almost no stake or power, American missionaries were freed from the political and moral complications and challenges that they faced in their work on the frontier, even as they carried colonial epistemologies to new sites of proselytization.

No matter their benevolent intentions, the mission project in any context took as a given Christianity's—and the West's—inherent superiority, and this assumption necessarily shaped the relationship between missionaries and (potential) converts. While American missionaries were not formally connected to European or American colonial projects, they benefited from the environment that Western colonialism created. This gave strength to their work in contexts such as the Ottoman Empire (Makdisi, 2011, p. 176). What's more, missionaries operated from the same cultural and epistemological frame of their Western colonialist counterparts. In his study of the history of the ABCFM, Paul Willaim Harris (1999) wrote, "American Board missions might act quite independently of the Western powers, might even act to wean their converts from dependence and promote their autonomy, and yet they still acted like colonialists" (p. 111). We see in the missionary project, then, the intractability of colonial logics, which—like invasive plants—reproduce and sustain systems of power.

Along the same lines, Porter (2002) pointed out that empires have held together not only through political and economic domination, but also through culture and epistemology. Missions parroted, produced, and sustained colonial discourse, which in turn constructed social hierarchies—including religious ones—in line with and in support of the greater colonial project. Porter (2002) argued that "the global expansion of evangelical Protestant activity not only reflected the worldwide distribution of relative material power. It assisted the definition of distinct religions, with clear theological boundaries and in competition with one another" (pp. 7–8). The construction of such distinctions allowed for some religious beliefs and practices to be named as superior to others, supporting the spread of colonial epistemology.

Missions and Local Populations

The history of missions in relation to Indigenous peoples in the United States provides important context for the orientation of American Protestant missionaries overseas, because the colonial logics that justified evangelism at home carried over to their approach abroad. Much more is known today than previously about the problematic history of the education of Indigenous peoples in the United States. Missionary organizations are deeply implicated in this history; the schools that they established in the early 19th century under the mantle of proselytization were precursors to the boarding schools established and supported by the federal government beginning in 1860. These schools are known today as instruments of genocide, in which Native people's culture, language, and humanity was violently oppressed.

According to Haselby (2015), missionaries initially set out to integrate Native Americans into U.S. society, believing that their primary focus should be to "civilize" before attempting to convert. In a forerunner to the government's boarding school movement, "earlier Anglo-American missions had taken 'the most promising children' from many 'tribes' and focused on their religious indoctrination" (p. 296). However, missionaries found that focusing on religion proved ineffective, because when these "purportedly indoctrinated Indians were sent back, as young adults, 'to their native tribes,' wrote a missionary, they 'became *Indians* again"—as though these students' cultural and ethnic identities were merely social characteristics that could be removed and put back on like clothing (p. 296). In the view of these early missionaries, religious indoctrination was unsuccessful because of Native Americans' supposed lack of "civilization"—they believed that Native American culture itself needed to change before they would be able to adopt Christianity, which in their view was a "civilized" religion.

It is important to recognize that American Protestant missionaries' views of Native Americans and enslaved peoples was more nuanced than a simple sense of superiority. According to Haselby (2015), American Protestants generally combined nationalism with liberalism to see those outside of the Anglo-American community as divinely subjugated—that is, Protestants saw Indigenous peoples and slaves as endowed with a special spiritual primacy by virtue of their suffering. At the same time, of course, many Protestants viewed these groups as lacking "civility" according to their own Anglo-Christian standards, and therefore not equal. In other words, Protestants' perceptions of these groups were heterogeneous: Some saw and spoke out about the injustices inherent to the slave trade and the relocation of Native Americans, while others articulated justifications of inequality in their religious literature (Haselby, 2015, p. 268). Such justifications would have been supported in 19th century popular magazines, which highlighted scientific "proof" that attributed various mental and physical differences to race. Importantly, not everyone at the time believed that these differences were genetically transmitted, which offered the possibility of change—these beliefs justified missionaries' and educators' continuing efforts to convert and civilize these groups (Spack, 2002, p. 31).

In considering the relationship of missionaries with Native Americans, it is also important to remember that Native people were not harmoniously living with each other before settlers moved in and that they had agency in relation to missions. While missionaries took advantage of the existing tensions among different Indigenous groups to win allies and converts, Indigenous peoples also made use of these tensions for their own advantage. As Harris (1999) pointed out, "the Indigenous clients of the American Board were quite capable of borrowing selectively and wisely from the West," and indeed made use of the resources provided by missions for their own purposes (p. 8). Mary Stuckey and John Murphy (2001), too, noted that "the Indigenous peoples of the Americas accepted those elements of Christianity that caused the least damage to their resident cultures, while their 'conversion' may have helped them to resist the imposition of other elements of the colonial culture" (p. 76). We must therefore understand local populations as having some agency in relation to missions; the relationship, while often manipulated in favor of the missionaries, was never unidirectional.

Whatever agency local populations may have had, missionaries' complex, and often contradictory, perspectives about non-Anglo cultures, religions, and races were carried with them overseas. These perspectives also defined their relationships to the communities within which they settled. In the Ottoman Empire, for example, missionaries viewed Islam as inherently hostile to Christianity. Even as they developed good relationships with individual Muslims, "in their letters [the missionaries] spoke of systematically penetrating and 'occupying' Ottoman lands as if they were enemy territories" (Kieser, 2002, p. 145). These characterizations of Islam and Muslims intertwined with racist ideology and nationalist rhetoric of 19th-century America, resulting in discourse that "increasingly idealized America, orientalized the East, and presumed to speak for the natives in a conversation about missions conducted mainly with American critics and supporters rather than with the people the missionaries had ostensibly come to save" (Makdisi, 2011, p 13). Missionaries in the Ottoman Empire perceived the local culture as corrupt based in part on their perceptions of women's status and also a lack of "modern (Western) furniture, education, medicine, and knowledge" (Makdisi, 2000, pp. 89–90). In contrast to their approach to Native Americans, however, missionaries overseas attempted at first to provide education that would align with local customs and values. Their justification was still colonial, however, in that they withheld education about Western life and customs because they believed that the West would be too appealing. Missionaries abroad wanted converts to stay in the region and evangelize rather than leaving (Lindsay, 1965; Makdisi, 2000, pp. 89–90).

Missions and Language

Missionaries regularly studied and documented language, and they debated about which language was "best" to achieve their proselytization goals. This adds another complicating factor when considering Protestant missions' role in colonization. Evangelicals sought to transmit—inoculate—Christian (Western) beliefs and values to the Indigenous population; they were the "'human vehicles of a hegemonic worldview . . . engag[ing] [Indigenous peoples] in a web of symbolic and material transactions that would bind them ever more securely to the colonizing culture'" (Comaroff & Comaroff, 1991, as cited in Porter, 2002, p. 8). How best to inoculate their targets was an open question, and ultimately, in some contexts, neither the locals' home language(s) nor English produced a great number of converts. Many 18th- and 19th-century missionaries were highly educated (at a time when higher education was rare), and with this education they became what we would today call linguists and anthropologists. Some saw their primary work as documenting—literally transcribing—Indigenous languages and cultures around the world. They used this linguistic and anthropological knowledge not only to support their evangelical work in the field, but also to educate Western populations about non-Western cultures and ways of life.

Part of the project of Protestant evangelism, then, relied on articulating not only religious difference but also linguistic difference—and this articulation of difference contributed to the colonial social hierarchy that missionaries sought to maintain. It is important to remember that American missions emerged within multilingual contexts where English was not inevitable and was not intrinsically tied to the nation.[2] At the same time, as I discuss more deeply in Chapter 3, English was promoted by both Protestant missionaries and local populations as a valuable commodity, one that the missionaries could choose to share or not, depending on how they viewed the mission's purpose.[3] Some American missionary organizations, including the ABCFM, grounded their early educational programs on the belief that their targets would adopt Christianity (and in turn become more "civilized") if they were

---

2   As Kimball (2021) pointed out, the English-only ideology that permeates American educational and cultural contexts today was not inevitable. The government-sponsored Americanization movement of the early 20th century likely helped cement the connection between nation and language in the US, as it sponsored English-language teaching for immigrant and Native communities. Spack (2002) pointed out that this movement offered many promises through the English language that were not ultimately fulfilled: "The reality of the Americanization movement was that Native people were being asked to reject the ways of their ancestors and families without being offered the benefits of full participation in the European American way of life" (pp. 37–38).

3   For more historical context about this tension as it arose in the context of the British Empire, see Stephen Evans (2002) on the English Education Act of 1835, and also see Willinsky (1998, pp. 97-98).

exposed to scripture in their native languages.[4] At the same time, other missionaries in the early 19th century believed in—and asserted—the superiority of English as a vehicle of a more "civilized" Anglo-Saxon culture. In the context of missions targeting Native American communities, the 19th-century doctrine of individualism, reinforced by Darwinism, promoted the belief that "English was . . . capable of breaking [the] barrier [of communalism in Native tribes] and thus of improving students' lives" (Spack, 2002, p. 29).[5] It is evident that, no matter the approach to the medium of instruction taken by missions during the 19th century, all approaches are founded on colonial epistemologies that assert and maintain the superiority of the West.

Missionaries' articulation of religious, cultural, and linguistic differences was also inevitably tied to constructions of race and racial hierarchies. Within the context of the British Protestant mission, "[d]oubts were often expressed as to the ability of Indigenous peoples to attain the ethical standards acceptable as the hallmark of genuine conversion. . . . Racial concern often underlay missionary reluctance . . . to surrender control and authority to local Christians" (Porter, 2002, p. 12). Such racial differentiation was not, of course, limited to British Protestants—in any foreign mission context, missionaries generally shared a common belief in the superiority of the Anglo-European "race" and its culture and, according to Kieser (2002), a rigid understanding of what constituted appropriate beliefs and behaviors (p. 162).

Even facing these beliefs, however, local populations must be understood as having agency in the context of English-language education. They made use of and negotiated colonizers' languages (including English), as well as missions' transcription of Native languages (Porter, 2002, p. 9; Spack, 2002, p. 11). Spack (2002) saw this agency as decidedly translingual and transcultural, providing the Native American students she focused on in her study with the tools to understand the discourse used to describe them and, in turn, to take up the work of representing themselves in the language

---

4   This approach was reinforced under the oversight of Rufus Anderson, secretary of ABCFM from 1832-1866. He favored vernacular education because it saved money for the mission and also maintained Western hierarchies of power. Students who learned English were more marketable for jobs outside of the mission and therefore were less likely to remain in their home regions. This disrupted Anderson's three-self doctrine of producing self-supporting, self-governing, and self-propagating churches. Additionally, students who learned English might eventually consider themselves equal to the missionaries and demand similar salaries and lifestyles if they remained (Harris, 1999, p. 8).

5   Haselby (2015) notes that this attention to language—in the Native American context—was coupled with a conviction that American Indians also needed to secure rights to their land; in fact, the ABCFM wrote that "The doctrine that Indians cannot be civilized . . . is the . . . slander of men who covet their lands" (qtd. in Haselby, 2015, p. 297).

of the colonizers (p. 112).[6] The three chapters that follow this one highlight this agency as part of its decolonial approach. Tracing the agency of local populations as they engage with colonial language policy and literacy education allows us to imagine pluriversal perspectives and possibilities that may otherwise be buried.

The American Board of Commissioners for Foreign Missions

The ABCFM was established in 1810 by graduates of Williams College (Massachusetts) and became one of the largest American Protestant missionary organizations in the 19th century. Prior to the establishment of the ABCFM, American missionary activities were mostly limited to proselytizing to Native peoples and some financial support of the British mission in India (Lindsay, 1965, p. 10). The ABCFM's first missionaries were sent to India in 1812; later, the field expanded to include North American Natives as well as stations as far afield as Ceylon (Sri Lanka), the Sandwich Islands (Hawaii), China, Singapore, Thailand, Greece, Cyprus, Turkey, Syria, Persia, Liberia and Sierra Leone in Africa, and the Zulus in southern Africa. Following in the footsteps of the Wits, the ABCFM's founding documents reinscribe the nation-mission narrative, using it to justify the organization's existence (Haselby, 2015, p. 197).

The ABCFM grew to have an extremely powerful influence at home and abroad in the 19th century. As an institution, it was built and developed through strategic bureaucratization and consolidation of various missionary efforts (for example, it absorbed the United Foreign Missionary Society in 1825; see Haselby, 2015, p. 240). In 1820, 62 men and 48 women had been sent to eastern and western Asia, the Sandwich Islands (Hawaii), and locations in the US with Native populations. The ABCFM founded 40 schools with 3,000 children and 300 boarding students enrolled. In spite of these efforts, the organization was not particularly effective in its proselytization mission, as it spent $200,000 to ultimately convert 50 people (Lindsay, 1965, p. 21). Haselby (2015) noted that "by 1830, the ABCFM was spending $100,000 a year, almost twice Harvard University's 1830 total annual income, to support a missionary force of 224 ordained ministers, 600 native teachers, and 50,000

---

6   Spack (2002) offered a definition of translingualism that should be seen as an important precursor, with strong similarities, to Horner, Min-Zhan Lu et al.'s (2011) discussion of the concept. Her definition is as follows: " . . . here I use [translingualism] to capture the translinguistic process students underwent as they moved back and forth between languages making qualitative decisions about which aspects of language to incorporate and which to reject or transform. Translingualism involved not only students' language use and choices but also the transformation of their linguistic and cultural identities, for their worldview was now being mediated through a new language" (p. 112).

students" (p. 252). By 1860, according to the ABCFM's report, the organization's budget was approximately 8 million dollars; they claimed 415 ordained missionaries and 843 unordained missionaries located in 269 stations within 31 missions (Lindsay, 1965, p. 21). There were 458 local "helpers, preachers, and pastors"; 149 churches with 55,000 members; and 369 seminaries and schools with more than 10,000 children enrolled (Lindsay, 1965, p. 21).

Rufus Anderson is an important figure in the history of the ABCFM and of SPC because of his role leading the ABCFM's overseas work from 1832 until 1866. During his tenure, Anderson narrowed the organization's scope and mission to conversion from the broader "civilizing" mission that the ABCFM had previously assumed (Makdisi, 2011). Initially, the ABCFM allowed local converts to join the mission only if they professed the faith and were educated—this high standard was prohibitive for the expansion of foreign missions (Harris, 1999, p. 6). Anderson changed mission policy to focus primarily on conversion and believed that Christianity itself would do the work of "civilizing" converts (Harris, 1999, p. 7). Ideologically, Anderson was anti-imperialist and explicitly resisted any training that would produce missionaries who were "agents of imperialism" or "collaborators for Western commerce and diplomacy" (Harris, 1999, p. 99). Instead, Anderson strongly promoted a "three-self" doctrine for church creation, arguing that missionaries' key responsibilities were to establish churches that would eventually become "self-supporting, self-governing, and self-propagating" (Stowe, 1998/n.d.). As a result, there was a great expansion of the ABCFM abroad under Anderson, but those educated by missions became dependent on them for employment (Harris, 1999, p. 99). The ultimate success of the "three-self" doctrine is questionable, particularly in the context of the Ottoman Empire and present-day Middle East, which saw few converts but led to many becoming interested in the education that Western missionaries could offer.

The ABCFM and the Ottoman Empire

As mentioned previously, the ABCFM was founded in 1810, and its first mission site was located in Bombay in 1812 (Masters, 2001).[7] The ABCFM Syria Mission in the Ottoman Empire was established in Palestine in 1818. The

---

7   After 1870, all Presbyterian missionaries affiliated with the ABCFM moved to the Presbyterian Board of Foreign Missions (PBFM); at that time, the Syria Mission was also transferred to the PBFM (Global Ministries, 2023). The PBFM merged with other organizations in 1961; present-day organizations that trace their lineage to the ABCFM include the United Church Board for World Ministries (United Church of Christ, today Wider Church Ministries), the Division of Overseas Ministries (Christian Church, Disciples of Christ), and Global Ministries.

Beirut site was established in 1823 and grew to become the most important, and permanent, site in the region for the ABCFM[8] (the Palestine mission closed in 1844[9]). The ABCFM was not, however, the first missionary program in the Ottoman Empire. The Society of Jesus, or the French Jesuits, founded a mission in Syria in 1626, and it continued until 1773, when Rome ordered it closed (Thompson, 2002). During this time, the Jesuits "converted many Orthodox Christians to Catholicism, guided the reorganization of the Maronite Church, and established two seminaries in Mount Lebanon" (p. 73).

American Protestants entered the Near East for several reasons. First, the region was outside of British control. Therefore, the field was untainted by British colonialism and potential converts did not have this association with the missionaries. Additionally the mission did not have to negotiate with America's settler colonial ambitions; as Makdisi (2011) put it, missionaries in the Ottoman Empire "could simply bask in American glory one crucial step removed from its inglorious underpinnings" (p. 176). There was also a high degree of literacy among the population compared to other parts of the world—from the perspective of the missionaries, the region was more civilized and developed than other foreign posts.[10] What's more, Syria proved to be an ideal location for its proximity to the West and for the hospitable living environment it provided to the missionaries. According to a late-19th-century retrospective history of the Syria Mission published by the ABCFM:

> . . . it is interesting to see how Providence directed the pioneers of the mission to locate it in just that point where the Arabic-speaking portion of our race has attained the highest degree of development, where the body has drunk in vigor

---

8   According to Masters (2001), American and British missions targeted the Middle East under the auspices of converting "the Jews of the Holy Land" and began their work in Jerusalem for this reason (p. 147). However, Ottoman Jews proved difficult to convert and "faced with indifference or open hostility . . . the Americans moved their operations to Beirut in 1823 where they began to proselytize among the local Christians," such as the Greek Orthodox and Maronites, who were considered "nominal Christians" (Masters, 2001, p. 147).

9   The Palestine mission eventually closed due to sickness, "lack of faithful native assistants," and less desire for education than in Beirut (Lindsay, 1965, p. 109); the Cyprus mission opened in 1839 but closed in 1842 (Laurie, 1862). A separate mission in Turkey was established after Syria and included the northern part of Syria, previously part of the Syria mission.

10   However, the degree of "civility" was relative only to other parts of the world—it was understood that non-Anglo cultures and non-Protestant religions were inherently inferior: the missionaries "discoursed on the national matters, customs, and traits of the Syrians, Turks, Armenians, and Arabs, sometimes sympathetically and sometimes not, but always with the knowledge that theirs was not simply the more righteous civilization but also the most powerful" (Makdisi, 2011, p. 177).

from the cool springs and bracing air of goodly Lebanon, and the mind has learned manliness under the inspiration of the freedom long maintained in those mountain fastnesses, after it had been swept away from more accessible regions by the merciless oppression of the Turk. Here, too, in this home of energetic and thinking men, is the commercial center of Syria, offering every facility for the diffusion of truth; while constant communication with Europe rouses inquiring minds to search into the causes of the prosperity of nations so much more favored than themselves, and the healthy atmosphere of Lebanon offers itself to sustain the vigor of missionaries sent there from a northern clime. (Laurie, 1862, pp. 3–4)

Moreover, the region held a historical, religious affinity for Christians as the holy land. There were already many Christians (such as Maronites and Greek Orthodox) in the region, though they were considered "nominal."[11] Jews and Muslims already accepted the Old Testament, providing a potential foothold for conversion, and the Druze population initially seemed open to conversion (though later this proved not to be the case).[12] These first American missionaries did not expect to be able to easily convert Muslims; however, they believed an indirect approach, through schools, books, and scriptures, could eventually influence them.[13]

According to Samir Khalaf (2002), the mission in Syria "came to occupy a special place in the hopes and aspirations of New England missionaries . . . their inroads into Lebanon turned out to be the most seminal and far-reaching in terms of the socio-cultural transformations they generated in the lives of the people they touched" (pp. 16–17).[14] Because of the unstable

11   In a historical retrospective of the ABCFM's Syria Mission, the Reverend Thomas Laurie wrote in 1862: "Good people in America are often at a loss to understand how there can be so many Christian sects in Syria, and no religion" (p. 8).

12   The Druze expressed interest in mass conversion to Protestantism primarily to be protected from being drafted into the Egyptian military when Egypt occupied Syria (c. 1831–1840) (Masters, 2001, p. 152).

13   They also hoped for the collapse of the Empire, which would remove the legal restrictions that prevented the mission from proselytizing directly to the Muslim population (Lindsay, 1965).

14   There were a variety of responses within the Ottoman Empire and Syria to the presence of Protestant missionaries. According to Khalaf (2002), the secular elements of Northeastern Puritanism were received well from the beginning: " . . . it was the diffusion of such practical precepts—those of temperance, moderation, sobriety, frugality, industry, silence, cleanliness— that was less obtrusive and hence more penetrating in its impact" (p . 43). Syrian Muslims held a variety of attitudes about non-Muslim schools in the region, some of which are discussed further in Chapter 4: While more conservative Muslims rejected the presence of Muslims in

geopolitical landscape in the Ottoman Empire at the time, missionaries in the Levant continually adapted their approaches to evangelism in ways that were distinct within the global mission field.[15] Indeed, Makdisi (2011) noted that as they negotiated their work in relation to the broader regional context, missionaries ultimately "abandoned [the] millennial enthusiasm [of the early nineteenth-century evangelists] for the much harder task of accommodating themselves to foreign realities" (p. 217). While they generally failed to convert the masses, American missionaries continued to enjoy support within the region in part because they provided education and modern medicine (Murre-van den Berg, 2007, pp. 15–16).[16]

By the time the Jesuits returned to Syria in 1831, Protestant missionaries dominated the field, and the ABCFM had already established a printing press and schools (Roper, 1999; Tejirian & Simon, 2002).[17] The two groups often saw themselves in competition with each other throughout the 19th century. This battle for conversions manifested itself in the continued growth of schools and printing presses throughout the region. The French Jesuit Université Saint-Joseph (USJ), for example, opened in Beirut in 1875 and is often seen as the Jesuit missionaries' response to the opening of SPC less than a decade earlier.[18] In the first decade of the 20th century, nearly half of the

---

non-Muslim schools, others welcomed the introduction of modern sciences through Christian education (Haddad, 2002, p. 257). Proponents of this view warned Muslims who entered Christian schools not to be affected by the Christian indoctrination they were sure to be exposed to. Others, such as Arab Ottoman nationalists, held that secular education was against the community's distinct religious and national identity. During the reign of Sultan Abdulhamid in the late-19th century, as noted previously, the Ottoman government established state-funded schools in major cities. Some Muslims also established schools "in Beirut, Jerusalem, Aleppo, Damascus, and Baghdad to provide a modern education for their sons that would equal that on offer in the missionary schools" (Masters, 2013, p. 196).

15   For example, Syria was the site of Egyptian and Ottoman conflicts in the first half of the 19th century, and American missionaries had to leave Beirut temporarily when Britain attacked in 1840 to force Egypt out (Harris, 1999, p. 102).

16   American missionaries were extremely limited in their success, in part because communities would shun those who converted—the threat of social isolation was high, with dangerous implications for the convertee (Masters, 2001, pp. 148-49).

17   In the Ottoman Empire, the ABCFM Press helped produce texts for the mission as well as local schools in the native language (Lindsay, 1965, p. 60). The American Mission Press was established in 1822 in Malta and moved to Beirut in 1832 (Lindner, 2013). The Press, which in Malta collaborated with the English Church Missionary Society's press, initially published in Greek and Italian, and later in Arabic (Roper, 1999).

18   USJ is an important site for post-secondary literacy education in Syria, and its curriculum was similar to SPC's in its offering of "modern" subjects such as history, geography, math, and sciences alongside languages and rhetoric. If I had 10 more years to develop French-language skills (of which I currently have none) and to conduct archival research, I would love

Syrian immigrants who arrived in the United States were literate, and many had been educated in Protestant schools (Masters, 2001, p. 151).[19]

Common schools were the first American schools established in the region—these were elementary, teaching basic literacy (Lindsay, 1965). The earliest American school was established in 1824 in Beirut, which had become the center of American missionary activities, and educated the children of local people employed by missionaries as well as neighborhood children. By 1825, the school enrolled 80–90 students, the majority of whom came from Greek Orthodox families. A second school was established a few miles away from Beirut in 1825 and enrolled 20 boys (Lindsay, 1965). Generally speaking, at the beginning of this period, the educational approach of the ABCFM in Syria was conservative, focusing on memorization and recitation of scripture and religious texts. Literacy was viewed as an important way of spreading Protestant Christianity (p. 60).

Between 1830 and 1860, missionary presence in the Ottoman Empire brought in many changes, but the most widespread was the establishment of mission common schools in the region (Makdisi, 2000). By 1835, 11 schools had been established by the ABCFM in Syria, enrolling 323 students including 75 girls (Lindsay, 1965). Between 1845–1860, the policy of the ABCFM under Rufus Anderson led to an effort to make schools more religious. By 1862, local schools enrolled 1,925 students. For the remainder of the 19th century, enrollment in missionary common schools in Syria increased dramatically—perhaps because Rufus Anderson was no longer at the helm of the ABCFM's overseas work. According to Lindsay (1965), there were 2,840 students enrolled in 1876; 5,180 in 1884; and 6,087 in 1891. Missionary Henry Harris Jessup, however, reported that in 1897, enrollment was closer to 17,000 (including 8,000 girls) in all the Protestant schools in Syria and Palestine, with 150 American schools in Syria (Makdisi, 2011, p. 168).[20]

---

to consider USJ's curriculum alongside SPC's. However, I have not mentioned USJ extensively in this book as it remains outside the purview of my current expertise. A few relevant sources include Adil Baktiaya (2008), Susanna Ferguson (2018), Julia Hauser, Christine Lindner, and Esther Möller (2016), Rafaël Herzstein (2007, 2008, 2020, 2024), Idir Ouahes (2017), and Lorella Ventura (2014, 2018). I invite others to pursue this research!

19   Signs of the battle between Protestants and Jesuits in their pursuit of converts remain in present-day Lebanon in well-respected American-style and French educational institutions, as well as churches, which are prioritized and patronized by many elite and middle-class Lebanese families.

20   There is some discrepancy here, with Jessup's account likely being somewhat exaggerated in his memoir, *Fifty-Three Years in Syria* (1910). Whatever the case, the larger point—that enrollment was increasing significantly around the turn of the 20th century—stands.

While schools initially tried to provide religious education only, the local community wanted a modern, secular education. This affected the structure and focus of missionary schools (Makdisi, 2000, p. 90). In the beginning, the majority of the students who attended mission schools were from Christian sects, but this changed in the latter half of the 19th century (Masters, 2013, p. 195). By the first decades of the 20th century, American missions had broadened their approach to education significantly: ". . . by the eve of World War I the American schools were designed with the hope that they would help civilize, elevate, and enlighten the people of the Levant not only through religious instruction but also through a broad curriculum designed to create independent thinking and a broad spectrum of enlightening knowledge" (Lindsay, 1965, p. 112).

In addition to the common schools, which provided a relatively temporary basic education, the ABCFM also invested in opening several boarding schools, which were more costly and provided long-term education. In Lebanon, these schools included the Beirut Boys School (1835–1842), Abeih Seminary (c. 1844–1875), and others in Sidon (Sidon Evangelical School for Girls, est. 1862; Sidon Academy/Gerard Institute, est. 1881 and today merged as the National Evangelical Institute for Girls and Boys), Souk el Gharb (1882), and Zahleh (1885–1886) (Lindsay, 1965). The curriculum at these schools included a larger variety of subjects than those offered at the common schools. Like the missions' boarding schools for Native people in America, these schools were meant to separate students from their families and enculturate them in Protestant values and beliefs. Missionaries believed that these schools

> would diffuse Christian knowledge more widely. . . . A boarding school could train translators, native preachers, teachers, and assistants for the mission as well as offer men for public service who could later exercise an enlightened influence in the government. By providing well-trained young men for the government, the prestige of the ABCFM would be enhanced. (Lindsay, 1965, p. 141)

The language of instruction also proved important to mission schools. Prior to Rufus Anderson's tenure at the ABCFM, English was the medium of instruction at most schools because this allowed students to read religious texts as well as be exposed to Western knowledge (Lindsay, 1965, p. 145). When Anderson became the ABCFM's secretary, the language of instruction at the ABCFM schools changed to Arabic only, with education focused primarily on the Arabic language, math, and geography. Western knowledge was thought to have a corrupting influence, and it was feared it would encourage students to leave their home country (p. 155). In spite of the ABCFM's official policy, however, the Abieh Seminary succumbed to the demands of parents and local stakeholders and offered training in history, astronomy, natural philosophy, and English. Later, after SPC was founded, these secondary schools served unofficially as preparatory schools for the college.

The ABCFM and the Founding of Syrian Protestant College

In 1860, in large part due to the U.S. Civil War, the ABCFM was insolvent; financial support had been reduced dramatically for education and the Syrian mission in particular (Lindsay, 1965). At the same time, thousands of people migrated to Beirut due to conflicts between the Druze and Christians in Mount Lebanon, with European powers intervening and taking sides (the Druze were supported by the British whereas the Christians were supported by the French). Traditional familial, tribal, and religious hierarchies were broken and new economic structures requiring new skills and knowledge emerged. These developments, in combination with increasing contact with the West, led to an increased demand for modern education in Syria, especially in metropolitan areas such as Beirut. The Jesuits had also increased their activity in Beirut, which in turn amplified pressure for the American Protestant mission to respond. The French schools were growing rapidly, while the Protestants' stagnated, presumably because they did not provide exposure to the Western languages and culture demanded by the local population.

As enrollment in ABCFM's schools decreased in the early 1860s, the missionaries began to consider the possibility of establishing a college.[21] The missionaries reported to the ABCFM that, from their vantage point, "a more just appreciation of the value of education is rapidly spreading through the

---

21   The Syrian Society of Arts and Sciences (1847–1852, الجمعية السورية للعلوم و الفنون), founded by missionaries Eli Smith and Cornelius Van Dyck as well as native Syrians Butrus al-Bustani and Nasif al-Yaziji, is a good example of the intellectual work that preceded and, in part, motivated the founding of SPC (American University of Beirut Libraries, 2025, *al-Nahda*). Smith is credited for bringing the first Arabic printing press to Syria and beginning the first Protestant translation of the Bible in Arabic; Van Dyck was one of the founders of and a medical professor at SPC; al-Bustani was a Protestant convert who taught for the Syrian mission; and al-Yaziji later became a teacher at SPC. Smith and al-Bustani began the work of translating the Bible into Arabic, a project that Van Dyck and al-Yaziji continued to fruition; it was published in 1865. This Protestant translation of the Bible into Arabic was the most popular version of the Arabic Bible until the late 20th century. Van Dyck learned Arabic from al-Bustani and al-Yaziji, and he wrote many math and science textbooks in Arabic which were used in Syrian schools. al-Bustani is considered one of the major writers of the Arab *al-Nahda* (النهضة, or the Renaissance) movement.

Arab community generally" (Salibi & Khoury, 1995, p. 57).[22] In response to the Syrian mission's request for the project's approval, the ABCFM worried that offering the local population a more expansive education would risk alienating the students from their home communities, writing that "it is difficult to educate without, to a certain extent, denationalizing" (as cited in Jessup, 1910/2002, p. 301). The ABCFM offered their endorsement—but not official support—of the college only if the missionaries continued "emphasizing the vernacular part of the educational course" (as cited in Jessup, 1910/2002, p. 301). Therefore, SPC was officially founded separately from the ABCFM, but the college remained closely aligned with the ABCFM. The first faculty and administrators, including Daniel Bliss, George Post, and Cornelius Van Dyck, were in Syria as ABCFM missionaries prior to becoming faculty and administrators of the college, and the college's Board of Managers included missionaries living in Syria.

The original goal of the college, like the ABCFM's goal for its mission churches, was to create an institution that would eventually be locally run and self-supporting: Daniel Bliss (1920/1989), SPC's first president, wrote in a retrospective account toward the end of his life that the college was founded with the assumption that

> . . . the native Arab element should be introduced as fast as possible into the professorships and other teaching positions, in all departments of the College, in order that the Syrians might have every facility for qualifying themselves to assume, at no distant day, the entire management of the institution; that care should be exercised to prevent the students from becoming denationalized; that, in the interests of the independence and self-respect of the student body, the principle of self-support should be fostered as far as possible. (p. 68)

For this reason, Arabic was the medium of instruction for nearly two decades after the college was established (see Chapter 3 for a discussion of the college's decision to change the language of instruction to English). Although the decision about the language of instruction aligned with the conservative

---

22   The establishment and ultimate long-term success of institutions such as SPC and Université Saint-Joseph (the French Jesuit university opened in 1875) substantiates the missionaries' claims. However, it is likely that these claims were exaggerated. Alternative explanations could be that the establishment of the schools by French and American missionaries spurred a growing interest in education in the region, or, as Fortna (2002) pointed out, the value of education and enlightenment ideals was growing throughout the Empire simultaneous to the development of mission schools.

principles held by the ABCFM since the 1840s, the curriculum was modern, similar to that of the American colleges where the founders had been educated.[23] Writing, rhetoric, and literature were taught in Arabic, English, and French (with a focus on translation and conversation in English and French). Greek and Latin were electives, and Turkish was introduced in the third year. Mental and moral philosophy, mathematics, and science were part of the literary curriculum; the medical department included courses in anatomy, chemistry, physiology, medicine, and surgery.

Conclusion

This chapter illustrates the complex sociopolitical conditions in which SPC was founded in 1866 and forecasts the significance of SPC as a site of analysis for the discipline of rhetoric and writing studies. In the second half of the 19th century, Syrians were the subjects of a vast empire, the Ottoman Empire, with a language and culture distinct from the government's. This led to conflict and demands for autonomy that, at least in Beirut, were eventually granted. Compared to the rest of the region, Western influence was strongest in Syria because of its religious diversity, which included several Christian denominations. Education was largely private in the Empire until the turn of the 20th century, but there was a shared belief, especially among the rising middle class, that education could facilitate progress and prosperity. Most subjects of the Ottoman Empire were tied by a shared religious identity and saw the Empire as a ruling power that was preferable to Western imperialism.

Beginning in the 18th century, language and writing—including the fixing or standardization of language—became tied to the modern nation-state, with global colonialism underwriting this change. In the young United States, writing was used, alongside violence, to take land from Indigenous peoples, to map out a "newly discovered" country, and to trade humans as property. American Protestant missionaries held mixed views of the settler colonialism that pervaded their home country. But no matter their ambivalence, colonial epistemology informed a rewriting of history, ultimately producing a rhetoric of American exceptionalism—a belief that America was a nation chosen by God—that justified a missions movement that reached far beyond U.S. borders to "civilize" and convert the "lost."

The American missionaries who settled in the region in the early 19th century were indistinguishable from the British to most locals. The ABCFM

---

23   Daniel Bliss, SPC's first president, was educated at Amherst College, graduating in 1852, and Andover Theological Seminary, graduating in 1855.

targeted the Ottoman Empire for missionary work because it was outside of British control, the people had high rates of literacy, and so-called "nominal" Christians could be targeted for conversion. The ABCFM was an important sponsor of modern (Western) education, literacy, and the press to the region.

Haselby (2015) called the founding of SPC "the greatest achievement of the American missions movement," in large part because its founding put religion in a backseat position to the nationalism that was fundamental to the American Protestant evangelical movement (p. 244). Indeed, as Haselby (2015) pointed out, SPC—and later, AUB—"has never taught theology, nor had a seminary, nor even a religious studies department" (p. 244). Instead, its focus from the beginning was on providing a solidly Western education to the region, through which American (Christian) nationalism could be transmitted by virtue of its Protestant founders and Western (mostly American) professoriate. Indeed, as the first institution of higher education like it in the region, SPC represented for the local population, as well as the college faculty, an unofficial but important extension of an otherwise distant America. The success of SPC—and later, AUB—can be credited, at least in part, to the college's success in persuading the local population that its aim was not to force conversions through religious indoctrination. Rather, the college succeeded in presenting the knowledge it transmitted as universal and universally valuable—a hallmark of colonial epistemology.

But how did the college succeed in promoting its universal value in the context of the Ottoman Empire? To answer this question, we must consider that the Empire itself was undergoing a great deal of change, both in terms of updating its approach to education to become more "modern" (Western), and in interacting with—even relying on—European powers in order to survive. Exposure to Western innovations and epistemologies, therefore, would have primed the regional population to be open to Western schools. Undoubtedly, too, the college's location in Beirut was advantageous. Arab subjects had historically experienced conflict with each other and with the Empire; they saw themselves, and were seen by others, as distinct from Ottoman Turks. Relatively recently, they had begun to realize their autonomy as the Empire's grip over the region weakened. And, although the majority viewed themselves as Arab, the local population was highly diverse, including the "nominal" Christians that American Protestants had worked with frequently and with whom they occasionally had success. These experiences of precarity and independence, as well as regular encounters with difference, may have made some parts of the population more open to the education on offer by SPC.

As the rest of this book attests, SPC operated as a space where the Ottoman political sphere, the Arab world, and the American Protestant missionary movement converged. At SPC, language, culture, and identity were continually in flux and up for negotiation. SPC invited students to convert—or "come over"—to American Protestant culture and epistemology through its education. A decolonial analysis of the curriculum, student protests, and student writing at SPC—which comprises the coming chapters—offers scholars a more nuanced understanding of how literacy and rhetoric propelled SPC students' co-construction of identity in relation to the imagined America offered in and through the institution. Negotiation of the struggle over who *did* or *could* belong in this imagined America—and how literacy education is key to understanding this struggle—is the focus of this book.

In the upcoming chapters, I show how an imagined America—including the colonial epistemology underlying it—was always at the center of the college's approach toward literacy education. This centering of colonial epistemology, I argue, shaped not only how the college educated its students in and through literacy, but also how its students identified themselves rhetorically in relation to it. Analyzing SPC as a site of *colonial* literacy education—perhaps especially because it operated outside the formal processes of colonization—is valuable because it exposes the processes by which colonial epistemology has been, and continues to be, transmitted and sustained through literacy education. This analysis should also prompt scholars in rhetoric and writing studies to more purposefully examine the field's disciplinary history—as well as its disciplinary present and future—through a decolonial lens. The forthcoming chapters show, through analysis of several specific moments in the history of SPC, how colonialism has shaped (and continues to shape) approaches to literacy education, as well as how approaches to literacy education have shaped (and continue to shape) students.

3 Syrian Protestant College and the Exportation of America

One goal of this chapter is to show how Syrian Protestant College's (SPC's) curricular and language policy decisions complicate rhetoric and writing studies' Harvard narrative, which I discuss in Chapter 1. A more important goal of this chapter is to reveal how transnational and translingual discourses circulating outside of SPC prompted within it specific curricular and policy changes rooted in specifically American nationalist and monolingual ideologies. The existence of transnational and translingual discourses—hidden in the majority of rhetoric and writing studies' disciplinary histories—highlights the colonial underpinnings of the history of writing instruction, not only outside of North America but also inside of it. Perhaps anticipating critiques such as mine, Horner and Trimbur (2002) called for the "develop[ment] [of] an internationalist perspective capable of understanding the study and teaching of written English in relation to other languages and the dynamics of globalization" (p. 624). In this chapter, I answer this call by examining SPC's evolving language policies, curriculum, and extracurriculum. The evidence I present illustrates, first, that colonial epistemology served as a foundation for multiple, seemingly contradictory justifications for the medium of instruction (which was initially Arabic and later changed to English).[1] Second, I offer a provocative complication of Horner and Trimbur's (2002) assertion that languages other than English were pushed aside during the shift to the modern liberal arts curriculum by showing that multiple languages remained at the heart of SPC's curriculum. I argue that English, even as it gained prominence in SPC's curriculum as the medium of instruction in the 1880s, did not carry universal or uniform power. Finally, I offer implications of this chapter's historical account that links to the work of contemporary writing instructors, program administrators, and researchers.

Spack's (2002) exploration of Indigenous students' use of English in U.S. government schools and beyond—which she labeled translingual a decade

---

1   Jimenez (2023) arrived at a similar conclusion in her analysis of two differing approaches toward language policy in Filipino educational contexts during colonization: The first approach, under Spanish colonization, favored the vernacular, whereas the later approach by the US. sought to eliminate the vernacular and instituted English-only education. Both approaches, Jimenez argued, are inherently colonial (p. 113).

earlier than the term gained popularity in rhetoric and writing scholarship (see Chapter 2)—demonstrates that language use, even in highly oppressive contexts, provokes multidirectional change. In the American context of settler colonialism, "English-language teaching served to reinforce the United States government's linguistic, cultural, political, and territorial control over Native people" (Spack, 2002, p. 38). At the same time, Indigenous people "used English to speak for themselves and represent their own lives. . . . [They] manipulated the English language for their own purposes and played with it. . . . [They] took ownership of English to fashion a critique of a monolithic European American world view" (Spack, 2002, p. 112). In the context of SPC, where languages other than English remained a part of everyday communication as well as the curriculum, students and faculty alike continuously negotiated English and what it signified. As we can see here and in the chapters that follow, this negotiation changed students, administrators, faculty, and the institution itself.

The archives suggest that the issue of language(s)—including which language(s) should be taught and why, the effect of language(s) on students' identities, and the power and cultural value attached to language and education—was of central concern to the college's founders, ultimately determining the pedagogical approaches taken and curricular decisions made at SPC in its early years. Indeed, the founders' attitudes about and personal experiences with language learning and its politics, particularly in relation to the multi-sectarian, multicultural, and multilingual context of the region, shaped language policies and curriculum at SPC.

This chapter denaturalizes the role that English has played in the history of rhetoric and writing studies. In other words, this historical account resists taking English as a "given" in the history of the discipline. Instead, I argue, study of SPC's curriculum and language policy highlights the ways in which English has always interacted with multiple languages and transnational perspectives, even in seemingly monolingual contexts of writing pedagogy. This argument supports a larger claim: Language policy and curricular decisions within institutions have always been constructed in relation to transnational and translingual discourses in or outside of those institutions, even when those discourses are suppressed. The constructed power of English, in other words, is deeply related to its positioning alongside other languages. This chapter takes up Cushman's (2016) questioning of the discipline's "presumption that *English* is the *only* language of knowledge making and learning" (p. 234). Ultimately, this chapter reveals the pluriversal understandings of our history, present, and future that become possible when English is made *visible* as one of many languages at work, both in and outside of the US.

Shifting from Arabic to English at SPC

At the college's inception, SPC's American missionary founders wrote and translated textbooks for and taught their courses in Arabic. But in 1880 for the Collegiate and Preparatory Departments and in 1887 for the Medical Department, the language of instruction at SPC officially shifted from Arabic to English. In 1902, at the end of his 35-year tenure as founder and president of SPC, Daniel Bliss remarked that, "[i]n the intellectual development of the College, the most important step was the change of the language of instruction from Arabic to English" (*Annual Reports*, p. 225). Examining the decisions of SPC to change the language of instruction in relation to the specific context in which the shift took place underlines You's (2010) critique that American rhetoric and writing scholars generally lack "cognizan[ce] of the geopolitical differences and stakes involved in the teaching of English writing" (p. xi). Indeed, the complex multilingual, multicultural, and sectarian context of Beirut and greater Syria suggests that there is much for rhetoric and writing scholars and practitioners to learn from SPC's decision to move from Arabic to English instruction in the 1880s about the colonial epistemology underlying literacy curriculum.

What is the significance of the region's sociopolitical history to SPC's decision to teach in English instead of in Arabic? In contrast to You's (2010) history of the teaching of English in China, which suggests that English was often disconnected from and irrelevant to larger Chinese culture, decisions to teach (in) any language, including English, at institutions of higher education in Syria were deeply intertwined with the ever-evolving political and cultural landscape of the Ottoman Empire around the turn of the 20th century. The language of English as the medium of instruction pointed to an imagining of the West that was deeply connected to empire and colonialism. Languages carry a different value, or weight, depending on where they are used and promoted, and by and for whom. In the context of Syria, where the British Empire had previously intervened (see Chapter 2), the language of English (like the language of French) would have signified for locals new routes of employment and emigration, access to new and valuable forms of knowledge—particularly scientific and medical knowledge—and potentially, a loss of ties to home, friends, and family. In the context of SPC, the language of English also created (new) ties between the language and American and Protestant ideals, including democracy and personal liberty. For SPC students, the stakes of acquiring English were high, and SPC's founders held the keys to this acquisition. In articulating these stakes—this "weight"—through a historical lens, scholars in rhetoric and writing studies can identify parallels between this history and the high stakes of literacy education, particularly in English, today.

It is useful to first examine SPC's decision to change the language of instruction in light of its ties to the American Board of Commissioners for Foreign Missions (ABCFM). As discussed in Chapter 2, Rufus Anderson, who led the ABCFM's overseas work from 1832 until 1866, shifted the focus of the missions away from providing broad educational and civic opportunities to a focus on conversion only (Harris, 1999; Lindsay, 1965; Makdisi, 2011). This meant that most missions under the ABCFM offered education narrowly focused on religious matters in the local vernacular. The vernacular was prioritized as the language of instruction within the missions for several reasons: First, Anderson believed that the local language(s) could carry Christianity more directly and more effectively to potential converts. Additionally, Anderson believed that Christianity itself was enough to "civilize" potential converts—there was no need, therefore, for education in English or other subjects. And finally, Anderson worried that potential converts would take advantage of non-religious education and use it to obtain jobs outside of the mission or region, which would work against the "three-self" doctrine that sought to produce churches that would be self-supporting, self-governing, and self-propagating.

This decades-long approach to the work of missions was echoed when Syrian missionaries proposed the founding of SPC in the early 1860s to the ABCFM. One member of the Board argued that "a smattering of English fills men with conceit, makes them unwilling to labor in the villages, and [makes them] dissatisfied and heartless grumblers" (as cited in Jessup, 1910/2002, p. 301). In 1872, six years after the founding of SPC, President Daniel Bliss wrote, "Our experience thus far . . . though short confirms us in the opinion that young men, educated in the country and through the vernacular tongue, will use their education for the good of the country" (*Annual Reports*, p. 24). Arabic, in other words, was seen as the best means through which Christianity's "seeds" could be planted and eventually grow. The college founders imagined that SPC-educated students would convert to Christianity, graduate, and become leaders who would further propagate the region in support of the mission's purpose.

SPC's founders, particularly those faculty who taught science and medicine, were fluent in the Arabic language because the majority of them had lived and worked in Syria as missionaries for the ABCFM prior to the establishment of SPC. These faculty translated their knowledge from West to East, from English into Arabic.[2] As such, the use of Arabic as the language of instruc-

---

2   What was considered Western or modern scientific knowledge was a construction that emerged during the 19th century and should not be understood as neatly divided between East and West. Historians of science see Arabic/Islamic, Greek, Roman, and Medieval European scientific traditions as largely interconnected. Marwa Elshakry (2010) pointed out that in the 19th century, missionaries in Beirut redefined terms such as علم (*'ilm*, as science), معرفة

tion during SPC's early years played an important role in "the diffusion and translation of science. . . . For a moderate charge, students received instruction in all the latest scientific disciplines, from engineering and astronomy to medicine and natural science" (Elshakry, 2011, p. 180). Those faculty who were less experienced with Arabic were also required to receive training in the language. Even if teaching a foreign language such as English or French, before 1880 each faculty member studied Arabic, worked alongside local Syrian instructors, attended religious services in Arabic, and communicated in the vernacular with their students and within the local community daily.

The founders of the college initially supported providing education primarily in Arabic on the grounds that this would ensure that students (potential converts and future graduates) would stay in the region and, presumably, support the college and help it achieve its original self-sustaining goal. While English was taught as a language from the beginning, the founders' choice of Arabic as the medium of instruction rested on paternalistic views of what would serve the students of the region best—whether that meant students would avoid becoming "dissatisfied and heartless grumblers," as one Board member put it (as cited in Jessup, 1910/2002, p. 301), or would "use their education for the good of the country," as Daniel Bliss originally opined (*Annual Reports*, 1872, p. 24). For the founders, SPC had the potential to achieve what the ABCFM mission in the region did not—conversion of the masses. SPC offered an American-style education, supplemented with exposure to the "good word" through required religious services. Offering this education primarily in the Arabic language meant that, if local students converted at SPC, wider proselytization might be possible and the mission's vision of a "civilized" Middle East might be achieved. From the beginning, in other words, teaching in Arabic was rationalized as in the students' best interest, when in fact such an approach served the goals of the mission.

Although English eventually became the language of instruction for the college, the archives suggest that the faculty were split in the decision. The split emerged along the lines of those teaching science and medicine versus those who taught "literary" subjects such as rhetoric or foreign languages. The tension can be explained in part in practical terms: Newly hired English-speaking

---

(*ma'arifa* as knowledge), and حكمة (*hikma*, as wisdom): "In this formulation, knowledge was equated with matters of fact; science represented a higher order of truth in that it was the systematization of these facts through the derivation of natural laws; and, finally, wisdom, which was established by suprarational means, involved the Ultimate Truth" (p. 103). Such a redefinition allowed missionaries to create clearer divisions between "facts" and "belief"—even though the original Quranic meaning of علم includes both. In both Arab and Chinese contexts at the time, local scholars also traced "modern" Western science to their own knowledge traditions (Elshakry 2010, p. 104).

professors required private tutoring in Arabic. Efforts were made to recruit new faculty who already had a background in Arabic, such as Edward Van Dyck in 1870, whose "birth in, and . . . connection with [Lebanon], [whose] acquirements in the Arabic . . . [and] abilities and studies in other directions" made him an ideal candidate to teach at the college, but these efforts were not sustainable (*Annual Reports*, 1869, p. 6). As the school and its curriculum grew, finding faculty with both the appropriate amount of education and a background in Arabic became impractical: English-speaking faculty who were hired had to engage in intensive study of Arabic, in addition to fulfilling their other duties, as can be seen in the examples of Harvey Porter and Edwin Lewis, who, according to the 1871 *Annual Report*, "since their arrival have assisted in giving instruction in English and Latin but the greater portion of their time has been devoted to the study of the Arabic language" (p. 18).

With Arabic as the language of instruction, SPC faculty were also responsible for the translation of textbooks from English to Arabic or for writing new textbooks in Arabic for their courses. These activities were time- and labor-intensive. As early as 1869, Daniel Bliss expressed concern about how Arabic-language instruction might be maintained as students progressed through the college curriculum, reporting that

> the corps of teachers in the literary department is now barely able to carry out the programme of studies prescribed for the three first years. When these classes are advanced to more difficult studies, of which there are no text of books in the Arabic language, and another class enters, the present force of teachers will be inadequate. (*Annual Reports*, p. 6)

Even those prolific in Arabic and translation would have been burdened by the amount of time these activities required. Jessup (1910/2002) reflected that "Van Dyck and others had published in Arabic works on geography, arithmetic, pathology and the higher mathematics, but before a scientific textbook could be translated, printed and bound, it might be quite out of date, and the enormous expense of publishing Arabic books with their slow and limited sale made it impossible to keep up with the progress of science" (p. 304). Moreover, as Jessup's remarks indicate, publishing textbooks in Arabic was costly. David Stuart Dodge, a professor in the Collegiate Department, expressed skepticism about the cost in a letter to Daniel Bliss in 1875: "If English is to be so large an element hereafter, is Dr. Wortabet's *Physicology* in Arabic needed? Is it worthwhile to get out so expensive a book now? The plates and publishing cost heavily and the [publishing] fund may never see any return adequately" (Bliss, 1852–1956, D. S. Dodge to Bliss, April 12, 1875).

We can see in these materials how the rise of seemingly practical concerns—labor, time, and cost—pushed some administrators to advocate for a shift in the language of instruction at SPC. What does not seem to have been considered is how SPC had limited itself by creating narrow definitions of who could comprise the college's faculty: First, all faculty members at SPC were required to be Protestants, and as Antoine Benjamin Zahlan (1962) explained, "since qualified Protestants were limited in Syria, teachers had to be imported in increasing numbers as the College grew. The need for a carefully planned program for the recruiting and language training of additional staff was never met" (p. 71). Second, for local graduates to acquire the level of education needed to hold professorships at SPC, they would need the privileges of time and mobility, which many were hard-pressed to find: A. L. Tibawi (1967) wrote that while "[w]ith the graduation of the first class in 1870 it became possible to take American-trained native teachers or to send promising graduates to America for further training with view to their future employment in the College . . . it seems that this second method was too novel and expensive to have been even considered" (p. 283). And finally, while the college did allow Arabs to hold teaching positions, only foreigners held professorial-rank positions; in fact, Arab faculty were informally disallowed from the professorial ranks and did not hold any official power within the college until the 1920s (B. S. Anderson, 2011).[3] Zahlan (1962) pointed out that

> as late as 1897 six out of twenty teachers at SPC were Syrians and not one of these Syrian teachers had any voice in the affairs of the College. It seems quite possible that those faculty members who opposed the promotion of natives to professorial status desired the change to English in order that the linguistic ability of the Syrian teachers and the difficulty in recruiting sufficient British and American professors would not force the elevation of native teachers. (p. 84)

While SPC administrators created limitations on who could hold professorships, they did not explicitly deny the possibility that locals could hold such positions in the future. In fact, SPC could point to the goals set out by the college's founders to thwart any criticisms of its actual practices.

SPC faculty began making the case for switching the language of instruction to English just a few years after the founding of the college, in part

---

3   Arab instructors were not given professorial-rank status until 1909 and did not receive voting rights or professional equity until the school changed its name and dropped its religious affiliation in 1920, when it became present-day American University of Beirut (B. S. Anderson, 2011, p. 48).

based on the idea that English would provide students with greater exposure to Western ideas and epistemology. Discussion about the topic is evident as early as 1873, when some argued that providing students with consistent instruction in English meant that students would have direct "access . . . to nearly all that is valuable both old and new" (*Annual Reports*). In a letter to Daniel Bliss in 1874, Dodge wrote:

> I consider English as the essential thing now. We are running sciences into the ground. A knowledge of one foreign language, so that it is really understood and can be used with comfort and pleasure, will be actually of more service to any of our graduates than the general and indistinct smattering of chemistry, geology, astronomy and zoology which they carry away or are able to retain for twelve months. . . . Making thorough Eng[lish] or Fr[ench] scholars would, I am convinced, be as much or more advantage than the present notion that we teach foreign sciences, [of] which we have little practical use and for which people care little and know nothing. (Bliss, 1866–1902, D. S. Dodge to Bliss, August 5, 1875)

Although the argument Dodge made never mentioned Arabic, it was rooted in the colonial belief that European languages are inherently valuable, over and above any curriculum that would require Arabic to communicate knowledge.

In 1878, the faculty voted to give up the college's original mission and make the switch from Arabic to English (actual implementation would occur in the Collegiate Department in 1880, and in the Medical Department in 1887). They voiced reluctance to do so while at the same time articulating a belief that teaching in Arabic had not proven to be "the best means of Christianizing and civilizing the East" (*Annual Reports*, 1878, p. 45). For example, some faculty argued that students who

> . . .lay aside their English studies have little access to the thoughts of the great men of our age; they are shut up to the worst part of the dead past. After entering upon their professions instead of reading in a language permeated with the spirit of progress in all departments of life, they either read not at all or are confined to books, saturated with errors in religion, morals law [sic], politics, medicine, and social life. (*Annual Reports*, 1878, p. 45)

Thus, SPC faculty drew on the rhetoric used by the pre-Anderson ABCFM in the early 19th century to justify providing instruction in English, not Arabic.

They argued that English was instrumental in not only Christianizing but also civilizing the region. Instead of being "shut up to the worst part of the dead past," English would expose students to the "thoughts of the great men of our age." Instruction in English, they insisted, would correct the "errors" of local cultures and ways of life and instead promote the "spirit of progress" that was celebrated as a universal good throughout the West.

What's more, as other historians have pointed out and as discussed in Chapter 2, the missionaries continually failed in their efforts to convert the local population, and this also justified a switch to English as the medium of instruction. Zahlan (1962) explained that

> By 1882 the missionaries had explored all possibilities as to means by which to attain their ends. They had translated the Bible into Arabic. They had opened schools for both boys and girls, established seminaries and founded SPC itself. They had supplied medical aid to the populace. They had established churches. None of these projects had brought about the great wave of conversion that they had dreamed of. There was one factor left to vary, however, and this was the language of instruction at the College. (p. 79)

Despite SPC President Bliss' optimism about Arabic at the founding of the college, instruction in the language had not translated into an increased number of conversions. Therefore, the English language seemed to be the only path left if the college were to be successful in proselytization.

At SPC, English won out not only for its ability to "correct" and "civilize" but also because it provided a practical solution for the college in maintaining a balance of power that supported the college's American faculty and administration. The justification for English as the language that would bring students closest to presumed universal (Western and Christian) truths seemed to contradict the administration's (and the ABCFM's) earlier stance on Arabic as the best medium of instruction for "civilizing" and "Christianizing" the locals. However, the justifications expressed for both languages ultimately relied on deeply colonial logics that centered and upheld Eurocentric ways of knowing: On the one hand, Arabic was seen as a more direct conduit to the hearts and minds of the local population and therefore was potentially more effective for the mission's evangelism. On the other hand, English could more directly support and transmit the colonial epistemology that constituted the heart of the college.

What's more, as the student population grew year after year, SPC's need for more faculty grew—and this too became a justification for switching to

English as the language of instruction. Foreign hires were recruited because locals—who generally had not had access to the Western education so prized in the American college—were not seen as qualified enough to hold faculty positions. Most of these foreign hires, who primarily hailed from America, were not proficient in Arabic and would require years of language training before they would be ready to teach. College faculty argued that it was simply inefficient to wait for these native speakers of English to gain Arabic proficiency. And although the college had indicated a desire to eventually turn its leadership over to locals, it clearly did not see this transfer of power happening any time soon. We can see, therefore, that decisions about the language of instruction at the college served the needs of the college's American administrators and faculty rather than putting the local population at the center. The materials preserved in the archives also do not reveal consideration of students' needs or desires regarding the language(s) of instruction or the extra burden they were forced to take up after the switch to English took place. Faculty and administrators seemed to assume that students would agree that English carried with it a universal good and a higher value than students' native language.

Language and the SPC Curriculum

Despite the colonial epistemology that drove SPC administrators and faculty to make key decisions regarding the college's language of instruction, ultimately they could not wipe away the multiple languages that characterized everyday life for the local Syrian population. In fact, no matter the language of instruction, the college's curriculum was decidedly multilingual at its founding and throughout its history. The materials preserved in the archives provide evidence of a multilingual curriculum that complicates dominant disciplinary historical narratives in rhetoric and writing studies, which have ignored translingual practices or have focused on institutions, such as Harvard, that indeed minimized the value of multilingualism by shifting from a classical to liberal arts model of education (see Horner & Trimbur, 2002).

Before and after the shift from Arabic to English instruction at SPC, students studied Arabic, English, and French intensively, and in fact, for the students enrolled in the Collegiate Department, language study occupied much of their time at least until the turn of the 20th century. Latin and Greek were offered until the mid-1880s, and Turkish was offered as the college's first elective (to substitute for French) in 1898 (Syrian Protestant College, *Catalogue*). According to the details provided in the course catalogues, the central language-based courses—Arabic, French, and English—focused on the consumption and production of texts at all levels. In every language, students read not only literary and rhetorical texts, studied grammar, and practiced penmanship, but they also wrote original essays—"extempore compositions"—gave performances of memorized texts, delivered "original orations," and practiced conversation in the target language. The examples of the curriculum that are available suggest that students were expected to be able to work across languages, an approach that scholars in rhetoric and writing studies might today call translingual.

Examples of end-of-year exams for all subjects and all years—including exams for Arabic, French, and English—were published in the course catalogues for academic years 1871 and 1872 (المدرسة الكلية السورية الإنجيلية [Syrian Protestant College]). While each English exam focuses, perhaps predictably, on providing definitions ("What is the meaning of vice versa?" Senior Year, 1871) and explaining grammar ("Into how many parts is English Grammar divided and what are they?" Freshman Year, 1872), students were also asked to translate short texts from English to Arabic, and from Arabic to English. At times, students were asked to translate a text and also provide examples of the correct usage of a particular word in the same passage. Take the following two questions from a Sophomore-level exam, published in the 1871 course catalogue:

> Having no money I was obliged to beg.
>
> - Translate this into Arabic; and give a few examples of this kind of construction.
>
> No thank you I have one already.
>
> - Translate th [sic] sentence and explain the ward [sic] *already* and give sentences showing how it is used.

Sample French exams required students to demonstrate similar kinds of knowledge, including the ability to translate, while exams in Arabic assumed a more complex understanding of the grammatical nuances of the language.

At least two interpretations can be made from the exams: On the one hand, the examinations appear to rely on a monolingual ideology, in that they focus primarily on surface-level concerns. Although translation is requested, the elements of a "good" or "correct" translation are not articulated—and understanding the expectations is imperative, as a literal, word-for-word translation is a different (and presumably simpler) kind of project than a meaning-based, or idiomatic, translation, which is focused on intelligibility for the recipient. What's more, the exams do not ask students to write anything beyond what is required to answer each question. On the other hand, the exams can be understood as evidence of translingual practice: The exams demonstrate that, at least in the early years of the college, students were being asked to think and write in multiple languages simultaneously—even within the constraints of an exam.

While no other course materials from this period at SPC have been preserved, we do know that the curriculum required students, in addition to studying grammar and learning vocabulary, to actively engage with texts and produce their own, in multiple languages. Just as English-speaking faculty were forced to negotiate language, formally and informally, on a daily basis, Arabic-speaking students at SPC were also regularly working across language to make meaning as writers, readers, and speakers of multiple languages. However narrowly language norms may or may not have been presented and upheld in the classroom, students and faculty at SPC were likely aware of the "heterogene[ity], fluid[ity], and negotiab[ility]" of language as it was encountered in multiple contexts and used for multiple formal and informal purposes (Horner, Lu, et al., 2011, p. 305). For those living in multilingual contexts, it is impossible to ignore the malleability of language and the linguistic and extra-linguistic resources available to make meaning. This suggests that in practice if not in pedagogy, SPC represents an institutional location in which a translingual approach was fundamental, as Horner, Lu, et al. (2011) would characterize it. Importantly, as discussed earlier in this chapter, translingual practice was not neutral in this space: American faculty and administrators during this period ultimately created language policy that maintained the dominance of the English language. This dominance constructed a colonial educational space that delivered a clear message to students about the seemingly inherent value of English, while also working to construct a vision of America for which students, it was implied, should strive. At the same time, this dominance was troubled not only by the recognition of multiple languages in SPC's curriculum, but also translingual practice in the context of the college's extracurriculum.

Extracurricular activities at SPC, which I discuss here as well as in the next two chapters, suggest that students and faculty alike understood language as a rhetorical and evolving practice. Specifically, in 1871, the medical students formed a literary society, which the following year became two (one Arabic and one English), in which weekly "exercises were both oral and written upon literary[,] scientific[,] and moral subjects. The society celebrated its first anniversary meeting by an oration and a public debate" (Annual Reports, 1871, p. 21). One faculty member reflected that "the work of the year" for the Arabic literary society attracted the interest of the college and local community; the society's activities "always culminated in a grand annual open meeting when Assembly Hall was crowded to the doors with friends of the Society and with those from the city who wished to encourage activity in Arabic literary work"

(*Founding*, n.d., p. 12). By 1878, the faculty saw the literary societies as so useful in their "contribut[ion] to the development of the minds of the students and their readiness in extempore speech" that they moved to require all students to participate in the activities of the societies (Syrian Protestant College, p. 323).

In February 1871, the faculty minutes report that the students enrolled in the Collegiate Department wished to start a journal—and although it is not clear whether the request was approved, students' interest in pursuing such an activity did not wane (Syrian Protestant College, *Minutes of Faculty*; see also Chapter 5). For graduation in 1873, students gave orations in English, French, Turkish, and Arabic on subjects as varied as "Labor, Love of Country, The Immortality of the Soul, Advantages of History, The Sun, [and] Growth of Plants" (p. 162). According to historian Betty Anderson (2011), "students published a magazine or newspaper for part of almost every year between 1899 and [the present]" (p. 22)—student writing in these publications is the focus of Chapter 5. Also at the turn of the 20th century, a prize for writing was established and awarded annually for at least a few years.

While these extracurricular activities occurred in multiple languages, it is important to consider the place of Arabic in SPC's curriculum, as it never disappeared, even after the switch to English as the language of instruction. It is difficult to make a causal connection between SPC's initial and continued emphasis on Arabic and النهضة (*al-Nahda*, literally "the Awakening" but often referred to as the "Arab Renaissance)—a pro-Arab and sometimes nationalist movement that aimed to revive the Arabic language and led to the translation and appropriation of Western knowledge, literature, and philosophy into Arab and Muslim contexts. However, most historians note that instruction in Arabic, at SPC and the mission schools, at least indirectly supported the larger movement occurring throughout the Arab world (see B. S. Anderson, 2011). Some of the first SPC instructors, as well as early graduates of SPC were active as professional writers and editors throughout the region.[4]

---

4   Nasif al-Yaziji (1800–1871), Butrus al-Bustani (1819–1883), Ahmed Faris al-Shidyaq (1805/6–1887), Ibrahim al-Yaziji (1847–1906, son of Nasif), and Rashid Rida (1865–1935)—all considered pioneers of *al-Nahda*–were born in Greater Syria. Nasif al-Yaziji and Butrus al-Bustani were both Protestant converts, and Nasif al-Yaziji was an instructor at SPC, as were Faris Nimr (1856–1951) and Ya'qub Sarruf (1852–1927), both of whom were also alumni of SPC. Bustani taught with the ABCFM and wrote Arabic and math textbooks. In 1863, he founded his own school in Beirut and started a daily newspaper. He and Nasif al-Yaziji founded the Syrian Society of Arts and Sciences and translated the Protestant Bible into Arabic with Eli Smith and Cornelius Van Dyck in the mid-19th century. Nimr and Sarruf founded the periodical al-Muqtataf in Beirut and Cairo, and Jurji Zeidan, who was a medical student at SPC but did not graduate, founded *al-Hilal* in Cairo and went on to write 23 novels. For more on Nimr, Sarruf, and Zeidan and their relationship to SPC, see Chapter 4.

Zahlan (1962) pointed out, for example, that although the *al-Nahda*'s roots were centered in Egypt, "the size and influence of the Syrian Arab contingent in Egyptian journalism"—including Arabic-educated graduates of SPC between 1866 and 1880—"was overwhelming" (p. 73). Zahlan and others have emphasized the importance of Arabic education at SPC in terms of performing a kind of cultural transfer. Elshakry (2011) noted that "historians have . . . accord[ed] the missionaries a key role in the transformation of Syrian society and identity" (p. 168). At the same time, as discussed in Chapter 2, such transformation cannot be understood as determined solely by the missionaries—in other words, specific kinds of knowledge and resources were in demand throughout the Ottoman Empire, and whatever successes might be attributed to the mission, and later to SPC, is related to how the mission and SPC were able to fulfill the demands of the local population, most of which were not religious in nature. Missionaries were skilled at articulating justifications for the language and literacy education that they provided, and these justifications mostly followed the lines of colonial thought. However, the local population had their own reasons for taking advantage and making use of the linguistic resources offered through mission schools and SPC.

It is clear from the archives that the study of multiple languages—and the study of writing, oration, rhetoric, and literature within and across those languages—constituted the core of the school's curriculum. No matter a student's or teacher's language background, at SPC, all were engaging in a translingual type of negotiation with the school's official curriculum and policy toward language. We can only begin to imagine what those practices, and subsequent pedagogies, may have looked like on an everyday basis, but it would have been impossible for students or teachers to study grammar, oration, reading, or writing in one language without considering and negotiating others. The college's transnational curriculum, perhaps unsurprisingly, highlights the important role that multiple languages played for students and faculty. Adding this account to the disciplinary history of rhetoric and writing studies requires a rethinking of the centrality of English in the discipline's narratives. While the English language has undoubtedly defined the history of rhetoric and writing studies, it is the interaction of multiple languages (after all, one language cannot be prioritized without the existence of others) that has ultimately shaped approaches to literacy education, for better or worse. This history should push others to further account for how students and teachers of writing have engaged—and continue to engage—with language(s) and translingual practices, even in seemingly monolingual contexts.

Conclusion

This chapter's account of SPC's language policies and curriculum substantiates a transnational and translingual narrative about the history of rhetoric and writing studies. At SPC, an imagined America—constructed through common, specifically American, assumptions about literacy—was exported across national, cultural, and linguistic borders. The college's policies on the language of instruction changed over time but were consistently rationalized through an Anglophone, colonial lens. The curriculum, too, was clearly influenced by the founders' own experiences as students at Yale, Harvard, and Amherst in the early and mid-19th century. As they developed SPC, the founders would have been aware of the recent changes that reduced the study of multiple languages at Harvard—and yet, perhaps because they could not assume a monolingual stance in the local context, multiple languages remained at the core of the college's curriculum. SPC's unique position as a fulcrum among languages, epistemologies, and cultures should encourage scholars to reexamine those American institutions of the past, where the intermingling of language, epistemology, and culture may have been less than explicit but must have been a force to be reckoned with, requiring negotiation within and across languages, a negotiation that remains active in the present.

Exposure of the (mostly American) faculty at SPC to multiple languages and the local population meant, in turn, exposure to the local culture, along with its complicated religious beliefs, politics, and epistemologies. As they negotiated these differences, no faculty member or student—foreign or domestic—would have been unchanged. Languages at SPC, therefore, acted as instruments whereby various kinds of knowledge, formal and informal, were exchanged multidirectionally—and this exchange undoubtedly had an influence far beyond the grounds of the college. In other words, although the language of English and the colonial epistemology attached to it was dominant at the college, it was not hegemonic.

Arabic and English at SPC, therefore, can be understood as epistemological conduits that were anything but unidirectional. Indeed, English at SPC was—and continues to be today at AUB—laden with "a whole different constellation of values and practices" than those that tend to be attached to English in the United States (You, 2010, p. xi; see also Arnold, 2021). What it meant to teach, study, and write in English for students and faculty at SPC can only be understood in relation to the region's geopolitical history. For many, English provided a route to a better life outside the country, or it represented social or cultural privilege and power within the region. In contrast, for others, achieving fluency in English meant a break from distinct cultural and ethnic traditions, and perhaps irreparable departure from family and friends. At the same time, other languages, including Arabic and French, carried varied meanings in the same context. Languages, and in particular colonial *lingua francas* such as English and French, carry a value, or weight, that changes depending on the context.[5] In Greater Syria during the late 19th century, English signified a gateway to the West, including emigration to the United States or work within the British Empire.[6] At SPC, English shifted to represent America because it was used by the college's American administrators and taught by the American faculty. While the United States at the time was still a new nation and not yet the world power that it is considered today, the nation was represented in and through English at SPC.

This chapter reveals that SPC's decision-making about the language of instruction relied on deeply colonial logic. Like their students, college faculty and administrators understood that English provided knowledge and prospects that might not otherwise be available with Arabic alone. They initially withheld these resources in order to support their own belief that Arabic was the most direct route for conversion of the local population, and that English had the potential to move students away from the region rather than staying and spreading Christianity. Likewise, the decision to switch the language of instruction to English rested primarily on the basic premise that Western forms of knowledge were inherently superior to local ones. Instruction in English, college faculty and administrators believed, would allow students direct access to modern (Western) literature, science, and philosophy; as a result, students would surely leave behind "the worst part of the dead past," represented in and through Arabic, and move toward a more "civilized" future (*Annual Reports*, 1878, p. 45). A secondary rationale for the switch to English— that the college did not have time to train foreign faculty in Arabic—also relied on colonial epistemology, in that such a decision put the needs and interests of the college faculty and administrators above their students and assumed the superiority of foreigners over locals when it came to filling faculty positions (even though the founders had previously indicated that they intended for the college to eventually be turned over to local leadership).

The negotiations among college faculty and administrators about SPC's language of instruction, then, highlights the "weight" of English for those

---

5   For an extended discussion of the "weight" of English in the context of contemporary American University of Beirut (AUB), see my (2021) contribution to Silva and Wang's (2021) *Reconciling Translingualism and Second Language Writing*.

6   For more information on patterns of Arab immigration to the United States, particularly immigrants from Greater Syria during the same time period as this study, see Becky Little (2025).

who have historically been identified as outsiders to the language through colonial epistemology. At SPC, English—and the Americans who represented it at the college—carried considerable weight for students. The language represented a kind of power valued at the college, and faculty members held it out as a kind of promise for students—a promise that many of them later learned was false (see Chapter 4). Even those who graduated early on from the college and were hired there as instructors did not gain status equal to their foreign counterparts. They learned that, in spite of their best efforts, they could never gain the kind of power implied by English at the college. In creating these contradictory conditions, the administration held an imagined America at bay for local instructors and students alike. In this context, English was more than a language—it also served as a gateway to certain kinds of (Western) knowledge and social rewards. The founders of the American college knew this, and the debate about whether English should be the medium of instruction revolved around the kind of power and access that they wanted to offer to students. SPC, in other words, was constructed as an institution that mimicked exactly what America really was and continues to be: a country that professes democracy, equality, and liberty for all but that in reality makes the attainment of these ideals largely contingent upon racial, ethnic, linguistic, religious, and/or cultural identity.

Studying SPC's negotiations about the language of instruction raises questions about some of the field of rhetoric and writing studies' contemporary "structuring tenets" (Cushman, 2016, p. 239), such as what language(s) are prioritized in programs and classrooms and why, and the ability to recognize the different power dynamics at play when it comes to writing in English or in other languages (see Gilyard, 2016). Taking a historical perspective on the question of language in rhetoric and writing studies curricula suggests that the weight of English is more complex and more deeply rooted in colonial history for students enrolled in college-level writing classes than program administrators, instructors, and students might expect. For writing scholars, administrators, and teachers living and working in Anglocentric contexts such as the US, recognizing that English *has* a weight shifts the understanding of historical narratives, such as the Harvard narrative described in Chapter 1, that have rendered English, and its interaction with translingual and transnational discourses, invisible. As a result, teachers, program leaders, and scholars in rhetoric and writing studies tend to see writing programs and classrooms as largely linguistically homogenous spaces (see Matsuda, 2006), where translingual and transnational discourses are representative of difference rather than part of the norm and thus are treated separately.

Just as SPC students negotiated the complicated weight of English every day, so too do students today negotiate this weight, whether consciously or not. Writing program administrators and teachers should consider how to better adapt teaching to the reality of students' linguistic lives. Students today, particularly but not only multilingual and historically underrepresented students in the US, come into writing classrooms with different legacies of oppression that are often tied to language and language ideology. Their experiences and understandings of what English means, and has meant, can differ considerably from instructors' own experiences and understanding. The Indigenous languages of students' ancestors may have been violently suppressed through colonial educational practices or by withholding education altogether. Additionally, many students have faced teachers who hold onto harmful language ideologies that are deployed unpredictably in response to their writing. And some students face intense pressure from home to represent their family, culture, race, or ethnicity well in higher education. On account of their identities, these students are expected, and they expect of themselves, to achieve high levels of success, which oftentimes means adopting and staying within the bounds of dominant ways of thinking and being. How can writing programs and educators expect students to trust them when it comes to the deeply personal activity of writing? In the face of the power that literacy educators wield, while carrying weighty legacies and expectations of English, students cannot be blamed for resisting instructors' appeals to develop ideas, refusing to revise meaningfully, or keeping personal reflection to a minimum.

When multilingualism is understood as the historical norm (Yildiz, 2012)—as an always-already part of writing practices and pedagogies around the globe—writing program leaders, teachers, and scholars can better articulate the practical and problematic consequences of monolingualism in literacy classrooms. Just like the American missionary founders of SPC, writing programs in Anglocentric contexts are implicated in a monolingual and ultimately colonial framework that privileges English and mastery of it. Students of writing (in English) are always already working within and across languages; acknowledging that students have agency and desires in relation to language will enrich the writing classroom, enabling teachers to work with the "multiple origins, relations, and emotional investments [that] are possible and occur daily" for students, including those investments that do not align with our own (Yildiz, 2012, p. 205).

In addition, examining the history of language attitudes, policies, pedagogies, and practices at SPC highlights that the problems faced by contemporary rhetoric and writing scholars and teachers are not new. The archival materials explored in this chapter suggest that the SPC founders struggled with difficult questions related to language and literacy similar to those we face today. These difficult questions include: How should different languages and/or language varieties be approached and valued in the college classroom? In what ways might teachers, scholars, and administrators negotiate the complex relations among specific educational contexts and policies on or about language, and what do these decisions mean for students, particularly student writers? And how can researchers, teachers, and administrators address the politics of language and language difference in ways that acknowledge the concerns and needs of all those who have a stake in higher education? These questions are highlighted in contemporary discussions about "professionalism" in writing and what students "need" from writing courses. These questions are undermined when programs and instructors do not recognize the language resources and language legacies of students in writing classrooms, or when writing programs, educators, and scholars frame students' varied literacies as problems to be solved rather than resources to be valued.

Understanding the history, present, and future of rhetoric and writing studies as inherently transnational and translingual means recognizing that even seemingly monolingual students wrestle with what writing in English means. In every educational context, particular uses of English signify identification with and belonging to particular sociopolitical groups. Therefore, writing programs and teachers should take the opportunity to promote inter- and intra-language and cultural exchange. At the same time, instructors should always be aware that these opportunities will present risks as well as rewards for students depending on their (as well as their instructors') experiences, values, and desires. In other words, every programmatic, curricular, and pedagogical decision related to language practices and standards represents beliefs and values outside of the classroom—including implied, perhaps unfulfilled, promises—and thus carry consequences that will be neither predictable nor smooth.

Perhaps most importantly, this historical account pushes us to ask: How can we make *all* language practices—including the language of English—visible? Recognizing English as a language that carries ideological power, rather than taking it for granted as a "given," is one step we can take to delink the colonial legacy of English from the history of rhetoric and writing studies. The social justice goals that underlie much of rhetoric and writing studies scholarship will advance only if and when writing scholars, program administrators, and teachers recognize and work to undo the ties that have bound English to colonial epistemology as well as to Anglocentric language policies and curriculum in higher education. Such delinking, in turn, can expand the scope of the discipline and push us to recognize and value the existence of pluriversal literacy practices and pedagogies in the discipline's history, present, and future.

4 Specters of America in Students' Rhetorical Activism at Syrian Protestant College

Syrian Protestant College (SPC) experienced two significant moments of student protest and rhetorical activism between 1866 and 1920; together, these crises disrupted the usual workings of the college and demanded responses from the college faculty and administrators as well as from local and regional community members. These crises reveal how the college constructed an imagined America through its curriculum and policies and how students learned the limits of belonging to this idea(l) through their literate action. In this chapter, I analyze how the idea—or specter—of America was invoked rhetorically to forward these two moments of student protest. The first moment, known as the "Lewis Affair," occurred in 1882 as a response to the forced resignation of a respected professor, Dr. Edwin Lewis, in the medical school. The second, known as the "Muslim Controversy," occurred during the academic year 1908–1909 and was sparked after an Islamophobic sermon was delivered during the chapel service, which all SPC students, including Muslim and Jewish students, were required to attend.

Although the students who participated in these protests were not, ultimately, successful in changing SPC's decisions, both moments are significant for this study in the ways that they reveal the strong ties that bind literacy education to American nationalism and religious ideology. For example, during the 1882 crisis, students at first characterized America and its affiliated values in a positive light, as model citizens would, but their rhetoric shifted in a final petition to the administration, in which they critiqued the "noble, pious American people" who had unfairly broken the promise of equal opportunity that they believed an American education would afford (as cited in Jeha, 2004, p. 67). During the 1909 protest, students conjured what they knew of America to critique the administration's religious requirement. The 1909 controversy generated conversation—and controversy—beyond the college and throughout the region, inspiring anti-Western rhetoric grounded on a growing sense of Arab identity and Muslim unity.

This chapter adds to the evidence showing how literacy education has historically been used to maintain colonial markers of identity that determine who is included and who is excluded from an imagined America. As discussed in Chapter 1, literacy in the US has been linked to American nationalist ideology since at least the late 19th century, as Americanization educational programs were developed to create ideal citizens out of the waves of immigrants from outside of Western Europe who arrived in the US (see Kendall Theado, 2013; NeCamp, 2014) and as Jim Crow laws in the American South used (lack of) literacy as a weapon to prevent former slaves from exercising their right to vote. More recently, rhetoric and writing scholars and program administrators have used the idea of citizenship, according to Wan (2011), as an "ambient" (and ambiguous) label to describe a range of literate actions and behaviors that, they imply, can produce citizens (pp. 30–33). Wring scholars, program leaders, and teachers base this connection between literacy and citizenship on the assumption that literacy has the potential to lead to productive engagement with(in) democracy. Wan (2011) noted that this idea of citizenship is problematic insofar as it suggests that citizenship is achievable by individual behavior or activity and is a means through which equality and social mobility can be gained (pp. 29–30). This claim ultimately rests upon and reinforces a colonial epistemology that draws on a "rhetoric of modernity" in which individualism and the nation-state are privileged (Mignolo, 2007, p. 464). Ana Milena Ribero (2016) added the observation that in the US, citizenship is racialized through exclusion, in that it is "marked on the body through phenotypical characteristics (e.g., skin color, hair texture) and social traits (e.g., clothing, mannerisms, language use)" (p. 35). To be successful, the embodied performance of citizenship must fit dominant discourses of citizenship (Ribero, 2016, p. 40). When connected to literacy education, the idea of citizenship amounts to a mere "aspiration, a promise" that can easily be broken—which SPC students learned as they attempted to perform certain "habits of citizenship" but found them insufficient for provoking change (Wan, 2011, p. 46).[1]

During the two moments of crisis discussed in this chapter, SPC students articulated their sense of American cultural citizenship, something Wan (2011) described as a "state of being" rather than static legal category (p. 37), while at the same time finding the limits of belonging to the American

---

[1] It is important to note that there are some limitations in applying Wan's (2011) argument to SPC, in that Wan's focus is on U.S. contexts of literacy education, and SPC students generally did not aspire to emigrate to the US or to become American citizens (though some Syrians did emigrate to the US around the turn of the 20th century). The point I am making in this chapter, however, is precisely that the example of SPC shows how ideologies associated with American-style literacy education extend beyond national borders. American national, religious, and linguistic ideologies were promoted at SPC and sent the message that literacy itself would allow students to enjoy full rights and inclusion at the American college.

college. This citizenship by performance if not by law informed students' strategic construction and deployment of an imagined America in their responses to the crises. They used this construction to speak to college administrators and other stakeholders against injustices they perceived to be antithetical to the American values and beliefs espoused within the curriculum and also to critique America as it was symbolized in and through the college itself. The college's (American) faculty's and administrators' responses to the crises expose deeply held racist and xenophobic attitudes about Arab students, which in turn highlights the colonial epistemology—the specter of America that students discovered—underlying the college's curriculum and policies. This epistemology ran up against local values and beliefs that promoted Arab unity and, in the second protest, Muslim identity. Together, the crises reveal contradictory definitions of and desires for American-style literacy education and the impasse created when two competing epistemologies meet in the context of literacy education. These contradictions continue to shape contemporary literacy education in and outside of the US today.

The "First Student Rebellion in the Arab World:" The 1882 Lewis Affair

What has been called "the first student rebellion in the Arab world" occurred at SPC in 1882 (Zeidan, as cited in Leavitt, 1981, p. 97; Jeha, 2004, p. 52). Sixteen years after the college opened, 160 students were enrolled (see Appendix A for demographic details), and administrators, faculty, and students all held a stake in seeing the school succeed, albeit for different reasons. The crisis, alternately called the "Lewis Affair" (Farag, 1972; Leavitt, 1981) or the "Darwin Affair" (B. S. Anderson, 2011), occurred after a professor in the medical department, Dr. Edwin Lewis, gave the college's commencement address in July 1882. His speech, given in Arabic, was titled "Knowledge, Science, and Wisdom." In the address, Lewis set out to define the terms in the title, and he illustrated the term *science*—which he defined as the active construction of knowledge—with reference to the work of scientists Charles Lyell, Louis Pasteur, and Charles Darwin, the latter of whom had died only a few months before. In the speech, Lewis acknowledged the public controversy surrounding Darwin's theory of evolution, suggesting that "his theory was opposed by enemies and antagonists . . . because his doctrine led to the nullification of certain ideas strongly adhered to by the people as though they were part of their religion" (as cited in Leavitt, 1981, p. 86). Lewis gently promoted the validity of the theory in his speech, pointing out that Darwin's *On the Origin of Species* was based on 20 years of quantitative research. Darwin, Lewis argued, applied the high standards of the scientific method that had been used by Lyell before him, noting that Darwin was "an example of the trans-formation of knowledge into science by long and careful examination and accurate thinking," thus exemplifying the ways in which science would—and should—build upon pre-existing knowledge (as cited in Leavitt, 1981, p. 85).[2] Lewis was ultimately forced to resign by SPC leaders, and the majority of the medical faculty also resigned in support.

In the sections that follow, I examine the rhetoric surrounding the crisis, in which can be seen SPC faculty and administrators negotiating internal disagreements about the religious and moral identity of the college as well as the value of Western scientific knowledge. This dispute was relevant to the college's identity as an American institution and its relationship with the local American Board of Commissioners for Foreign Missions (ABCFM) Syrian mission and the region *writ large*. Perhaps more significantly, for students, the crisis represented a failure of the college to uphold its promise of offering an American education and to act according to what they assumed were American values—values represented in and through SPC's approach to education. In addressing and eventually resolving this crisis, students and faculty articulated these differences into contradictory visions about the meaning of SPC, arriving at a definition that many found unsatisfactory but that would outline the direction of the college for years to come. The contradictory assumptions and values that emerge in the rhetoric surrounding the crisis illustrate the devastating effects of colonial epistemology carried out in the name of education, particularly literacy education. Students' deployment of literate action during this crisis reveals their own agency while at the same time illustrating the impossibility of achieving the cultural citizenship seemingly on offer at SPC. In the following sections, I first discuss the faculty response, then turn to the student response, and then discuss how the crisis was resolved with implications for the discipline of rhetoric and writing studies.

---

2   Hisham Sharabi (1970) discussed the influence of John Stuart Mill, Charles Darwin, Herbert Spencer, and Thomas Henry Huxley on Arab Christian intellectuals in Syria; the ideas of these philosophers and scientists were mostly imported to the region by American- or British-educated Syrians (pp. 68-70). Darwin was translated into Arabic by Shibili Shumayyil, an 1871 graduate of SPC. In 1910, Shumayyil published a book on Darwin's theory of evolution (called *The Philosophy of Education and Progress*). He also wrote multiple articles about Darwinsim in the regional Arabic-language magazines *al-Muqtataf* and *al-Hilal*. Sharabi noted that there was controversy surrounding Darwin in Syria in the 1890s and 1900s, and the points raised against Darwin were similar to those of British Victorians a generation earlier (1860s and 1870s). See also Albert Hourani (1983).

Faculty Response

The varied responses to Lewis' address by SPC faculty and administrators expose the lack of consensus regarding the identity and mission of the American college among local and international stakeholders. Lewis' speech was published in the Cairo-based Arabic-language journal *al-Muqtataf* (المقتطف, or "The Extract"), which was founded by Syrians (Jeha, 2004).[3] After the speech's publication, Dr. James Dennis, an ABCFM missionary, wrote a letter to the editors of *al-Muqtataf* deriding Lewis's speech. The journal then published defenses by Lewis as well as a recent graduate of SPC in the following issue. Shortly after Lewis's speech and as the debate in *al-Muqtataf* advanced, Dennis, President Bliss, and Dr. George Post, the only faculty member in the medical school who did not support Lewis, wrote to David Stuart Dodge, secretary of SPC's New York-based Board of Trustees (BOT), to call for Lewis' dismissal from the faculty (Farag, 1972, p. 78). Meanwhile, Lewis translated his speech into English, received approval of its contents from a Protestant clergyman in the United States, and sent both to Dr. William Booth, President of the BOT, for his assessment (Farag, 1972, p. 79).[4] Ultimately, Lewis' proof—while perhaps persuasive to Booth—was not enough to overpower the pressure of the local mission, in combination with the opinions of Bliss, Post, and Dodge. The BOT accepted Lewis's resignation on December 2, 1882.

The fallout from Lewis' forced resignation was rapid: On December 18, Cornelius Van Dyck and his son William, a new member of the medical faculty, submitted their resignations (Jeha, 2004).[5] Dr. Richard Brigstocke, a member of the medical faculty and also of the local Board of Managers (BOM), resigned in March 1883 after his attempts to request a meeting

---

3   Khalidi (1991a) described *al-Muqtataf*, among other Cairo-based journals, as influential in the development of Arab nationalism: "More immediately relevant, several influential Arabist political groupings, such as *Hizb al-lamarkaziyya al-idariyya al-'uthmani* (the Ottoman Administrative Decentralization Party) were founded in Cairo. Journalists prominent in the press of Syria and Istanbul wrote in the Cairo press and often spent long periods in that city, as did many Arabist politicians during periods of repression by the CUP [Committee of Union and Progress]. Egypt was the home of a number of highly influential publications founded by Syrians—for example, *al-Manar, al-Muqattam, al-Ahram, al-Muqtataf,* and *al-Hilal,* all of which contributed significantly to the development of Arabic-language journalism and of Arabism" (p. 61). See also Hourani (1983).

4   It is not clear whether the speech was sent to Reverend Sell of the Union Theological Seminary or Julius Seelye at Amherst College; Nadia Farag (1972) cited the former while Shafik Jeha (2004) cited the latter, and the archives do not provide any additional evidence.

5   William Van Dyck is credited for being the first to bring Darwin—through *On the Origin of Species*—to campus in 1880, when Van Dyck was hired (Jeha, 2004, pp. 35-36).

between the BOM and Bliss were ignored (Jeha, 2004, p. 86). John Wortabet also protested the administration's actions loudly and officially resigned from the medical faculty after Lewis was dismissed.[6] Within several weeks of Lewis' resignation, then, SPC's medical school was reduced to only one faculty member: Post. While SPC dealt with the potential closure of the medical school, it was also forced to confront internal and external pressures demanding a clear definition of the college's identity as the most prominent American college in the region, particularly in relation to local and global stakeholders.

There are a number of reasons why Lewis' address led to a controversy at SPC: First, and perhaps most obviously, the theory of evolution was new and controversial—but in the region, perhaps this was only true for Protestants. Shafik Jeha (2004) noted that it was unlikely that Darwin's theory of evolution would have been controversial to anyone but the Protestant members of SPC, who constituted a minority of the student body (the Christian students were mostly Maronite or Orthodox; others were Muslim and Jewish; see Appendix A).[7] In contrast, the entire faculty and administration of SPC was Protestant. While the text of Lewis' speech does not appear to promote the theory as a matter of fact, some of the more conservative members of the commencement audience—particularly those affiliated with the ABCFM— may have been troubled by any reference to Darwin, as it could presumably be misconstrued as a subversion of the Protestant mission of the college.

Second, the publication of the speech presented a number of problems for the SPC administration: The speech became publicly available for the local community beyond the college, and the journal in which it was published was directly affiliated with SPC, as it was edited by two Syrian SPC graduates, Ya'qub Sarruf (B.A. 1870) and Faris Nimr (B.A. 1874), who were also instructors in the medical school. Probably torn between the expectations of international and regional sponsors and local realities, it is likely that SPC administrators worried that the publication of the address and subsequent responses would signify for a wider audience institutional support for, or at least serious consideration of, Darwin's controversial theories—and this suggestion could inflame the college's financial and religious sponsors in the region and abroad.[8]

---

6   After his resignation, Wortabet remained as a lecturer under special arrangement with SPC until 1890. Also note the discussion later in this section on Sarruf and Nimr's appointments after the 1882 crisis, which were later rescinded.

7   Jeha (2004) asserted this to contradict Jessup's claim that the administration was worried about the local Muslim community's response.

8   For further information about SPC's financial supporters, see Tibawi (1967).

Third, and as Chapter 3 explicates more fully, the college faculty had voted in 1878 to change the language of instruction from Arabic to English, but the medical faculty were resistant to the change. The majority of faculty in the medical department were fluent in Arabic and several had deeper connections to the region than the newer hires in the Collegiate Department.[9] Lewis was fluent in Arabic by the time he gave his speech; he had been hired only four years after the college's founding. What's more, the medical faculty had been producing teaching materials and translating textbooks from English to Arabic for the benefit of their students since the founding of the college, and they were not ready, at the time of the 1878 faculty vote, to give up Arabic as the language of instruction (*Annual Reports*). In short, the medical faculty's resistance to the change in language of instruction at SPC represented a deeper divide within the faculty about the role of the American college in Syria, as well as the kind of literacy education the college intended to provide for its students. While I show in Chapter 3 that the justification for either Arabic or English as the language of instruction was premised upon colonial thinking, the medical faculty's commitment to translating Western knowledge into Arabic can also be seen as a commitment to providing the local population with access to resources that could benefit them. When SPC changed the language of instruction—and thus its orientation toward literacy and student identity—perhaps the medical faculty felt that the college had distanced itself and the education it provided from the local population it was meant to serve.

What's more, the revised language policy explicitly privileged foreign faculty and underlined the lesser role that local faculty were meant to play in SPC's educational project. The son of an Armenian Protestant, Wortabet was the only professorial-rank faculty member born in Syria at SPC, and after his resignation, SPC would not assign any Syrian faculty member professorial rank status until 1909, nor would any locally born faculty member at any rank gain voting rights until 1920 (B. S. Anderson, 2011, p. 48).[10] This shift in policy,

---

9   In particular, Cornelius Van Dyck, who was well known in the region for his role in translating the Bible into Arabic while an ABCFM missionary, and John Wortabet, who was a native of Syria, were both notable in their ties and contributions to the local culture and community. Cornelius Van Dyck was trained in the United States as a physician and began work as a missionary to Syria in 1840. He was well known for his impressive proficiency in Arabic, which culminated in a modern translation of the Bible into Arabic (with Eli Smith, who died before the translation was published in 1865). Wortabet was an Armenian Protestant who was ordained as a preacher in 1853 by the Syrian ABCFM mission. Both were involved in the founding of SPC in 1866. For further information on these figures, see Jessup (1910/2002) and Brian VanDeMark (2012).

10   According to Jeha (2004), following the 1882 crisis, Sarruf and Nimr, editors of

too, went against SPC's original intention of establishing a college that would eventually be run by local faculty (Salibi & Khoury, 1995, pp. 56–57). The language change, therefore, maintained a power differential between local and foreign constituents of the college and sent a clear message to all that they must perform a foreign cultural identity—and thus strive for a kind of "cultural citizenship" (Wan, 2011, p. 37)—in order to succeed at SPC.

All of these factors contributed to the controversy surrounding Lewis' speech. At stake, then, was the college's identity as the American college in the region, as well as the identity of its students. The faculty's and students' responses to the controversy help illuminate the false promises of American-style education abroad and the limits of the cultural citizenship students tried to adopt through their rhetorical performance. Colonial epistemology dictated the boundaries of what action, particularly literate action, was "acceptable" and within the bounds of the American national imaginary (see Ribero, 2016). The exchanges and interactions among faculty, administrators, and students rhetorically constituted a vision of America that was inseparable from the college founders' American Protestant identity. In turn, this definition of America framed the college's expectations for its "ideal" student, who would adopt and employ American ways of thinking and knowing—in part through English literacy—within the Arab world. This "ideal" student was certainly not expected to use the discourses or ideologies of America to critique American institutions such as SPC.

Student Response

In addition to the resignation of its faculty, SPC was faced with another, perhaps more immediate, crisis: a student strike. The day of Lewis' resignation, between 40 and 50 students, most of them from the Medical Department and a few from the other branch of the college, the Collegiate Department, organized to protest the administration's decision (Jeha, 2004). The students acted quickly: On Sunday, December 3, they attended required chapel services but refused to sing the hymns. On Monday, December 4, the students stopped attending classes. The students met in the college halls or at the city's Prussian Hospital, which at the time hosted the medical department, and they quickly elected a president, a treasurer, writers, and a speechmaker for the group. Together, they began to write.

---

al-Muqtataf, were promised adjunct professor appointments in chemistry and physics (Sarruf) and mathematics (Nimr) by SPC in three years, on October 1, 1885. But at the end of the academic year 1883-84, SPC terminated the contract and dismissed both. In 1890, SPC awarded honorary doctorates to both, but neither attended the ceremony (Jeha, 2004, pp. 121-36).

Over the course of a few weeks, between December 5, 1882, and the end of the month, the students wrote a series of seven petitions to the faculty and the college's BOM.[11] According to Jurji Zeidan (1924–25), the students also presented their case in person to the governor of Mount Lebanon, the consuls of England, the United States, Germany, France, Italy, and Russia, as well as other local missionaries and teachers in Beirut (as cited in Jeha, 2004, p. 60). In the petitions, the students structured their appeals to the SPC administration around a number of grievances, including but not limited to Lewis' abrupt dismissal from the college. Their complaints, some of which have been preserved as a single Arabic-language document in the American University of Beirut archives, are framed as defenses of Lewis and the remaining faculty (whose resignations they anticipated) and concerns about the value of their diplomas and certification to practice medicine in the Ottoman Empire (see translations of the petitions published in Jeha, 2004, pp. 55–70).[12]

The group requested a meeting with the administration on December 4, and in presenting this request, they appealed to what they assumed was a shared concern for the medical school's ثبوتها وتسقوطها or "stability and potential downfall" ("To the Dean," 1882). Reflecting a keen rhetorical awareness, the students framed themselves as thoughtful and rational in their decision to strike: They introduced the first full petition, presented to the administration on Tuesday, December 5, with the qualification that they had "hope [the SPC administrators] will not consider [the strike] as the result of passion and folly, but of reflection and consideration, albeit the exciting cause is sudden" (as cited in Jeha, 2004, p. 55). Describing the relationship between the college and the students as a contract or promise that had been broken, the students wrote in the same petition that "we came to study medicine in your college under certain professors and defined conditions . . . and in as much as

---

11   Jeha (2004) provided a useful chronological account of the petitions. The full texts of these petitions have been translated in the English edition of his book, and it is because of the clarity of presentation that I have chosen to rely primarily on these translations rather than the translations included in the President's Annual Report of 1882–83, which did not reprint the whole series of petitions. A few of the petitions were translated from Arabic to English by Yahia Hamadeh on my behalf; not all of the original petitions were available in the archives. When the original petition is one that I worked with in the archives in Arabic, I present Arabic alongside the English translation.

12   As depicted in Jeha (2004), on December 5, the students presented two separate petitions: One made several educational requests related to the Turkish government's examination requirements for certification to practice medicine, which was at odds with SPC's curriculum and language of instruction. This first petition also discussed Dr. Lewis' dismissal. The second was focused entirely on the dismissal of Dr. Lewis. Later petitions also brought up the problems with the examination and SPC curriculum in tandem with Lewis' dismissal, though they focused more on the latter than the former (see Jeha, 2004, pp. 53–70).

the bond between us and you is those conditions and some of them are now wanting, we have come to fear that they will all fail" (as cited in Jeha, 2004, p. 55). Continuing, the students argued that they

> entered on condition that our Professors should be Doctors Van Dyck, Wortabet, Post, Lewis, Brigstocke, and William Van Dyck. This agreement has also been broken in a very strange manner, the like of which has not been heard of, by the removal of one of them from the College, notwithstanding that we need him. Can we be blamed if we fear greater trouble than this? (as cited in Jeha, 2004, p. 55)

In another petition submitted the same day, the students articulated the educational promise held by SPC as a right they were entitled to—in "not allow[ing the students] to know of what was coming before [they] entered" their studies at the beginning of the academic year, they characterized the college's decision to let Lewis go as one that has "caus[ed]" them "injuries" (as cited in Jeha, 2004, p. 56). The students apparently sought to demonstrate through their petitions that they shared the same concern for SPC's success in the region as the administration surely did. They suggested that the removal of one of their professors pointed toward an instability within the school that would affect everyone's collective progress and success. They also saw the situation as clearly unjust. As I discuss in Chapter 3, SPC students received a decidedly rhetorical education, one that emphasized linguistic, literary, and oratorical skills in multiple languages, and this education would have prepared the striking students to constitute themselves through the petitions as representative of SPC's model student-citizen: critical, autonomous, and empowered to speak. Perhaps because SPC promoted these values in its curriculum, the students felt authorized to adopt this seemingly American identity in the petitions.

Although Lewis' resignation was ostensibly based on his public support for Darwin's theory of evolution, the students never expressed in the petitions a concern over Lewis' beliefs. Rather, the petition that expressly protested Lewis' dismissal, which was submitted at the beginning of the strike, was framed as a defense of his character, a defense that would have resonated with what the students had learned in the (American) Protestant chapel services on campus, which they were required to attend regardless of their religious sect or beliefs. As in the petitions in which the students articulated their individual rights to SPC's promise of an American education, the students appealed in their defenses of Lewis to what they believed the administration would value. They defended Lewis based on their understanding of the

college's emphasis on moral and Christian conduct, as well as its commitment to just treatment for all.[13] Specifically, the students characterized Lewis
as "pious and excellent" (as cited in Jeha, 2004, p. 56). They argued that no
one would believe the administration's charge against Lewis of "setting forth
Darwin's infidel opinions in the last annual address" if they "underst[oo]d his
speech and [knew] his Christian deportment and upright example and piety"
(as cited in Jeha, 2004, p. 56). What's more, they pointed out, Lewis' service as
"President of the religious society and leader in good works" contradicted the
administration's accusation against him (as cited in Jeha, 2004, p. 56).

After several unfruitful exchanges with the SPC faculty and administrators,
as well as with political representatives and other local community members,
the students seemed disillusioned by what they perceived to be a gap between
the values espoused by SPC and its actions. As a result, the rhetoric of the petitions changed. As the situation escalated and it became clear that Lewis would
not be reinstated, the students presented a complaint targeted at President
Bliss and Post to the local BOM on December 16. Cornelius Van Dyck was
responsible for reading the complaints of the students at the BOM meeting
that evening. As Zeidan explained later, while he and the rest of the students
"walk[ed] around the school waiting for the end of the session," Van Dyck was
asked to read the petition, "given his good knowledge of Arabic. As soon as he
started reading, a member of the audience asked that he be silenced because he
regarded the subject as personal defamation" (as cited in Jeha, 2004, p. 64). Van
Dyck left the room, and Zeidan reported that he "saw [Van Dyck] riding away
in his carriage and anger was clear on his face" (as cited in Jeha, 2004, p. 65).
The remaining members of the BOM demanded that the students rescind their
names from the offending petition or be expelled. There could be no clearer
message that the students' assumed "right" to free speech and other benefits
afforded to American citizens were not theirs to assert.

Two days later, coinciding with the Van Dycks' resignations, the college
administration posted an announcement in response to the students' petition
in front of College Hall, located at the center of SPC's campus. Instead of
addressing the students' concerns about their education or their professors,
the announcement stated that the offending students were to be suspended
for one month if they did not sign a redaction of the petition (Jeha, 2004, p.
65). This response—similar to what students would receive in the 1909 protest

---

13   At the time, there were very few, if any, Muslims enrolled at the college, so it is tempting
but inappropriate to analyze the students' rhetorical practices here in light of Islamic principles
such as أمانة (*amanah,* or "upholding and fulfilling trusts") (see Tamara Issak & Lana Oweidat,
2023). While Islamic principles have undoubtedly influenced Arab culture generally, the students
at SPC at the time would have identified more closely with Western and Christian values.

discussed later in this chapter—attempted to disempower the students. It was hardly the fair and balanced response that the students had hoped to receive and believed they would get as they performed their role as cultural citizens. The announcement only strengthened the resolve and frustration of the protesting students. Only three medical students signed, and the remaining students maintained the strike.

In their final petition, composed several weeks after the first, the students indicted SPC faculty, administration, and the local BOM for refusing to fully respond to their complaints or reconsider the decision regarding Lewis (Jeha, 2004, pp. 66–68). While the students' rhetoric in previous petitions purposefully characterized America and its affiliated values in a positive light, this final petition marked a turning point in the students' rhetorical representation of the America they imagined. Instead of portraying America as an ally in this petition, the students identified America, with its affiliated colonial epistemology, as an entity that had failed them and was, apparently, a fiction. In this final petition is seen a heightened sense of agency based in students' shared Arab, rather than American, identity.

The students' indictment in this final petition referred explicitly to the false promise of America that Syrian students and the local community had assumed in their relations with SPC. They wrote that

> it never occurred to the minds in Syria or in the Syrian Protestant College that noble people like you who belong to the American land of freedom would issue judgments without considering the related evidence. You refused to listen to students whose acts did not convey any signs of rashness and who claimed their just rights. . . . Sirs, we thought that presenting our requests to noble, pious American people who came to serve our countries in the name of the good and the right would assure us about all that we are struggling for. (as cited in Jeha, 2004, p. 67)

In this petition, more than in any other, the students composed a rhetorical distance that separated their inherited identity from the American cultural citizenship they had previously performed. Indeed, the students identified themselves in terms of a specifically *Syrian* identity: Those who claimed this identity, according to the students, had imagined America to be a "land of freedom," full of "noble, pious . . . people." Americans, in the Syrian imagination and as represented through SPC until the 1882 crisis, were a people who would recognize and uphold "the good and the right." But here the students articulated clearly that such a construction was false.

The students substantiated their argument in the same petition by stating that their complaints "[had] been found reasonable by natives and foreigners" alike (as cited in Jeha, 2004, p. 67). Here, the students highlighted that SPC had acted not only against American values, but also against values that were shared by the local Arab community, as well as other "foreigners," perhaps referencing the British missionary and several American teachers in the local community with whom the students consulted during the protest (Jeha, 2004, pp. 60 and 67). At the end of the petition, the students noted that three of their classmates had signed the written apology. Identifying these students as "traitors," the group pointedly asked its audience, "Do you think all the Arab medical students are like [the students who signed the apology]?" (as cited in Jeha, 2004, p. 68). In posing this question, the students asserted a collective Arab identity, distancing themselves from the American cultural citizenship they had previously assumed.

In this final petition, in *dis*identifying with the college—and thus disidentifying with America and the colonial epistemology that exposed them to unjust treatment—the students inscribed themselves as the subjects, rather than the objects, of the conflict and thus their education. This petition represents the moment when students learned the limits of literate action for attaining cultural citizenship within the college as they realized that the college was grounded upon an exclusionary colonial mentality, no matter how well they expressed themselves in line with this mentality. Indeed, in describing their American education as a promise that had been denied to them and in subsequently rejecting the institution's (assumed) desire that they pursue American cultural citizenship or belonging, the students identified and rejected the deeper ethnocentric attitude that laid at the heart of the conflict and, perhaps, at the heart of American identity. In other words, in rejecting the false promise of citizenship—in refusing to pursue the "American dream"—the students ultimately exposed the social inequality that was and still is promoted and maintained within American nationalist discourse, then as much as now. Instead, the students asserted a collective Arab nationalist identity that rhetorically reasserted their agency in the face of colonialism.

Resolving a Failed American Revolution

The resolution of the crisis, dissatisfactory for all, illuminates the complicated commitments of the American college in the late 19th century, torn between colonial epistemology and local needs and desires. By the end of the 1882–1883 academic year, SPC would lose five of six of its medical faculty when it refused to reinstate Lewis.[14] The student "rebellion" complicated the affair, as the students involved comprised nearly a third of all the students enrolled at SPC at the time. It was in the best interests of the college to keep its medical students; if SPC were to lose the whole cohort—voluntarily or through expulsion—as well as its faculty, SPC would be forced to close the medical department. It would be difficult for SPC to convince students to remain if it could not satisfy their demands and guarantee that they had enough faculty to cover the curriculum. At the same time, the local BOM did not want to send a message to students, stakeholders, or the surrounding community that SPC would cave to local (Arab) pressure. By the time the students sent their final appeal to the college administrators, SPC had already chosen a course of action that would assert the superiority of the American administrators, maintain distance between local and foreign stakeholders, and, ultimately, uphold the college's distinctly American (colonial) identity.

When the students continued their strike, SPC administrators were both surprised and worried. Wortabet, the last remaining member of the medical faculty who did not resign until March 1883, was asked to visit the local students and convince them to sign a "clarification" statement rather than an apology, but the majority of students refused (Jeha, 2004, pp. 74–78). After Christmas break, SPC managed to find temporary faculty to cover the medical school's courses, and by the end of the academic year, a majority of the striking students—31 out of 50—signed an apology and returned to their studies.

When confronted by its own students and faculty, the college's attempts to resolve the 1882 crisis forced it to come to terms with tensions that already existed between its foreign and local constituents. SPC's decisions during this moment of crisis foregrounded and affirmed the college's position as a foreign entity, as well as its representation of America in the region. SPC ultimately chose a colonial path that privileged its foreign faculty over locally born, a trend that would continue for the next 40 years. The resignations of the Arabic-speaking medical faculty, too, paved the way for English to become the language of instruction throughout the college.[15] Although, as I discuss in

---

14   John Wortabet was the last of the medical faculty to resign in March 1883. Upon Wortabet's retirement, David Stuart Dodge, the secretary of SPC's Board of Trustees in New York, wrote to Daniel Bliss (apparently in reply to a letter from Bliss that hasn't been located): "What a blessing to be rid of the last of that half-hearted, half-educated (in the best sense), unwilling, un-American, missionary line of Professors" (as cited in Jeha, 2004, p. 90).

15   The Collegiate and Preparatory Departments agreed to use English as the language of instruction beginning in 1880, but the Medical Department did not officially make the switch until 1887 (*Annual Reports*).

Chapter 3, multiple languages remained central to SPC's curriculum after the crisis, the shift from Arabic to English also established a clear connection between English-language literacy and American nationalism for the local population. Additionally, the crisis reveals that there was disagreement about what it meant to be Protestant, which was closely affiliated with American national identity: Following the crisis, the Board of Trustees required all faculty to sign its Declaration of Principles, a document that highlighted the religious mission of the college and outlined a moral code that all faculty were expected to follow (Jeha, 2004, p. 101).[16] And finally, SPC chose to assert a single-minded authority over its students, even when confronted with well-reasoned arguments grounded in the same American values that the college espoused in principle.

According to Jurji Zeidan, whose memoir accounts for his role as president of the protesting student group, the students felt empowered to speak and write in protest specifically because of the American values espoused by the college, among which he included critical thought, freedom of speech, independence, and human rights (as cited in Jeha, 2004, p. 65).[17] In other words, according to Zeidan, the students' sense of empowerment, with which they questioned SPC through literate action, was made possible thanks to the literacy education they had been introduced to at SPC.[18] Zeidan characterized the college faculty's actions during the crisis as driven by "racial discrimination and . . . scorn for Arabs" (as cited in Jeha, 2004, p. 65). The faculty's response to the crisis, according to Zeidan, suggested that "they . . . want[ed] to prohibit [the students] from complaining against their American professors, who themselves had taught personal freedom and moral courage" (as cited in Jeha, 2004, p. 65). Zeidan's account highlights the contradictions and confusion experienced by students as they attempted to draw upon an imagined America in their protest but were unexpectedly met with resistance

---

16   Local faculty, none of whom were (or would become) professorial-rank faculty, were not required to sign the declaration but were required to be Protestant and to be supporters of the mission of the College (Jeha, 2004, p. 101).

17   At the time of the strike, Zeidan was a second-year student in the medical department at SPC (Jeha, 2004). After he was expelled and refused to sign an apology, he and another expelled student went to Egypt to continue their studies in medicine. However, they were unsuccessful, and Zeidan remained in Egypt (Jeha, 2004, pp. 75 and 77). There, he became a prolific writer of history, literature, and autobiography; he is well-known today as the author of 23 novels, the founder of the journal *Al-Hilal*, and an early voice of Arab nationalism, or النهضة (*al-Nahda*, which translates to "the renaissance" or "the awakening," which is discussed in Chapter 5).

18   By naming these values "American," I do not mean to suggest that these values can only be attributed to America. However, Zeidan specifically attributed the students' understanding and deployment of these values to the American education provided by SPC.

by those who had constructed that image. Such experiences of confusion and, undoubtedly, disappointment can help begin to reveal the implications of educators' promises for those for whom success or failure is most at stake.

Beyond Zeidan's account, the petitions themselves can be understood as a rhetorical rendering of the epistemological conflicts that students experienced throughout their literacy education at SPC. The students deployed this understanding of America strategically in an effort to persuade the American faculty and administrators to reinstate Lewis. Examining these students' strategies can help shed light on the epistemological conflicts that students experience, today and in the past, when they are asked to perform as American cultural citizens in and through literacy.

Initially, the petitions represented America and American colonial epistemology in a positive light, which underlines students' understanding of American nationalist rhetoric that they learned through their literacy education. At the same time, the early petitions articulated the students' disappointment in what they perceived to be SPC's failure to provide an American education—an education that matched the values it espoused—and which they saw as embodied by faculty such as Lewis, the Van Dycks, and Wortabet. In one early petition, the students wrote, "We did not come to the College save to study with distinguished professors whom we know, and the College to us is these professors" (as cited in Jeha, 2004, p. 56). Importantly, these faculty were educated in the United States but were tied through language and experience to the local community. The students' protest, therefore, can be understood as a response to the loss of faculty whose perspectives married the local and the global in their pedagogical approaches, which for students represented what they might call an "ideal" American education.

The students' defense of Lewis in these petitions illustrated a belief among the students that the college valued fairness, equity, and moral (Christian) behavior—values tied to American conceptions of citizenship. The students assumed that the American education at SPC, which they espoused in their own rhetorical practices, would be valued. The students believed that they had the *right* to speak out about a perceived injustice specifically because the right to free speech was fundamental to the American identity they had learned to imitate in and through their literacy education. In adopting the behaviors and actions of American citizenship and its associated values in their rhetoric, the protesting students expected SPC to reflect the same values and behavior in its actions toward its faculty, as well as in its interactions with students. The problem, of course, was that the college's espoused values were grounded upon a colonial epistemology that would always assert the superiority of the college's American administrators and faculty over local ways of knowing.

In effect, in critiquing the administration, the striking students rhetorically constituted themselves according to what they imagined to be SPC's "ideal" student body—a body that acts and speaks according to the American values embedded within the school's curricular and extracurricular requirements. As the students were to learn, however, SPC administration did not respond favorably to this application of students' literacy education. Three years later, Ya'qub Sarruf and Faris Nimr, who were themselves Syrian graduates of and former medical instructors at SPC but who were now the editors of *al-Muqtataf*—the same journal that originally published Lewis's offending speech—would write what Makdisi (2010) characterized as a "scathing article about the college" (p. 68). In the article, Sarruf and Nimr criticized SPC for abandoning its original mission, which was "to turn over the college to local hands as soon as the nationals of [Syria] had proved themselves qualified" (Makdisi, 2010, p. 68). As Makdisi (2010) explained, the editors "lamented" in the article "that the . . . American professors who remained at the college after the Darwin affair had decided that the college was 'American through and through'" (as cited in Makdisi, 2010, pp. 68–69).

As can be seen from the petitions as well as later accounts of the 1882 crisis, the SPC medical students addressed their audiences directly, establishing a clear sense of agency in relation to their rights as students and also in articulating what they saw as an injustice. They demanded answers, frustrated by a lack of transparency on the part of the administration. It was the absence of clarity or dialogue—values that the students learned through their education at SPC were American and should therefore be shared by the institution—that justified, in their view, the continuation of the strike. As the crisis deepened, the students' rhetoric moved away from the model-citizen script with which they had begun the protest. The shift in rhetoric suggests students' turn to their own local values and beliefs when their American appeals failed. This departure is key to understanding how and why promises made by literacy educators have such high stakes: In coming to terms with the illusion that American education provides equal access and equal opportunity, students may find the promises of social mobility and social justice that are held as an ideal of American literacy education to be disingenuous.

Studying the exchanges between students and faculty and the dissatisfying resolution of the crisis helps expose the reality that literacy education does not necessarily produce an active or engaged citizenry. We can see in this case competing specters of America and conflicting desires for an American literacy education—as represented in and through SPC—at work in Syria and the region more generally in the late 19th century. These contradictory definitions and desires, which represent larger epistemological conflicts at work, created a simultaneous sense of belonging and exclusion. As will be seen in the next section, which focuses on a larger student protest at SPC in 1909, these epistemological conflicts grew stronger as the college grew and as the geopolitics of the region shifted.

"This Is No Summer Cloud . . . ": The 1909 Muslim Controversy

Twenty-seven years after the Lewis Affair, during the Spring 1909 semester, students at SPC once again organized to protest college policy during a period of crisis for the college that became known as the "Muslim Controversy." In this part of the chapter, I present the background for the crisis and details of the crisis itself, followed by an analysis of the internal and public documents surrounding the crisis, including those authored by SPC students, SPC faculty and administrators, and community members. Many of those voices were represented in newspaper articles published throughout the region, which form the basis for this analysis. The written exchanges about the 1909 crisis illustrate how SPC students and the local community articulated and negotiated conflicts about what the American college and the education it provided meant, or should mean, to the region. Such conflicts were, at their heart, epistemological, and local discourse undoubtedly reflects local concerns about the impact of Western colonial epistemology and its attendant religious ideology on the region. Just as we saw in the 1882 crisis, SPC students' literate action again called into question what it meant to "belong" to SPC or whether they could, in fact, claim the cultural citizenship that their literacy education seemed to promise was available to them. The 1909 crisis, however, brought a protracted debate among students and community members around whether the risk that the college's colonial and Christianizing mission presented for Muslim and Jewish students was worth the potential reward of acquiring a Western education. This part of the chapter sheds light on the kinds of epistemological and ideological conflicts that many historically underrepresented students experience in literacy classrooms today.

To understand the crisis, it is necessary to first understand the larger context in which it arrived. The year of 1908 was a revolutionary year in the Ottoman Empire, as the Young Turks reversed Sultan Abdul Hamid II's suspension of the 1876 Ottoman constitution and reinstated the Parliament, effectively ending the Sultan's power after 33 years. "Liberty, equality, and fraternity"—key words in the 1876 constitution inspired by the French Revolution—became the motto for the Young Turks' July 1908 revolution. The period marked, for many throughout the Empire including in Syria, the promise of a new era and the potential of democracy.

At around the same time as the Young Turks succeeded in overturning the monarchy, several articles were published in Beirut and Cairo openly criticizing the religious requirements at SPC. In "The Moslems in the American College, Beirut" (1909). the Egyptian newspaper *Moweyid* (المؤيد or *The Advocate*) reported that Suleiman Effendi Bustani, representative for Beirut in the Parliament, had met with the presidents of the foreign schools in the city, including the Université Saint-Joseph (USJ, the French Jesuit university which opened in 1875) and SPC, urging them to drop the religious requirements for non-Christian students. USJ's decision to follow Bustani's request earned praise from various newspaper editors and provided ammunition for the same as they criticized SPC's insistence on maintaining its requirement.

Presumably in response to these articles and the changing mood of the region, Muslim and Jewish parents began requesting that their children be exempted from the religious requirement at SPC. These requests were denied by the SPC administration (Moore, 1909a). During the 1908–1909 academic year, 128 Muslim and 88 Jewish students were enrolled out of 876 total students, making up approximately 15 percent of the student body (see Appendix A for demographic details). In the fall 1908 semester, apparently under the advisement of community groups such as the Society for Religious Liberty, the Muslim students made a number of requests of the SPC administration to form sponsored groups based on their religious identity.[19] Specifically, Muslim students first appealed to the faculty requesting permission to form a Muslim union. This request was denied on the grounds that no religious organizations besides the YMCA were allowed on campus. Students next requested to form a "somewhat select" literary society, which they said would be focused on the study of Islamic literature, but which would be open to anyone—according to Professor Franklin Moore (1909a), "this was smothered in committee" (p. 9). The students also requested that a student representative be allowed to "conduct pourparlors," or discussions, regularly with the SPC administration, but this was denied "seeing that to recognize a representative was tantamount to organizing for them a society, a matter already declined" (Moore, 1909a, p. 9; see also Mahmoud Haddad, 2002). According to Moore (1909a), "During all this time they frequented the mosques of the city, and many speeches were made by students and by Moslems of the city" (p. 9). Finally, the Muslim students requested permission to attend mosque for prayers. At last, this final request was approved (B. S. Anderson, 2011, p. 85; Moore, 1909a).

---

19   See "The Beirut College and Isla"m (A. of the Syrian College, 1909) for specific mention of the Society for Religious Liberty and Moore (1909a, pp. 8–10) for reference to a committee of Muslims in Beirut.

With this series of requests behind them, SPC administrators likely believed they had sufficiently addressed the non-Christian students' demands while upholding the mission of the college. In the college's annual report, President Howard Bliss retrospectively noted that, "With a Constitution proclaiming Islam as the religion of the State and at the same time pronouncing that there was to be everywhere liberty in religious belief . . . it is small occasion for wonder that the spirit of eager restlessness has entered the educational institutions of the Empire" (*Annual Reports*, 1909, p. 4). Indeed, the students' requests during fall 1908 demonstrate a growing awareness of, and response to, the sociopolitical context surrounding SPC. As they proceeded with high stakes requests to honor their religious identities, students developed an awareness and frustration at being denied the religious freedom presumably promised to them by the Empire, and which they believed was foundational to American society. This set the stage for SPC's next crisis, the 1909 "Muslim Controversy."

The Sermon and the Storm

In January 1909, shortly after the beginning of the spring 1909 semester, a sermon was given by a missionary named James H. Nicol, who was visiting SPC from Tripoli, a city in northern Lebanon. All SPC students were required to attend Sunday chapel services during which sermons were given. It was reported that Nicol said during the sermon that:

> We the Christians are surrounded with great walls of enemies, the Moslems and others. They prevent us from spreading the true call and await the opportunity to devour us. It is our business then, our sacred duty to break down these walls and tread upon them. . . . These obstacles to our faith and to our religion are doomed if we will only fight them as we should. (Nickoley, 1909)[20]

---

20   It is important to point out that faculty did not agree with students' interpretation of Nicol's sermon. The summary presented here by Edward Nickoley, an SPC professor who also served as the acting president while Howard Bliss was in the US, was presented in a letter to Bliss while he was out of the country. Nickoley's purpose in the letter was to defend Nicol's speech, writing that "there was not the slightest implication of hostility or animus in the address or in any of the talks of the week." Professor Franklin Moore, too, in a speech to faculty on January 25, 1909, suggested that the students misrepresented Nicol's address—Moore (1909a) called it "a malignantly false interpretation of portions of the address." Professor William Hall's summary of the event, as well as Bliss' April 1909 letter to parents, also suggest that Nicol was misunderstood (Hall, 1909; H. Bliss, 1909a).

Nicol's sermon provoked an immediate response from the students, as it suggested that members of the Muslim population—which comprised a majority of the Ottoman Empire—were "enemies" of the Christian missionaries. And, if the report was true, Nicol seemed to be sending a message to his audience that Christians were called by God to "fight" these groups. Given this message, it is no wonder that within the week, 98 students had signed a petition protesting the requirement of Christian religious services and more than 200 refused to attend chapel services (Moore, 1909a, p. 7). In an action reminiscent of the 1882 crisis, the faculty responded to the petition by posting the college's policy on religious instruction in both Arabic and English on a bulletin board in the library. The policy, which was also published annually in the College catalogue, read,

> Morning and evening prayers are held daily in the College. Each Sunday, there is a church service in the morning, and a Bible school in the afternoon, with classes under the care of various professors and instructors. All resident students are required to attend all these services, except that resident medical and pharmaceutical students are required to attend only evening prayers and Sunday morning church. Non-resident commercial, collegiate, and preparatory students are required to attend only morning and evening prayers, and non-resident medical and pharmaceutical students only evening prayers. There is a Sunday evening service for the Preparatory Department in Daniel Bliss Hall, attendance on which is voluntary for students of all other departments. (H. Bliss, 1909a)

Moore (1909a) later reported in a speech to the faculty that students reacted negatively to the administration's posting and took quick action:

> During the day or two following, several regrettable incidents occurred, each one inevitable by itself, and the students, roused by an outburst in the opinion of the city, irritated by the public delivery of the document, on a bulletin board, and by the regrettable incidents mentioned, finally engaged in a sacred oath on the Koran, swearing never again to attend services or Bible classes under compulsion, and swearing further not to leave the College if expelled. (p. 10)

In the same speech, given about two weeks after Nicol's sermon, Moore reported that the students had almost immediately begun telling their side of the story outside the walls of the college, even communicating with government officials. Moore (1909a) explained that the students

> . . . fired a powerful battery; they saw the Governor General; they telegraphed their case to the American Ambassador, to the Deputies in Parliament representing Beirut, to the Ministry of the Interior, whose present chief is said to be the leading man in the Party of Progress, and whose first utterance on this subject will be significant; and they telegraphed a long message to the Sultan direct, not as the Monarch of the Empire, but as the Caliph of the Moslem world. (p. 11)

Moore's overview of the actions taken by the students so quickly after the offending sermon must have caused anxiety among the audience of college faculty and brought to the fore how serious the crisis really was. Compounding the situation, newspapers in Beirut and Cairo became embroiled in the controversy: Editors, community members, and current and former students weighed in, siding with and against SPC. More than 60 articles related to the crisis were published in at least 15 regional newspapers between January and October 1909.[21] Thus, a student strike—and a college crisis—began.

While the strike was underway, the students behaved perfectly in all other contexts, demonstrating not only their own self-respect and dignity, but also that they understood well what it took to "belong" in the American college. In his account of the strike, Moore (1909a) remarked that the students were extremely well-behaved, noting that they "scrupulously observe every other regulation. They do their academic duties, up to this moment, with carefulness and with manifest good-will. They protest their love for the College. They do not wish to go" (p. 6). The controversy arose while President Howard Bliss was out of the country on a visit to the US, so the faculty were left to contain the strike as best they could without their president. They chose not to take any drastic action until he returned in late February 1909. In a letter to the Board of Trustees describing the crisis, Howard Bliss (1909b) noted the protesting students' admirable behavior, writing that upon his returned to Beirut, he

> received a very warm welcome. . . . Among those who met me at the steamer was a boatload full of Moslem students who had been most active in connection with resisting the regulations of

---

21　The newspaper articles related to the "Muslim Crisis" are preserved together as a collection in the AUB Jafet Library archives. All the newspaper articles were written originally in Arabic, but the articles preserved in the archives are only preserved as translations in English (the original Arabic articles are not preserved in the archives). According to B. S. Anderson (2011), Professor Harvey Porter translated the articles himself (p. 211n149).

> the College relating to religious exercises. This action of theirs
> was indicative of their desire to show their loyalty to the Col-
> lege. . . . All the students involved have been, almost without
> exception, scrupulously careful in matters of conduct and atten-
> tion to their class duties.

As will be seen in the next sections, the students' behavior in front of the American faculty and administrators who had the power to change the college policy contrasted with the Arabic-language discussions among students and the local community. In other words, students seemed to understand that the cultural citizenship that was implicitly promised by the college required adopting and adapting to American expectations for the role they should occupy.

There is evidence that the SPC faculty took the student protest seriously, which contrasts with the faculty's response to students during the 1882 controversy. In a summary of the strike in a letter to Bliss on February 5, 1909, Moore (1909b) wrote, "This whole issue may be a mere 'summer cloud' as some of the Syria Mission freely proclaimed at one of our meetings in conference with them. If so, then heaven help us in the time of a winter storm." After outlining what he saw as the basis of the conflict in some detail, however, Moore urged the President to return to Syria at his earliest convenience, warning, "This is no summer cloud; it is not child's play."

In the next three sections, I analyze the rhetorics deployed by students, faculty, and community members during this controversy. Specifically, stakeholders during the controversy deployed rhetorics of Muslim identification and rhetorics of protest against Western colonial epistemology as they debated the religious requirement at SPC. These debates exposed key ideological conflicts that ran to the heart of SPC's colonial presence in Beirut. These conflicts illustrate the difficult choices faced by the local population as they weighed the opportunities for mobility offered by the college against the challenge that the college posed to their religious and ethnic identities. Similar debates continue to resonate in literacy education today. Current and former SPC students and the local community, the archives show, engaged rhetorically in the questions underlying the conflict; this deep engagement highlights the agency held by local populations and deployed through literate action, even in the face of colonial epistemology.

Rhetorics of Muslim Unification and Identity

During the 1909 crisis, the students called upon a rhetoric of Muslim identification and unity, which was sometimes, but not always, also anti-Western or anti-American. As I elaborate in Chapter 2 and as Masters (2013) discussed extensively, the relationship between the Arab population in Syria and the Ottoman Empire was a complicated one. Like most of the Arab population, students tended to support the Empire after the 1908 revolution because of the Young Turks' perceived potential to exert power in support of the Muslim population. Although they identified ethnically as Arabs, distinct from their Turkish, Greek, and Persian counterparts, most of the local population identified readily as Ottoman subjects.[22] Even as the Empire faced challenges from outside, few Arabs expressed a desire to form a separate Arab state. This is likely because, until the Empire began to exert its power through linguistic and legal restrictions more forcefully in the face of its dissolution, the local population was largely allowed to govern itself and speak Arabic. Until the Empire's dissolution during World War I, most of the Empire's subjects perceived the Empire as valuable in the sense that it could speak for and preserve the interests of Muslims.

In the articles published during the crisis in magazines circulated throughout the region (Beirut, Damascus, and Cairo), students and community members appealed to Arab nationalism, Muslim unity, and resistance to the West or to America. These discussions, held amongst each other rather than in dialogue with the Americans, revealed tensions between the expected behavior and literate action of SPC students and the Muslim and Arab identity that was integral to this group of students' belonging in the region. The writers worked to persuade readers to accept and understand the student protest.[23] Although they did not use the term أمانة (*amanah*, or "upholding and fulfilling trusts"), the writers seemed to rely on this shared Islamic principle, which "requires Muslims to speak up against any injustice" (Issak & Oweidat, 2023, p. 187).

One writer, El-Ghalieni (1909), called upon readers' sense of Arab nationalism and shared Muslim identity to defend the students' perspective. He argued that the dispute was justified because of the new Ottoman government's stance on religious liberty, writing that "religious liberty demands that man should be free in his belief and worship without being compelled to

---

22   At least two articles referenced a secret student society called the "Society of Ottoman Students Union"—see "The College in Beirut and Islam" (1909) and Himmet (1909).

23   Khalidi (1991a) discussed the role of newspapers in Beirut, Damascus, and Cairo in the rise of Arab nationalism, writing, " . . . the newspaper that was arguably the most influential voice of the Arab movement, *al-Mufid*, was published in Beirut (its closest rival in this respect was *al-Muqtabas* in Damascus). . . . Other Beirut Arabist papers included *al-Ittihad*, *al-'uthmani*, *al-Haqiqa*, and *al-Iqbal*. It seems that most Beirut papers were Arabist and that this city had more Arabist newspapers than any other in *bilad al-sham*" (pp. 55–56).

attend the worship of another or learn his doctrines." An anonymous author, writing a month later in the same magazine, argued against the presence of "foreigners" in the Ottoman Empire, suggesting that writers who defended the college were unpatriotic (*The College and the Moslem Students*, 1909).

Other writers took a different approach, suggesting that the best solution would be for Muslims to create a university of their own instead of relying on SPC for higher education. For example, Safar Towfik (1909) of Egypt called on readers to consider establishing their own university rather than depending on foreigners to grant religious freedom. Similarly, Mahmoud 'Asmet (1909) called on "Egyptian Moslems" to give money, presumably for the establishment of a new college to "unify the course of instruction" and ultimately release their children from dependence on SPC for their education.[24]

These writers' appeals to Arab nationalism and resistance to the West were, more often than not, also tied up with appeals to the Muslim identity and Islamic principles they shared with sympathetic readers. One former student who wrote a number of articles critical of SPC during the course of the crisis, Mohammed Zeki (1909), addressed a letter to the "Honored Fathers" of Muslim students. Zeki opened the letter by appealing to the readers' shared Muslim identity, writing,

> . . . your sons (God preserve them) comprehended the matter and perceived the danger and refused to attend church where they had heard themselves despised and scorned, morning and evening. Are you aware what your sons do and what of toils and troubles they suffer? Your sons in that college (I refer only to Moslems) who are sent for the sole purpose of picking the fruits of knowledge not of preaching (which is one of the duties of a religious school) against their will, have raised complaints to heaven in supplication for help but there was no one to help, and they groan but there is none to have mercy.[25]

An anonymous writer for the *Ittehad* (الاتحاد or *The Union*) also appealed to Muslim identity, arguing that Islam "requires us to declare also that it is unlawful for any Moslem to place his child in the American College . . . as long as this is its policy" ("The American College," 1909). The implication in

---

24   These different stances were typical of Muslim discourse surrounding the topic of non-Muslim education in Syria at the time; see M. Haddad's (2002) discussion of four different attitudes surrounding foreign education during the first half of the 20th century (p. 257).

25   Also see the article "In Lighter Vein" (1909) for an imagined conversation between the SPC president and students, which presented the conversation as one of strength and unity rather than division.

this article and in others is that SPC was a space in which Muslims were unwelcome.

Similarly, in an article published in late February in *Ittehad* (الاتحاد or *The Union*), a student writer named Himmet (1909b), one of the presumed leaders of the movement, expressed strong conviction that "they"—those who urged the students to desist in their protest—underestimated the unity binding the Muslim students together.[26] Like Zeki (1909), Himmet (1909b) appealed to a broader Muslim readership in his rhetoric. Unlike Zeki (1909), however, Himmet's (1909b) rhetoric was less critical of the college, expressing a conviction that the college faculty would act on the matter wisely and highlighting his authority to speak from his perspective as a student:

> *They say* [emphasis added] that the college will take every means to bring the Christian students to support it in case of need against the Moslem students, not understanding that the Faculty will employ only the most honorable means to defend its rights and that they are superior to measures causing any such factions among their sons. *They say* [emphasis added] that the president of the college, who has recently returned from America, will use every means to frighten the students and induce them to break their oath through fear of punishment, not realizing that the students will not turn from anything they have sworn to as long as any power or device lies in their hands and that they will lose worldly good but will not lose their honor and its glory.

In this article, alongside another article by Himmet (1909a) published a week prior, Himmet (1909b) suggested that, from his perspective as a student, he did not think it would be productive to exacerbate tensions between the protesting students and the college administrators.[27] He threaded the needle, so to speak, between legitimizing the students' protest as a member of it, while also insisting on the value of the college for the local community. He strategically used his writing to criticize those who sought to increase the tension in other publications.

In an article titled "No Danger to Islam," Dr. Musa Zakhariya (1909) expressed his support for SPC as an institution and highlighted the unity of Muslims. He suggested, through a series of rhetorical questions, that SPC's

---

26   Edward Nickoley (1909), who served as acting president while Howard Bliss was in the US, identified Himmet as one of the leaders of the student movement.

27   In the article published in the same magazine on February 17, 1909, Himmet (1909b) expressed anger at other writers who had spread false rumors that "the honorable faculty of the college has asked for the presence of an American battle ship" in response to the students.

efforts to convert students were relatively innocuous due to the strength of the Muslim faith:

> Has any Moslem heard of one of his faith adopting Christianity in the College? Has he seen one entering a church after leaving college? You should have seen him asleep in the college chapel or occupied in reading some novel, and after having seen this, would you say or believe that there was any danger to Moslems in the American college?

Zakhariya (1909) also defended SPC by citing a number of ways in which the school "respects [students'] religious feelings"—specifically, "in the month of Ramadhan [the college] aids students who desire to fast, in every way. It allows them to go to the mosque on Fridays and gives them three holidays for the feast."[28]

Other writers echoed Zakhariya's (1909) downplaying of the effects of SPC's religious requirement, arguing that Muslim unity would provide protection from proselytization. In an article published in early February, former student Wadi' Abu Fadhil (1909) summarized the debate as it had appeared in various publications at that point. Like Zakhariya, Abu Fadhil (1909) called upon his readers' shared Muslim identity to support the college, suggesting that no Muslim students had ever converted to Christianity after attending the college. Most likely referring to Zeki's (1909) article, Abu Fadhil (1909) criticized the language used in it, arguing that the author had "reiterate[d] the word 'clergyman' to induce the reader to suppose that the college contained only clergymen." Providing evidence similar to Zakhariya (1909), Abu Fadhil (1909) referred to the positive experience he had as a Muslim SPC student, writing that

> . . . the professor of Arabic was constantly urging us to read the Minar, a Moslem journal, although he is a Christian professor, and he advised us to read the Koran and the "Nahij al-Bilagha," by Ali ibn Abi Talib, and other distinguished Moslem writers that we might be well grounded in the art of composition.

The reference to *Nahij al-Bilagha* (نهج البلاغة, literally translated to *Peak of Eloquence*) would have been a particularly compelling example for Abu Fadhil's readers because of the text's religious value to Muslims and its value as a literary and rhetorical Arabic text (*Nahj al-balagha*, 2024).

---

28   As mentioned earlier, however, this concession was only recently provided: SPC administration had agreed in the fall 1908 semester to allow students to attend prayer services on Fridays, in response to demands by students and their families.

As we can see from these examples, students and stakeholders held a range of attitudes about the student protest at SPC, particularly related to SPC's place as a Western institution in the Middle East more generally. In spite of the range of perspectives on the issue, writers were unified in identifying themselves as Muslims, and their rhetoric demonstrated a keen awareness of SPC's symbolic power in the region.[29] Writers rhetorically constructed a representation of America with both positive and negative connotations, and in doing so they highlighted their shared identity and apparent unity as Muslims. While Nicol's sermon might have been the inciting incident, it was not what motivated the controversy on a deeper level. These writers demonstrate how the sermon brought to the surface underlying epistemological tensions that had circulated within the college since its founding—tensions that prompted the 1882 student protests. The expression of these tensions was perhaps more pronounced in the post-revolutionary context in which the local community was writing in 1909.

As the archives illustrate, current and past SPC students involved in the 1909 protests expressed agency in relation to the college's colonial epistemology, which is an important reminder that coloniality, for all its power, does not actually eliminate the voices of the oppressed. Rather, the expression of agency may emerge in other contexts and, as in this case, in other languages. In and through the Arabic-language publications, students sought to negotiate the cultural citizenship that SPC seemed to offer but which did not include them as Muslims. Current and past SPC students drew on their multiple literacies—importantly, in Arabic rather than in English—to search for a path forward. The writers made appeals to a shared Muslim identity in these publications, which was important for their collective resistance to the American colonial epistemology that was integral to SPC's American identity. As evidenced by current students' use of first names only or pseudonyms, it seems that the writers understood implicitly that the discussions carried out in the

---

29   Another important figure who weighed in on the conflict at the time was Salafi Sheikh Rashid Rida, a Syrian who was the founder, editor, and primary writer of al-Manar (المنار, *The Lighthouse*), a popular periodical published in Cairo between 1838 and 1935 (Nile Green, 2020, in his review of Leor Halevi's *Modern Things on Trial* in the *LA Review of Books*, suggested the periodical was "the most influential magazine in Muslim history"). According to Haddad (2002), Rida visited SPC in early 1909 and met with the Muslim students there. At the time, the students recalled, he urged them to "learn from [the college's approach] and improve ourselves so that we should be more qualified for this achievement than they are today" (p. 259). Because the AUB archival collection of articles surrounding the 1909 crisis did not include Rida's contributions to the conversation, I have not included them in the discussion of other published conversations, which the involved faculty at SPC translated and transcribed. However, Haddad's (2002) account of the protest and Rida's involvement is worth reading, and digitized copies of the 1909 *al-Manar* are available in Arabic online at the Internet Archive at https://archive.org/details/Almanar/almanar12/mode/2up).

Arabic-language publications would not be considered an acceptable use of literacy in English at SPC. As Muslims, they all agreed that SPC's Christian national ideology worked against their own identities. They disagreed about the extent to which this conflict posed a risk and whether the risk was worth the reward of an American education.

Coloniality and the "Idea of America"

SPC faculty were aware of the potential for students and stakeholders to deploy anti-Western rhetoric. They knew that the college was understood by many in the region as a symbol of the West. Additionally, they knew that SPC's policies could be interpreted as conflicting with the freedoms represented in and through the idea of America. Although some faculty sympathized with the students' point of view, the faculty ultimately could not escape the colonial epistemology within which they were enculturated and upon which SPC's existence was justified. We can therefore see negotiation of the crisis unfold as a response to the colonial attitudes held by SPC faculty and administrators; students and stakeholders examined these attitudes in order to engage their audiences in the Arabic-language publications throughout the strike. For the students as much as for the faculty, the negotiation that unfolded was ultimately about who belonged in the American college and what kind of religious and ethnic identity was required in order to access the cultural citizenship held out by SPC.

One of the underlying tensions within the college was related to the hierarchical positioning of American over Syrian faculty at the college. Even before the crisis emerged, writers in regional newspapers had criticized SPC's lack of Syrian faculty and staff holding positions of power in the college. Salim, in September 1908, wrote the following after reviewing the SPC catalogue:

> I found that within the names of the faculty, staff, and teachers, that amount to 18 teachers, all are American and none who are Syrian who teach there. There are only 8 [Syrians] who are literature based and all who are assistants to Professors. . . . There is Jaber Efendy Doumit, for example, who has not been promoted even though he has attained a school degree in the year 1876, i.e., 32 years ago. And Bouli Efendy Khooly, the "Professor's Assistant," hasn't either, even though he received his degree in 1897, i.e. 11 years ago. At the same time, you find Mansour Efendy Jeradik and Khaled Efendy Thabit both titled as "Professor's Assistant," even though they both attained their degrees in the year 1901, i.e. 7 years ago. I

> would think that 32 years of teacher experience, publishing, and practice is enough to allow for a "Professor's Assistant" to be an actual Professor; perhaps Jaber Efendy's time spent teaching after attaining a degree is the equivalent of the age of some of the American "Professors" within the College, so what is the reason that the local cannot be a Professor even after 32 years, 11 years, and 7 years? If you were to say that a Teacher every 7 years is promoted to Professor's Assistant, then Jaber Efendy, after 32 years of teaching, should have been promoted 4.5 times over. So am I to say that 4.5 times (Professor's Assistant) does not equate one full time Professor?

Salim (1908) pointed to an issue that SPC had hypocritically failed to address since its founding, the question of whether and when Syrian faculty might hold equal status in the college. In January, during his speech to the faculty, Moore (1909a) presented the difficulty of possibly expelling the striking students by force; he noted too the imbalance of power in the college that Salim (1908) pointed out, warning,

> It is not that we count only Americans, and count out our magnificent body of Syrian professors and Staff; but when it comes to the application of physical force of the problem of expulsion, *the affair becomes American* [emphasis added]. We 30 Americans, if we think it right, will undertake the task. But will it ever be right? (p. 8)

Moore noted in this speech that, should the college decide to physically remove the protesting students, that show of force would "*become[] American.*" In other words, it seems that Moore and other SPC faculty perceived SPC as occupying a liminal space that positioned them between America and Syria; this liminality allowed the college to conduct its work and attract the local population. But using physical force to remove the local, Muslim students would edge SPC to a decidedly American stance toward the population—a stance that would explicitly assert the college's power as an American, Christian, and colonial entity, when before this power was asserted somewhat implicitly through the education it provided. Clearly, Moore was uncomfortable with such an explicit display of power, especially as it would reveal an unpleasant truth about American identity.

Moore's (1909a) question to the faculty—"will [expulsion of the protesting students] ever be right?"—highlights the internal tension, felt by students as well as faculty, between SPC's soft assertion of power through education and religion and the potential power that the college could assert by virtue of the colonial epistemology underlying its American identity. The 1882 crisis, too, stemmed from this tension, but by 1909 the college had grown considerably—particularly in terms of the number of Muslim students enrolled—and neither the students nor the faculty were homogenous in their views about what an SPC education meant, what it should mean, and who belonged that space. While many SPC students, as well as many members of the local and regional community, held the college in high regard, they were not ignorant of the xenophobic and colonial attitudes that had formed the basis for the college's founding and its continuing hold on the attitudes of SPC faculty, administrators, and other stakeholders.

In the examples provided by Moore (1909a) and Salim (1908) above, we can see that the hierarchy between Syrians and Americans at SPC troubled not only outsiders but also some members of the faculty. In its report on the strike, SPC's Committee on Discipline (1909) failed to make a clear recommendation for action in relation to the students, but it tied the strike to the internal hierarchy and recommended

> . . . that the old-time distinction between American Professors and Syrian Adj[unct] Professors be stopped; further that the distinction between Americans and Syrians be stopped; that a discrimination be hereafter made not between Americans and Syrians but between Americans and Americans, thereby . . . adding to the administrative efficiency of the College.

The Committee's recommendation was ultimately not enacted—it took the college 11 more years to give full voting rights and equal standing to Syrian faculty (B. S. Anderson, 2011, p. 49). But the connection made between the strike and the college's power structure is significant, in that it brings into view the faculty's awareness of, and possible discomfort with, the consequences of maintaining the Syrian/American distinction within the college if they hoped the institution would remain influential within the region.

At the same time, in my review of the archives, I found that, no matter the benevolent intentions of some faculty, xenophobic and colonial attitudes were prevalent and entrenched. Rhetorics of coloniality are reflected in Moore's (1909a) summary of what he saw as the different views of the faculty on the crisis:

> To some it is a question of dealing with refractory, rebellious students; to others it is all of that plus a supposed or real threat of mob violence. To others, it is a question of the authority of the Faculty matched against what some would call the

> clamor of, and others would call the conscientious demand of, the united opinion of student representatives of two great non-Christian religions within our College. To some it is a question of the technical rights of the Faculty to make and enforce any law, to receive or dismiss any student, as weighed against the harassing, illegal, irritating hectoring of the Faculty and of our loyal student-body by irresponsible and fanatical insiders and outsiders in the city and country.

In Moore's ostensibly representative summary of faculty attitudes, the students' point of view was seen as inherently corrupt. Faculty views on the crisis characterized the students as, at best, disrespectful of authority and "harassing," and—at worst—potentially violent. These views were held even though the students had deliberately remained on their best behavior—displaying their best performance of cultural citizenship—and had merely refused to attend chapel services.

What's more, Moore's (1909a) speech suggests that even as faculty may have tried to understand the students' point of view, they kept returning to the threat to authority that the student protest represented. On the one hand, this insistence on authority could be seen as unsurprising no matter the context, since institutions tend to work to preserve the power of those who already hold it. But on the other hand, Moore's characterization of the faculty's view of the protesting students as "irresponsible and fanatical insiders and outsiders in the city and country" goes further than a relatively mundane insistence on power: Rather, such characterization had the effect of subordinating Muslim and Jewish students collectively, establishing a distinct hierarchy between faculty and students, Christians and non-Christians—even as the faculty were foreign to the place—and even among students themselves, based only on their religious identity. Such characterization, in other words, was grounded in a deeply colonial way of thinking—the very epistemology that students were protesting against.

Looking more closely at the accounts of the controversy reveals how deeply the SPC faculty—even those sympathetic to the students on strike—were entwined in colonial thinking, even as they apparently sought to serve the region by providing an American education. Accounts ranged from hostile to and fearful of the students, as can be seen in the summaries composed by the acting president Nickoley (1909) and Dodge (1909), the president of the SPC Board of Trustees, to sympathetic to the students, as represented in Moore's (1909a) and Professor William Hall's (1909) portrayals. All, however, dismissed the striking students' primary claim that Nicol's address during a required chapel service was offensive. For example, Nickoley's (1909) account focused on the actions of specific students, including two brothers with the last name of Khairi and a third student with the last name of Himmet (referred to in the previous section), in organizing the student protest. Instead of taking up the students' complaints about Nicol's address, Nickoley blamed the Muslim community—both in and outside of the college—more generally, arguing that "what has happened would have happened anyway . . . the Moslems were on the keen lookout for a peg on which to hang the garment on which they and their city friends had been laboring so long and so painstakingly." Likewise, Hall (1909), whose account belies a fairly sympathetic understanding of the students' point of view, particularly their feeling that requests for religious accommodations on campus had repeatedly been ignored, downplayed the students' interpretations of Nicol's words by calling them the "wildest rumors." None of the accounts written by faculty acknowledged the anti-Muslim xenophobia promoted by Nicol, and some accounts explicitly highlighted and forwarded colonial epistemology, underlining the prevalence of the problem that the striking students recognized in and through their protest.

Beyond their refusal to acknowledge the address that sparked the strike, faculty accounts of the controversy also reveal deeply held colonial views of the region and its people, particularly Muslims, manifested in fear. In a letter to the college's Board of Trustees, President Howard Bliss (1909b) relayed the many political discussions he had on his way back to Beirut from the US after the strike began; the account reveals just how fearful college leaders were of violence—administrators took "proper precautions," according to Bliss, to "safeguard[] the property of the College." Further, upon the President's return to the campus, faculty met with and interviewed each student involved in the strike to ensure that, as Howard Bliss (1909b) explained it, they understood the difference "between a question of conscience and an act of violence . . . any student maintaining the defiant attitude would be severely dealt with, while any one showing a spirit of submission would be dealt with leniently." In an unsigned letter to the American Consul-General (part of which was reproduced in the *Missionary Review of the World* in April[30]), control of the student strike was attributed to "secret Committees in the city, and perhaps in Egypt" (A Friend, 1909). Clearly, faculty and administrators were distrustful of the Muslim student body, in part because of its connection to the broader Muslim community outside of college walls.

---

30   *The Missionary Review of the World* was published as a monthly journal from 1888 to 1939 and was meant to provide its American readers with an overview of (Christian Protestant) missionary activity around the world; it was published independent of any mission organization (see Sherwood & Pierson, 1887; Simnowitz, 2022; for archival copies, see Christian Archives for Islamic Studies, n.d.).

The colonial epistemology underlying the accounts written by SPC administrators and faculty is not all that surprising, given American missionaries' efforts to colonize the region through educational institutions and native-language publications for more than 80 years. As President of the Board, Dodge (1909) explained to the U.S. Secretary of State in a letter written shortly after the crisis began, "[American Missions in Turkey have] been perhaps, the most notable contributions [America] has made for the enlightenment of other nations" through education, which included the Syria Mission's "five important centers . . . , educational Institutions of high grade and a long list of smaller schools. . . . Its press, in capacity and output, stands second among Mission presses in the world" (pp. 4–5). The missionaries and the SPC administrators alike, in other words, saw SPC as one arm of their work, a part of their broader project of colonization.

SPC students were well aware of the colonial and anti-Muslim attitudes of some of their teachers and members of the ABCFM's mission in Syria, and some of the claims the students made in their writing drew upon these attitudes to persuade their audience, who, it was implied, shared the students' understanding and experiences of implicit or explicit racism and xenophobia in their interactions with foreigners in the region. The tone of many of the articles published during the period of student protest suggests that writers were voicing concerns that had been long held: Repeated references to the "despotism" of the recent past, for example, suggest that the views and criticisms of the writers, and their audiences, had been silenced or censored by the Ottoman Empire prior to the 1908 Revolution. The language used also assumed a shared optimism about the future of the post-Revolution Empire. The writers involved in the 1909 debate projected a future for the Empire in which the local population would be autonomous, no longer dependent upon foreign institutions for cultural and social development. Critics and even supporters of SPC during the crisis regularly problematized the college's position as a foreign school funded (and founded) by American Protestant missionaries. Many of the debates about Western education articulated by the local community and SPC students during the protest paralleled the debates in Arabic-language magazines and newspapers published by students at SPC between 1899 and 1920. These publications and the rhetorics circulating within them are discussed in detail in Chapter 5.

Several articles represent well some of the strongest condemnation of SPC on the grounds of its foreign, potentially colonizing, influence within the local community. In one article, titled "Foreign Schools in the Ottoman Empire," the author, El-Ghalieni (1909), criticized "orators and writers" before him who had failed to "[strike] a blow at the doors of these foreign schools or shown what injury they have done to the customs of the people of this country of the Orient, their characteristics, their religious tenets and their political also." El-Ghalieni did not elaborate about the "injury" that foreign schools such as SPC had committed, but the tone suggests that the sentiment would be well understood by the newspaper's audience.

In a second article, titled "Bigotry in the American College," Towfik (1909), of Egypt, offered a strong critique of the college and directed his words to the school forcefully, putting them on the spot by using the second-person pronoun "you." In this article, Towfik argued that SPC had "bewitched us like the college of Carthage and Rom[e]." Doubling down on his references to well-known Westerne empires, Towfik complained that "you have dwelt in our hearts for half a century and conquered them as did Napoleon the Great." Additionally, in an appeal directed toward *The Mohammedan Nation*," an anonymous author commented on the politics of foreign educators in the region, writing,

> The Occidentals perceived the schools are power. They orga-
> nized societies and sent their mission to the east when they
> founded their institutions for the purpose of attracting our
> sons to them. They erected schools to educate the young not
> for our benefit but for theirs, and not to augment thereby our
> power but their own. (*The Mohammedan Nation*, ca. 1909)

In both of these articles, the writers not only constructed a clear division between Muslims and the Westerners who had brought schools to the region but also explicitly named and criticized the coloniality underpinning the Christian mission's project. In other words, they explicitly exposed and critiqued the false promises of the education offered by SPC.

In an article published much later, in July 1909, after the school year had ended and the college returned to its original policy of requiring attendance at religious services, the Committee of the Moslem Students in the Syrian Christian College (1909) addressed the "united Ottoman people" in order to "complain . . . about the hegemony of the faculty in your midst as well as your future men . . . who have been forced to silence their voices of conscience against their will." The committee characterized the experience as "submissive and humiliating to the Ottoman Empire where the foreigner stays in its midst corrupting the laws and regulations without impediment . . . while the days of disguise and ignorance are long past and our people are now free."[31] In a similar vein, Fouad Hantes (1909) outlined the ways in which he saw

---

31   This article was reprinted in at least four newspapers.

Western schools as having a harmful, denationalizing influence on the local population; he argued that "the youth that are brought up in these schools are raised for a purpose that wasn't entailed for them in the first place in light of their identity. Because they are made to believe that this land is not theirs and that its skies are not theirs. They are brought up with a partiality to those countries more so than that of their homeland." While sharing similarities to some of the other articles published during this period, these two articles went further in arguing that the American missionary presence in the region did psychological damage to the students who attended their schools.[32] This implication was rhetorically powerful in its own right and served as a call for Muslims to unify around this issue. Similar arguments also arose in the student-authored magazines and newspapers published at SPC at around the same time, a topic taken up in the next chapter.

Some articles accused the college not only of carrying a colonizing influence in the region but also of being deliberately harmful and nefarious in its religious ideology. An anonymous editorial in *Moweyid* (المؤيد or *The Advocate*) critical of SPC, for example, argued that "these places of learning are only churches under the guise of schools and . . . their professors and directors are merely missionaries under the guise of teachers" (*The Strike of the Moslem Students*, 1909). The authors of this editorial further suggested that the college purposefully deceived the local community, writing that the local population

> . . . cherished in [their] minds a lingering belief that these people were expending these funds and enduring the toils of travel and the burden of exile out of love for the service of humanity alone without the slightest blemish of partisanship, but . . . they do not bestow upon us Moslems these schools freely and are not giving to us science and knowledge as a gift but they are selling them to us at a high price, employing great fraud, like an avaricious trader.

In another article, an anonymous SPC student outlined three different kinds of schools: the "quasi-political" or nationalistic schools, the religious schools, and—the category to which the student said SPC belonged—schools that were "founded in the country in the name of humanity giving the people to understand that they seek the good of the country. They are thus enabled to drop poison unperceived into the nourishment they offer" (A Student, 1909). Another harsh critique of SPC was published later in the year, prior to the

---

32   This rhetorical approach is similar to that of the Iranian mid-20th-century writer Jalal Al-e Ahmad in *Gharbazdegi*, as described by Ahmadi (2023) and Raewyn Connell (2020).

start of the 1909 fall semester, by an author simply identified as "A Witness."
Opening with the line, "By God, he lies who says that despotism is dead," the
writer continued by arguing that even though the government has changed,
"[despotism] is still alive and stirring in many of the foreign institutions that
live on the money of the sons of this Empire, and in many of the Ottoman-
ized Western companies which, not content with wringing money from the
people, aim at their bodies and souls as well" (A Witness, 1909). Collectively,
these writers argued—significantly in Arabic rather than in English—that
SPC and institutions like it were fraudulent, poisonous, and destructive, particularly for Muslim students. Writers wrestled in explicit ways with the colonial epistemology that was transmitted through American literacy education
and its implications for the local community.

Even those who were supportive of the college did not deny its Christian
mission and Western influence, but these writers framed these characteristics
of the school as positive, not negative. Although seemingly contradictory to
their Muslim identity, the positive framing of SPC's American identity illustrates that Muslim views of the college were not homogeneous. In fact, many
who were aware of the college's coloniality accepted it as a foundational part
of its American identity. Towfik Abu Raad (1909), a former student, argued
that the required chapel services were "only . . . lessons in universal morality";
he also wrote, "This is the meaning of the American College. Such it has been
and such it continues to be, and I do not think it is to be blamed if it is fit
for the continuance of these lessons of universal morality as it remains firm
in the continuance of the English language." Abu Raad's defense of SPC on
the grounds that it was merely fulfilling its mission as an *American* college
explicitly illustrates how Christian colonial epistemology helped to justify
American missionary work and the college's mission in the region during that
time period. Abu Raad's defense explicitly promoted the colonial myth that
a "universal morality" exists, and he tied the English language to this myth.
For Abu Raad, the teaching of "universal" truths and the English language
were self-evident and fundamental components of American identity and,
therefore, American literacy education.

No doubt, Abu Raad's (1909) argument mirrored those made by SPC
faculty and administrators as they defended the school's religious requirement. They never wavered in their confidence that their mission—promoting
a Christian education—was "the meaning of the American College" abroad.
In other words, for all stakeholders, "American" meant "Protestant Christian,"
and some would therefore never have the opportunity to gain the cultural
citizenship that seemed to be promised in and through SPC. Moore's (1909a)
speech to faculty on January 25 argued that SPC administrators "frankly

desire to enroll non-Christians; not to swell our numbers, not . . . to toady to Moslems, —none of that; but because we believe the hour has struck when *we can reach just those who most need our work*" (emphasis added). Indeed, an American education, for leaders of the college and for some students and community members, was one that explicitly posed education—particularly education in English—as deeply entwined with Christian morals and values, thus forwarding the epistemological colonization that defined American missionary work in the region. However, the protesting students during the 1909 "Muslim Crisis" refused to accept SPC's exclusionary assumptions, and they drew on their Arabic-language resources to express their agency in the face of the oppression that they experienced at the college.

Reinscribing America

The appeals that the students and other stakeholders made throughout the strike provide clues about how American law and values were understood in the region, especially in light of recent sociopolitical transformations marked by the key words of "liberty, equality, and fraternity." Indeed, the Young Turk Revolution, which temporarily transformed the Ottoman government, motivated students to seek the religious freedom that they assumed existed in America based on the First Amendment to the U.S. Constitution and that they hoped the new Ottoman government would uphold. But the students' arguments pushed up against the reality that American "separation of church and state" only applied to the public sphere, and no Ottoman laws at the time favored the students' position. What's more, because the American imaginary was built upon a Protestant Christian and colonial foundation, Muslims were simply not accounted for in the formation of America's legal system.[33]

Some members of the faculty seemed to respect and understand the students' claims about the illegality of SPC's religious requirement as resting on a moral understanding of American law. Professor Moore (1909a) noted in his speech to faculty, for example, his understanding that the students "appeal[ed] from the lower ground of our technical rights and even of their anticipated law, to the higher sphere of broad humanity, and [they] state[d] with courtesy and perfect circumspection that such compulsion does not accord with claims of freedom of conscience which Christians so frequently

---

33   Take, for example, the fact that many religious people do not attend church but instead attend mosques (masjids), temples, synagogues, etc., but Thomas Jefferson's (1802) widely adopted description of the First Amendment to the U.S. Constitution as a "wall of separation between *church* and state" (emphasis added) within public institutions takes Christianity for granted (as cited in Bailey, 2020).

make" (p. 5). In other words, students' legal appeals were based on a sense of morality, which, even if not technically accurate, reflected their understanding of American democracy and, not incidentally, American Christianity. As such, these appeals represent the striking students' efforts to achieve the cultural citizenship that SPC's education seemed to promise—efforts that would ultimately fail.

Throughout the strike, students remained loyal to SPC and expressed their desire for an adequate resolution reflecting their understanding of what it meant to be an ideal American and to show that they belonged in the college. Students referred to SPC as "their Mother," whom they did not want to leave ([A student reply], ca. 1909). According to Moore (1909a), the students "liken[ed] the situation to a man who, in the desert, owns a well of pure water; travelers, faint with thirst, pass by, and the owner of the well serves only whom he will." And in a different publication, a graduate of the college referred to SPC as "the source of life" (A former student, 1909).

At the same time, students and other stakeholders recognized that in spite of their loyalty, SPC remained beholden to its financial backers in the US. Ultimately, it was the Protestant community based in the US—and therefore their ways of thinking—that allowed the college to exist. In 1909, the source of the college's funding was an important and telling reality: The college had a responsibility to its trustees overseas, and thus the American Protestant answer to the question, "What is the meaning of the American college [in Syria]?" won out: The American college was meant to produce American-like Protestants. In other words, the religious requirement was maintained. Recognizing the power of SPC's American supporters, some critics characterized SPC's decision to uphold its regulations as inevitable. In the summer of 1909, writers directed their appeals to the community rather than the college. Their appeals suggest that the local community wanted the kind of education provided by SPC. The graduate who referred to SPC as "the source of life" also argued that "we ought . . . to seek knowledge and to require learning" so as to remain on equal footing with "western nations" (A former student, 1909). Some writers felt that attending SPC and being present at religious services was worth the compromise, and the language they used suggests that they blamed themselves for their inability to provide a better education led by natives of the region. Dr. Ayoub Thabit (ca. 1909), for example, criticized his readers for remaining "dependent on the education that this College offers."

It was not until after Bliss returned in late February that the crisis was resolved. The students maintained their strike until a temporary agreement was reached between students and faculty in mid-March, when the striking students were allowed to attend alternate, non-religious classes until the end of the semester. At the end of the school year, Bliss announced that all new and returning students the following semester would be required to sign an agreement stating their understanding of, and consent to attend, required religious services at the college.

The tensions discussed in this section illustrate how the idea of America, as well as its colonial power, was not disrupted but *reinscribed* at SPC as a result of the student protests against the college's religious requirements. The material conditions supporting SPC's existence served as specters of America in a remarkably different geopolitical location. These material forces, it turns out, were more powerful than the philosophical ideals that the students relied upon to demonstrate their aspirations to belong to the American college. When these efforts to persuade their American audiences failed at the beginning of the protest, SPC students exerted their literacies in a new way, by turning to their local community and using their linguistic resources to examine and debate the epistemological conflict that they encountered on the grounds of the college. These debates illustrate the autonomy and resourcefulness of the students in the face of an epistemological crisis. In addition, these debates articulated for the local population—and for current scholars and educators—the very real contradictions and harmful consequences of the coloniality underpinning SPC's American-style literacy education, which can shed light on the tensions that some students in writing classrooms navigate today.

Conclusion

The description and analysis I have provided in this chapter of two student protests at SPC in 1882 and 1909 corroborates the central claims of this book: The history of rhetoric and writing studies is inherently a transnational and translingual one, and understanding it as such offers us one step toward a *delinking* of the discipline with its colonial foundations. The case of student protests at SPC reveals how Anglocentric literacy education has historically been linked to colonialism and nationalism and the conflicts that arise as a result. In their attempts to perform an American cultural citizenship—a "state of being" rather than a legal category (Wan, 2011, p. 37)—SPC students learned during the two protests that belonging cannot be achieved through individual actions or behaviors. In their protests, students used forms of literate action and rhetorical appeals that they had learned at the college were distinctly American. These uses—the promises—of literacy, they believed, would demonstrate their belonging to the American college and enable them to help shape college policy accordingly. The students were surprised and disappointed when their protests were met with resistance and even fear on the part of SPC administrators and faculty. As a result, the majority of the protesting students participated in critical and public debates about the college's value in the region, considered the risks posed to their identity and goals, and sometimes left the college altogether.

This account therefore gestures toward the negative consequences that can result from failing to address the "structuring tenets" (Cushman, 2016, p. 239) of the discipline of rhetoric and writing studies that have been informed by colonial epistemology—in this case, the link between citizenship and literacy education that has been made and promoted in much scholarship and writing curriculum. This principle can be traced in part to some of the discipline's foundational histories, which first helped construct the idea of "current-traditional" rhetoric and pedagogy (CTRP) and then characterized the contemporary discipline as resolving the problems attached to such practices through a commitment to critical literacy education with the aim of developing engaged (American) citizens. CTRP has been used repeatedly as a rhetorical trope in historical scholarship to measure the current discipline's progress and viability.[34] The discipline's foundational historians argued that CTRP could be traced back to 18th- and 19th-century rhetorical theory and that it was widely used at Harvard and elsewhere when first-year writing became a core general education course in U.S. universities in the late 19th century.[35] Foundational histories in rhetoric and writing studies, in other words, succeeded in "portray[ing]" writing instruction in the 19th century "as an intellectual and social abyss that swallowed up any and all ideas of rhetorical complexity" that could mostly be blamed on CTRP (Paine, 1999, p. 25).

However, many historians of 19th- and 20th-century writing instruction published since the 1990s have effectively complicated what scholars know about how writing was actually taught in the US, and they collectively show

---

34   References to CTRP in rhetoric and writing studies scholarship generally refer to an approach to writing that values product over process or surface features over content and implies a one-to-one correspondence between a writer's mind and their writing. Terms such as *product, grammar* (or *error, correct/ion/ness*), *form/al/ulaic* (or *system/atic, standard/ized, mechanic/al, schema/tic*), *exposition*, and *style* (or *surface*) often substitute for, or are combined with, explicit uses of the phrase *current traditional*. Further, references to CTRP are often paired with, or exchanged for, words or phrases that convey strongly negative connotations—e.g., *exclusion(ary), disappointing, pervasive, decay(ed), static, backward, contentless*, and, my personal favorite, "a recipe for pain" (Crowley, 1998, p. 227). Daniel Fogarty (1959) was the first to use the term "current traditional," but most references to CTRP in our foundational histories are tied to Richard E. Young's (1978) definition of the term.

35   The foundational historians I reference include James Berlin, 1980, 1984, 1987; John Brereton, 1995; Robert Connors, 1981, 1986, 1997; Sharon Crowley, 1986, 1990, 1998; Wallace Douglas in Richard Ohmann, 1976; S. Michael Halloran, 1993; Susan Miller, 1991; Thomas Miller, 1997.

that CTRP is a false construction based primarily on textbook evidence, White male voices, and also a limited number of elite institutions.[36] Yet writing studies scholars continue to refer to CTRP in explicit or implicit ways, using the trope as a rhetorical punching bag to present the discipline as progressive.[37] CTRP has offered the discipline an opportunity to claim a break from the past and to demonstrate contemporary scholarship and pedagogy as "new"—indeed, for Berlin (1987), the purpose of writing disciplinary history was to "vindicate the position of writing instruction in the college curriculum" (p. 1). Using these problematic narratives of CTRP, historians and others have disparaged past pedagogical practices as resulting from the rise of industrialization, scientism, and professionalism in the 19th and 20th centuries (Berlin, 1984, 1987; Clark & Halloran, 1993; Crowley, 1998) , which, they have claimed, led to higher education "serving the needs of business and industry" (Berlin, 1984, p. 60), ostensibly in opposition to serving the greater public good (notwithstanding problems with how the "greater public good" has historically been defined).

And it is this idea of literacy education serving the greater public good—the idea that "writing courses prepare students for citizenship in a democracy" (Berlin, 1987, p. 188)—for which CTRP has been used as a rhetorical foil in much contemporary writing scholarship and literacy curriculum. In "breaking" with a falsely constructed CTRP of the past and promoting contemporary literacy education as a means to develop an engaged citizenry, the discipline has relied on colonial epistemology to lay the foundation for its viability as a distinct and valuable academic discipline. Scholars in rhetoric and writing studies have rarely questioned or recognized the roots of citizenship as a colonial construction which serves as a marker of inclusion and exclusion (Ribero, 2016). Indeed, "citizenship, with its exclusionary underpinnings, serves to buttress nationalist discourses of fear and jingoism that constitute the nation-state—the organizing structure of colonial/modern power" (Ribero, 2016, p. 41). This calls for interrogating the "nation" as a modern construction supporting colonization (Mignolo, 2007, p. 455), the ways in which so-called citizens might belong (or not), and the complexities that emerge as a result.

---

36   Scholars who have complicated foundational narratives by presenting important microhistories include JoAnn Campbell, 1992a, 1992b; Jean Ferguson Carr, Stephen L. Carr & Lucille Schulz, 2005; P. Donahue, 2007; Enoch, 2008; Kathryn Fitzgerald, 2001; Gold, 2008; Greer, 1999, 2015, 2023; Byron Hawk, 2007; Susan Kates, 2001; Elizabeth Larsen, 1992; Kenneth Lindblom, William Banks & Rise Quay, 2007; Beth Ann Rothermel, 2003, 2007; Sue Carter Simmons, 1995; Robin Varnum, 1996; Heidimarie Z. Weidner, 2007; Kathleen A. Welsch, 2007.

37   The idea of "progress" is also a colonial construction; see Mignolo, 2007, pp. 462-463.

What's more, as Tendayi Bloom (2018) noted,

> Even critics [of the intrinsic value of citizenship] often focus on whether equality of citizenship is being realised, how to address barriers to it, or whether there is a need for new forms of citizenship. They seldom question the underlying assumption—and promotion—of liberal citizenship as the only legitimate relationship with a state. (p. 115)

Besides the obvious problems associated with promoting the ideals of (American) citizenship within U.S. literacy classrooms that include undocumented or international students, citizenship has also been used as a tool of settler colonialism in the United States. Bloom (2018) pointed to the 1887 Dawes Act and the 1924 Indian Citizenship Act to show that the United States government has historically imposed citizenship on Indigenous peoples as "a final step in the colonising process, forcing total submission to the American state" (p. 116).

Such complications disrupt the social justice orientation of the discipline, in which active citizenship and democratic participation are assumed to not only be *possible* for every student through literacy, but also to be a universal good. The case of student protests at SPC should prompt scholars, program administrators, and teachers to ask critical questions about the democratic potential of literacy education: How is "citizenship" defined; how does geopolitical context affect this definition; and who is included in or excluded from this definition? Who is allowed to be or act as a citizen within the framework of literacy education? What is at stake for those who are invited to participate as actual or hypothetical citizens? What are the risks and rewards associated with performing citizenship within the literacy classroom? If the idea of the nation—an imagined America—and citizenship itself is "aspirational, a promise" (Wan, 2011, p. 46), then literacy educators and program leaders who imagine themselves to be facilitators of engaged citizenship bear a great responsibility when such promises fail students, as they often do. Such failures were at work in the 1882 and 1909 protests at SPC. Taking a transnational view of the history of writing studies exposes the contradictions and conflicts that arise when colonial epistemology remains at the base of today's approaches to writing pedagogy.

Building upon the analysis presented in Chapter 3, this chapter shows that language(s) proved important to the two protest movements at SPC in 1882 and 1909 and carried significance for students as they wrote their way through the crises. Language and translingual exchange should therefore be both central and visible in rhetoric and writing studies' history, present, and future. The translingual geopolitical context of Beirut, Syria, at the turn of the 20th century contributed to SPC student agency during these protests. The 1882 protest occurred before SPC had fully transitioned to English as the language of instruction, and students primarily appealed to SPC administrators using Arabic to object to the dismissal of their beloved Professor Lewis. Students fought to keep Lewis and the other medical faculty, who also happened to be the last holdouts of Arabic-language instruction, at the college. After all but one of these faculty members had resigned, SPC administrators privately expressed relief, with the last member of the medical faculty characterizing his former colleagues as a "half-hearted, half-educated (in the best sense), unwilling, un-American, missionary line of Professors" (as cited in Jeha, 2004, p. 90). When considering the role of language(s) during this protest, it is possible to see that students may have chosen to fight for this group of faculty because their commitment to the Arabic language represented a commitment to the place and the people, in contrast to the rest of the college, which was turning toward English and upholding the power of foreigners over decision-making. As a result of SPC's refusal to reinstate Lewis, many of the protesting students chose to leave the college: Some took on important roles as Arabic-language writers in Syria and Egypt. I demonstrate in Chapter 3 that the college's stated rationales for first Arabic and then English as the language of instruction were both steeped in colonial epistemology. However, the Arabic language on its own carried sociopolitical power for local students that signified respect for their culture and identity. The removal of long-time faculty who were fluent in Arabic and willing to translate Western knowledge into the local language must have carried extra weight for the students who were affected, and it likely pushed them to leave the college as a result.

During the 1909 protest, SPC students negotiated with college administrators and faculty in English in an effort to change the policy that required all students to attend chapel services. At the same time, the students—along with many community members—participated in heated discussions about the college's place in the region in Arabic-language journals that circulated throughout the region. These debates reveal that the local community held a deep, almost intrinsic, understanding of what was at stake when Western educational enterprises entered the region. All seemed to understand that the colonial epistemology underlying much Western education ran up against local ways of thinking and believing, but they did not all agree upon the risks and rewards of Western education and the exposure to coloniality that was brought with it. Some vehemently opposed engaging with educational institutions such as SPC, while others saw the institutions as relatively harmless. Some resigned themselves to receiving a particular brand of education from SPC—instruction in English and the "lessons in universal morality" represented by SPC's controversial chapel services simply *was* "the meaning of the American college" (Abu Raad, 1909). Importantly, these discussions among the local and regional community were held in Arabic rather than English, demonstrating the value of centralizing language(s)—including languages that have been suppressed—in understanding the history of rhetoric and writing studies, as well as its present and future. The 1909 protest spread beyond the walls of the college, and students demonstrated agency in the conflict by drawing from their multiple linguistic resources, participating in the debates themselves in Arabic, while interacting with SPC administrators and faculty in English. As such, this case of translingual negotiation and exchange highlights how important it is to question the discipline's underlying tenet of monolingualism and recognize that "*English* is" *not* "the *only* language of knowledge making and learning" (Cushman, 2016, p. 234).

This chapter's decolonial analysis of the 1882 and 1909 student protests at SPC holds implications for productively *delinking* from the discipline's colonial foundations. Specifically, these protests provide us with a better understanding of why contemporary students may resist efforts to connect literacy with citizenship, democracy, and upward mobility. While literacy is undoubtedly a necessary tool for active participation in democracy, it also often fails to produce the idealistic outcomes that instructors sometimes espouse (see Lagman, 2018, and Lorimer Leonard, 2013). Suggesting that literacy—particularly writing in English—will lead to universally positive outcomes is unrealistic, and students may see these implied promises as disingenuous when they fail. What's more, as previously noted, writing programs and instructors cannot assume that students have equal access to citizenship or that citizenship is necessarily desirable for them. Making such assumptions can alienate or demotivate those students whom instructors are most interested in serving. In short, those of us in rhetoric and writing studies must be careful not to conflate citizenship with English-language literacy.

In addition, this analysis should remind us that students are agentive and autonomous and that they will use many linguistic, multimodal, and technological resources to negotiate and make sense of their literacy education. When this agency is denied, they may walk away from the opportunities that are on offer, as many of the protesting SPC students did when the college refused to change its policies. Or, even if they stay, students may ultimately feel excluded or alienated from the educational environment, even as they proceed through the curriculum. In other words, students may achieve a utilitarian goal in performing what is expected and receiving a degree but fall short of engaging deeply with course content. In order to facilitate critical engagement in the literacy classroom, programs and instructors must give students the opportunity to show where, when, and with what resources they use literacy outside of the classroom, and then work with them to develop rhetorical flexibility and skill in contexts that matter to them. We must also remain sensitive to the high stakes and contradictions that many students, particularly historically minoritized students, face as they navigate the writing classroom and all the promises it implies. Making these choices, as literacy educators and program leaders, has the potential to produce pluriversal definitions for the meaning and value of literacy that is free from the colonial baggage that has historically chained writing instruction with problematic constructions of citizenship.

5

Composing America at Syrian Protestant College

With Ghada Seifeddine (translator, Arabic to English) and Yasmine Abou Taha (Arabic-language transcription)[1]

Since 1899, students at Syrian Protestant College (SPC) "published a magazine or newspaper for part of or almost every year," and "in 1906 alone, the students published sixteen different papers, the largest output in any given year of the school's existence" (B. S. Anderson, 2011, p. 22; see Appendix B for a full list of SPC student publications between 1899 and 1920). As one student writer explained in the introduction to the first issue of الحظ (*al-Haz*), or *Luck*, magazine (published 1901–1903), newspapers went "viral" on campus at the turn of the 20th century (I. Attieh, 1901).[2] This chapter builds upon the previous two chapters to show that a decolonial understanding of the history of writing studies is fundamentally transnational and translingual. The evidence presented

---

[1]   Ghada Seifeddine and Dr. Yasmine Abou Taha were both undergraduate and, later, graduate students at the American University of Beirut when I was an assistant professor in the English department there. I could not have written this chapter without their contributions, which were supported by grants provided by the American University of Beirut. Yasmine identified Arabic-language student writing that was thematically aligned with my research interests, and then she transcribed those archival documents into a digital format. Then, Ghada translated those pieces from Arabic to English, with contextual notes to help me better understand the English-language translation. Ghada and I also periodically met to discuss her translations as she completed them. Both of these amazing women have gone on to pursue PhDs: Yasmine has earned a PhD in linguistics and now works at York University (Toronto). At the time of this writing, Ghada is in her final year as a doctoral candidate in rhetoric and composition at Purdue University.

[2]   A note on the Arabic-English translations throughout this chapter: I have presented the original passage in Arabic prior to each translation in English. My rationale is three-fold: First, I believe including the original Arabic highlights the students' original voices, making them accessible to readers familiar with Arabic. Additionally, presenting both English and Arabic emphasizes the transnational nature of the students' writing education. Finally, making multiple languages visible throughout the text disrupts scholars' tendency to discuss multilingual students and subjects in a single language. At times, the English translation does not match the exact wording of the Arabic original, because the translation aims to capture the contextual meaning of the passage rather than present a word-for-word or line-by-line translation. Because Arabic is read from right to left, all passages in Arabic are aligned to the right directly before the English translation. Titles of the publications are presented in the original Arabic (with the Arabic's transliteration in parentheses), next to the title's translation in English. I hope my presentation of the student texts and their translations serves to model the kind of multilingual academic convention that is necessary for transnational scholarship.

here illustrates students' construction of identity through writing, because and in spite of SPC's Americentric literacy curriculum and policy. I trace how SPC students negotiated identity in relation to their geopolitical positioning in nearly 50 English- and Arabic-language student magazines and newspapers published between 1899 and 1920 (for a complete list, see Appendix B). SPC student publications at around the turn of the 20th century operate as markers of linguistic, national, cultural, and political identity, not only in terms of their subject matter, but also in terms of their materiality as well as the languages in which they were written. In these publications, SPC students sought out the responses of their peers, drawing upon their multiple linguistic resources and engaging with diverse imagined and real audiences in rhetorically savvy ways. Additionally, as will be shown, SPC students' language use—in Arabic, English, and sometimes in French or Armenian—is central to the decolonial analysis presented here, exemplifying how understanding the history, present, and future of the field of rhetoric and writing studies can change when the monolingualism upon which much knowledge has been built is contested.

The reason(s) for the emergence of these student-authored publications—or even the prevalence of their circulation, who authorized their publication, and who read them—is not immediately clear, though there are occasional hints in the content of the individual publications themselves. It is likely that students chose to write because of the rise of print media in the local and regional community, as well as the legacy of the college itself. At the time, the newspaper industry was increasingly prevalent in Beirut, Damascus and—as the Ottoman Empire placed restrictions on the local press—Cairo, where journalists enjoyed more freedom thanks to Egypt's autonomy (Dajani, 1992, pp. 26–31).[3]

As print media proliferated, so too did the promotion of what is commonly referred to as Arab nationalism and identity—what is known as النهضة (*al-Nahda*), which translates to "the awakening" or "the renaissance" and is often called "the Arab Renaissance." Throughout the 19th century, the Ottoman Empire struggled to maintain its colonial influence and power over much of the Arab world; Rasha Diab (2024) described this period as

> marked by Napoleon Bonaparte's invasion of Egypt and Syria, and a massive regional, national, and intellectual awakening. The military suffers from resounding defeat; the whole region becomes a proxy battlefield for British and French mercantile

---

3   Hourani (1983) identified two new kinds of periodicals in the region emerging around the 1870s: The first were independent political newspapers, and the second were literary and scientific periodicals, the latter of which translated European and American ideas and inventions into Arabic. Most of these periodicals were written by Lebanese Christians who were educated in French and American schools in Syria (p. 245).

and political rivalry; the colonization of Arab nations piles on
a palpable cultural gap. (p. 36)

Ideologies of Arab nationalism—or "the idea that the Arabs are a people
linked by special bonds of language and history (and, many would add, religion), and that their political organization should in some way reflect this
reality"—gained traction (Khalidi, 1991b, p. vii). Christian and Muslim writers from across the region helped articulate a nationalist self-view, largely
in comparison with, or in contrast to, "the West." The discourses emerging
at this time and in this context can be framed through a decolonial lens as
a form of what Raewyn Connell (2020) called "Southern theory," or theory
produced outside of the Global North.

Throughout the *al-Nahda* period, "presses and magazines thrive[d] and
literary salons proliferate[d] . . . hold[ing] the space for envisioning, deliber-
ating, and advocating for varied transformations" (Diab, 2025, p. 209). Elizabeth Kassab (2010) explained that the writing published during *al-Nahda*
revolved around questions related to civilizations' "rise and fall," political
justice, science, religion, and gender (pp. 20–22). Importantly, the *al-Nahda*
movement cannot be understood as divorced from Western epistemology. In
fact, as Hourani (1983) explained, Arab nationalism was also tied to colonial
ideas about universal truth and knowledge (although Hourani did not label
these ideas as colonial). The publications circulating throughout the region

> lay certain positive ideas about what truth was, how it should
> be sought, and what the Arabic reading public ought to
> know. That civilization was a good in itself, and to create and
> maintain it should be the criterion of action and the norm
> of morality; that science was the basis of civilization, and the
> European sciences were of universal value that they could and
> must be accepted by the Arab mind through the medium of
> the Arabic language; that from the discoveries of science there
> could be inferred a system of social morality which was the
> secret of social strength; and that the basis of this moral sys-
> tem was public spirit or patriotism, the love of country and
> fellow countrymen which should transcend all other social
> ties, even those of religion: it was largely through the work of
> these periodicals that such ideas later became commonplace.
> (Hourani, 1983, pp. 246–247; see also Khalidi, 1991a)

In many ways, the circulation of print media and the rise of Arab nationalism
was a response to coloniality, represented not only by the Ottoman Empire

but also by Western powers that were increasingly influential in the region (see Chapter 2 for a more extensive discussion).

At around the turn of the 20th century, SPC students would have been well aware of *al-Nahda* writers' calls to "reclaim [Arabic] history and language as pivotal elements defining who they were" (B. S. Anderson, 2011, p. 12)—these calls were published in local and regional newspapers and magazines. Additionally, by the time student-authored publications began to flourish at the college, a number of the college's graduates, including Jurji Zeidan, Faris Nimr, and Ya'qub Sarruf, had become professional writers in their own right (Holt, 2016, p. 273). Student writing then, circulated in a deeply transnational context.

This chapter builds upon the analysis of student protests presented in Chapter 4 by showing how SPC students used language(s) for different purposes in their everyday writing. As evidenced in the student publications examined here, SPC students often used Arabic to identify themselves as a part of the Arab local and regional community as they spoke directly to their peers and other native Syrians (such as their Syrian instructors, who were not considered faculty at SPC at the time). Their use of Arabic drew upon and responded to central themes of the *al-Nahda* movement, often in order to critique and praise their homeland. In contrast, students' writing in English (which would have been accessible to faculty and administrators at SPC) was often more neutral in describing the problems facing their local and regional community or accounting for Western history and culture. Sometimes, English was used to explicitly praise the West or to denigrate Arab society. In other words, students made rhetorical choices about content, tone, and audience depending on the language. Noticing this contrast can help scholars better understand how America was imagined by students in and through language, as English was the language of instruction and was therefore tied directly to the American identity of SPC as an institution as well as its administrators and faculty and the cultural citizenship that they were implicitly called to perform (see Chapter 4). On the other hand, the use of Arabic tied writers to the Arab identity of many SPC students, staff, and the local and regional community in which SPC was located though not always a part. Students' negotiation of identity through writing, in other words, is especially clear when considering the languages in which students chose to write. The analysis presented in this chapter substantiates the value of making language(s) visible in the history, present, and future of rhetoric and writing studies and the ways in which such analysis can push to *delink* the field from its colonial base.

I begin this chapter by providing a general overview of the student writing published at SPC between 1899 and 1920, providing a sense of the publications' diversity in terms of genre, purpose, and audience (see Appendix B for a full listing). I highlight three magazines that help illustrate SPC students' approaches to, and beliefs about, writing across languages. This overview provides context for the analysis that follows, in which I show how much of the student writing captured in these publications explicitly connects language with identity. To accomplish this, I first provide an initial overview of the interactions among student writing, language ideology, and identity by showcasing instructive examples from a representative range of publications. Then, to further illustrate how these interactions manifested, I focus on an example of marginalia composed in Arabic and English found in one student publication, the *SPC Commercial Paper* (published 1904). Finally, in the latter part of this chapter, I outline how the student publications help scholars better understand students' imagined America in relation to their Arab identity and multilingualism. Specifically, I highlight three rhetorical strands—a rhetoric of nationalism, a rhetoric of resistance, and a rhetoric of Occidentalism—that shaped how students navigated identity in and through these publications. This chapter shows how SPC student newspapers and magazines allowed students to identify themselves in relation to their geopolitical context as well as to negotiate with peers, faculty, and the broader community through writing. Additionally, this chapter challenges the Americentric and monolingual "structuring tenets" (Cushman, 2016, p. 239) upon which much of the discipline of rhetoric and writing studies has been based.

Overview of SPC Student Writing

According to educational historian Betty Anderson (2011), SPC students wrote in English, Arabic, French, and even Armenian for a variety of reasons—for student societies or class assignments, on their own or in groups (pp. 22–23). In their writing, students explored a wide range of topics, many of which aligned with *al-Nahda* themes, centering on questions about religion and morality, social and cultural behaviors and practices, politics and national identity, gender and education, and progress and modernity. They wrote in a multitude of genres—editorials, short informational essays, biographies, personal anecdotes, fables and allegories, poetry, fiction, photo essays, and more. The archives suggest that student publications were overseen by members of the faculty, but it is not clear what role faculty played in monitoring or censoring the content of each issue; due to most faculty members' lack of fluency in Arabic, Arabic-language publications were likely only read or reviewed by Arabic-speaking staff and students.

Between 1899 and 1920, nearly 50 English- and Arabic-language SPC magazines and newspapers were published by students (see the list of these publications in Appendix B). The publications proliferated in the first decade of the 20th century, with a slowdown, probably due to a shifting geopolitical landscape and World War I, between 1910 and 1920. A small number of publications were published in two languages, with one including a section in French as a "supplement." Many of these publications are preserved, in full or in part, in the archives at the American University of Beirut today.

The purposes and positioning of these publications varied. Some of the student writers were enrolled in the Preparatory Department—such as the authors of صدى الاستعدادية (*Sada al-Isti'dadiyah*), or *Elementary Echo* (published periodically between 1902 and 1908), and *Prep Progress* (published 1911)—whereas others were clearly writing from more advanced perspectives as students in the Collegiate Department or the School of Commerce—such as the authors of *Seniors of the SPC* (published 1906), *Chemical and Industrial Gazette* (published 1906), and *The Business Amanuensis* (published 1906–1907).

As mentioned previously, the documents preserved in the archives do not clearly reveal the context in which the publications were composed—that is, the student authors do not often explicitly state why they have decided to produce a given publication. However, it is clear that the publication of various magazines and newspapers was a relatively popular activity for students in the college, pushing some students to articulate a specific purpose. For example, in the first issue of *The Business Amanuensis*, an unnamed author distinguished the publication from others, writing,

> Another strictly student paper is about to be launched . . . [it] will carry a cargo of a little different nature than other student papers of the College. . . . It is the purpose of the Amanuensis to be a Commercial man's paper and to be such a good commercial paper that no business man can be without it: to be such a good paper that the time invested in reading it, will bring a profit or interest of a large percent. ("Introduction," 1906)

Iskander Makarius, the author of the bilingual and multimodal publication *The Kodak* (published 1903–1904), positioned himself as a student with specific abilities in photography and language that he wanted to showcase and share with others who might have similar interests. Others, such as the editors of الغادة (*al-Ghada*), or *Grace* (published 1903), and الدائرة (*al-Daa'ra*), or *Circle* (published 1903–1904), critiqued each other regularly within their articles, implicitly suggesting that these students and others like them saw their work in conversation and sometimes in competition with each other.

Students conceived of their audiences—and the interactions they expected from their audiences—in different ways. Many of the publications directly instructed their peers. For example, in *Life of Service* (published 1907–1908), the unnamed editors acknowledged that their "English is not what it might be," but they told their readers to "please overlook or at least refrain from using either pen or pencil on the pages of the magazine" if they found mistakes ("Editorial," 1907).

Additionally, a number of the periodicals invited contributions from readers. In المنتهون (*al-Muntahoon*), or *The Terminators* (published 1905–1906), the unnamed editors, though ostensibly addressing teachers, in fact asked students to consider what teachers might say in response to this question:

أيها الأستاذ!

ما هي صفات أفضل تلميذ في إدارتك؟

Hey Teacher!

What are the qualities of the best student under your supervision?

The editors explained,

نرجو من كل معلمي الكلية ان يبدي رأيه في الاجابة عن هذا السؤال فان اطلاع التلامذة على الصفات التي يرغبها الاستاذ و التي يراها في افضل تلميذ عنده قد يحثهم على إحراز تلك الصفات.

Again, we wish for all teachers at the college to provide us with answers to this question, as disclosing the qualities that the teacher desires and sees most clearly in his best student in class might urge other students to attain these qualities. (سؤال نوجهه للأساتذة [Question Directed to the Teachers, 1905])

Both *The Commercial Triumvirate* (published 1906) and the *Miltonian* (published 1903–1904) indicated that they would like to receive contributions from students. In *The Commercial Triumvirate*, the editors wrote that they would "be glad to publish any articles sent . . . from students, provided they are bearing on commercial, social and economical subjects, either in English or Arabic" ("The Triumvirate Will Be Glad," 1906). The *Miltonian* saw itself as an avenue for "our [Milton Society] members and of any

other student . . . to display their ability in the use of the English language"
("Editorial," 1903).

And some of the publications presented implicit and explicit criticisms of
readers, imploring them to adjust their habits. In حسناء الكلية (*Hasnaa'
al-Kulliyah*), or *Beauty of the College* (published 1903–1904), the unnamed
author discussed the purpose and value of magazines and newspapers in general, moving to the student magazines published at SPC in particular. Explicitly criticizing students in the Medical Department, he wrote,

> و لا بد لي من كلمة انتقاد على فجقرَّاء [sic] [قرَّاء] الجرائد من تلامذتنا
> الاطباء. و ذلك أن [الوسط] الأعظم من رفقائنا التلامذة لا يستحسنون
> أهم جرائد العربية لعدم وجود نكت مضحكة و أقوال هزلية. على أن عدم
> وجود مثل هذه الاقوال في الجرائد لا يتألى عن قصر [أو] باع محرريها
> انما إعراضاً عنها لعدم فوائدها. و إني في خجلٍ لما قد كتبته في هذا
> الصدد إنما حقوق الصداقة و واجباتي أجبراني على ذلك.

> I have to add a few words of criticism directed to the medical
> students, particularly those who read magazines. The majority
> of our fellow classmates do not find value in major Arabic
> magazines due to the absence of funny jokes and comic say-
> ings in them, knowing that the presence of this type of content
> does not stem from a shortage or weakness on part of its writ-
> ers; on the contrary, it reflects the magazine's opposition to
> include these sayings because they are of no benefit. I feel
> embarrassed about what I wrote with regards to this point, but
> the laws of friendship and my sense of duty force me to do so.
> (الجرائد [Magazines], 1903)

Similarly, the editor of *Cedar* (published 1919) provided a stern-sounding
reminder to his peers about the importance of their continued participation
in the publication of the newspaper, writing,

> This is our Class Gazette. It stands for us. It is considered as
> part of what we are. Let us therefore strive not to lessen the
> enthusiasm for the first number. But to keep the fire burn-
> ing slowly and surely. If we can do that, it shows that there
> is a reserve cool, sure and steady, which we can depend upon.
> Remember it is our gazette, and it is up to every man of us to
> see that its standard is kept high. If we could only cultivate
> the spirit of unity and interdependence which it stands for, we
> would be the gainers thereby as well as those whom we hope
> to interest and amuse. (Awad, 1919)

Viewed together, a range of purposes and approaches toward writing are seen in these publications. Clearly, students approached this extracurricular writing as a professional activity. Some exhibited playfulness and experimentation in their writing. Others saw writing as a collaborative and interactive activity, soliciting responses from their peers and teachers. Students also saw their writing as a way to position themselves as leaders of behavior, thinking, and writing on campus. Additionally, some of the publications offered a way for student writers to model the performances that they understood to be valued at the college. As I will explain throughout this chapter, the language(s) in which students wrote also proved important to what and how they communicated, as well as the audiences to whom they presumed to be speaking.

Reasons to Write: Three Notable Examples

With this general overview of the publications in mind, in this section I call attention to a few specific examples—*I.O.U. 5 Minutes* (published 1902), *The Kodak* (published 1903–1904), and *Happy Days at SPC* (published 1903–1905)—that illustrate the ways in which at least some students conceived of writing at SPC. Although there were a wide variety of publications produced by SPC students during this period, the examples I present here suggest that students saw writing as invitational, pedagogical, process-based, and sometimes collaborative. Further, these examples highlight the labor that student writers put into their publications; the ways in which students conceived of language as inclusionary and exclusionary; and the imagined and actual uptake by readers.

Taking a closer look at these three publications helps contextualize the excerpts of other publications that I analyze in the latter part of this chapter and perhaps helps better explain how and why students used these publications to express their positioning and identity in relation to the larger geopolitical context. The examples I present later in the chapter, of students' depictions of the West and American-style schooling when writing in Arabic, suggest that students' different language choices gave them space to express and support different epistemologies.

I.O.U. 5 Minutes

The only issue of *I.O.U. 5 Minutes* that remains preserved in the archives was published in June 1902 and was written wholly by a student named Selim M. Zein enrolled in the Preparatory Department. Although no other issues of the magazine survived, this issue references previous issues, so evidently it was part of a series. The magazine is subtitled *A Monthly Review of "Criticism" closing with a "French Supplement" and an "Arabic" one*. The issue is entirely handwritten with an introduction titled "Last but not 'Least'!", a proverb, several anecdotes and allegories, a relatively lengthy "French Supplement," and an "Arabic Supplement." Several other publications are preserved from the same year, but all of them were written in Arabic. *I.O.U. 5 Minutes* is, in fact, the earliest English-language student magazine that is saved in the archives.

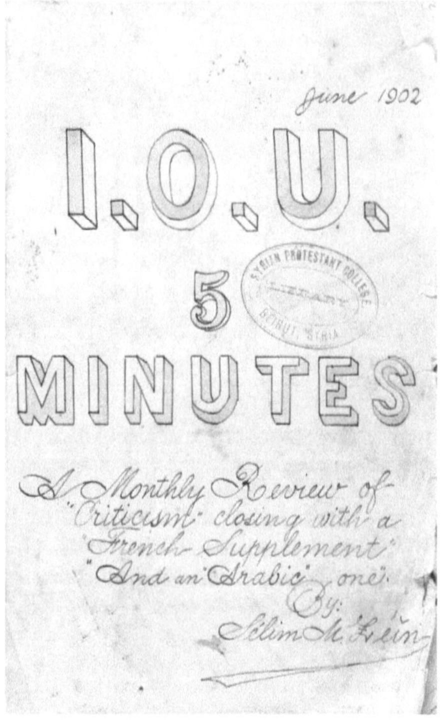

Figure 5.1. I.O.U. 5 Minutes (Zein, 1902). Permission to publish granted by AUB Libraries.

The introduction, reproduced in full here, provides some important context for how Zein (1902) conceived of the magazine:

> Last but not "Least"!
>
> This is the last time when our poor magazine will appear before you, most dear friends as you were!! . . . It is the last but not the least as you should know!
>
> I have been for a long time very thankful to you who have paid attention to what we have written in it.

Evidently it was not our purpose to show how little English that we know! Oh! Not in the least!! Our purpose has been only to encourage students in making practice in that language which till now students who have graduated from the Collegiate Department can not utter a few words without hesitating and making lots of mistakes. Doubtless you should not contract what is plainly known to you all.

Now it is time for you, Dear Friends, to write essays not minding whether they are poor in English or not because Rome was not built in a day, and Napoleon was not made Emperor from the first time over France? And infallibility is not expected in a beginner.

Look again to that French man. He was first a simple officer, then became general, and so on by his hard work he was made Emperor. It is so with you, at first, you would make many and many mistakes while you are young, but after that you would make no more when you would be men in the Collegiate Department.

I myself would never cease thanking the one who first had encouraged me to that work and till now I still remember his friendly advice saying to me:

"Go on, Selim, you would succeed if you work hard and I, myself, he said, would correct you all the little and big mistakes that you would make and help you more in making an English Club composed of all the strong Fourth Form students in English and call it the "Story Writers' Club" which till now goes flourishing and this being due to his care.

Oh! That man source of kindness how our College would have succeeded if it had many persons who would follow his example!!!

And now when I can address no more to you I close my speech in that number saying to you: Goodbye till we meet again! And may God accompany you in that vacation where, who knows, if we would all meet again in that Alma Mater which had fed us for a longtime from its moral and physical knowledges; and now Good-bye again, I hope you will have a good and pleasant vacation.

In this introduction, Zein indicated that the issue was the last in a series and was produced as part of his membership of an "English Club" or "Story Writer's Club" for the fourth-level students of the Preparatory Department at SPC. We can see, too, in this introduction Zein's deep engagement with imagined readers; he constructed an audience who would be attentive and appreciative of his message, and he also imagined himself as a teacher of sorts, providing encouragement for others at his level who were developing their language skills as they worked toward entering the Collegiate Department in the near future.

Zein's (1902) references to the French and Roman Empires—particularly his use of Napoleon's hard work as an example for fellow English-language learners to follow—provides a sense that students at the time held positive attitudes about Empire and colonization. However, he may have chosen to glorify colonizers and the West specifically because he was writing in English—perhaps such glorification seemed a particularly appropriate rhetorical strategy for writing in the English language for English-speaking readers such as his professors. Likewise, Zein's praise of the unnamed "man," who was likely his English-language teacher and perhaps assigned students to produce magazines such as this, seems similarly strategic and perhaps self-serving—it is difficult to imagine Zein praising an instructor in a language that the instructor couldn't read.

Toward the end of the issue, just before the "Arabic Supplement" at the end, readers encounter the following:

> A free page.
>
> I beg all those who find mistakes in my magazine, to note them down here in this page and put under their corrections their names, because politeness does not allow in our time, boys or gentlemen, to write with a pencil on any magazine, some mistake left by the editor without attention. By: Selim Zein (Zein, 1902)

The rest of this "free page" is blank; no one provided any responses in the empty space. Ironically, on the back cover of the issue, someone scrawled—without the requested identification—"Please look in a dictionary before you write." This "free page" indicates that Zein imagined his readers to be engaged and supportive of his efforts. He did not see his work as finished; rather, he invited his peers to help him improve his writing. However, Zein's "polite" imaginary audience is thrown into sharp relief against the reality of a sarcastic, unhelpful, and anonymous response on the back cover of his magazine, eerily similar in spirit to the marginalia found in the *SPC Commercial Paper*, which is discussed later in this chapter. It remains unclear why Zein's peers did not respond in the way he imagined—in all likelihood, Zein's peers simply found it easier to criticize than to contribute.

The two language supplements Zein (1902) created seem to serve as outlets through which he could practice and demonstrate his proficiency in languages other than English while also serving the purpose of entertainment for his readers. The French supplement, which spans 18 handwritten pages, contains a series of humorous anecdotes and proverbs. The Arabic supplement is much shorter—only two pages—and contains two love poems.[4]

The Kodak

Figure 5.2. The Kodak (Makarius, 1904). Permission
to publish granted by AUB Libraries.

---

4   Since the majority of the student writing preserved in the archives was in Arabic and English, I have focused my analysis in this chapter on Arabic and English only. I note other languages as present, but I did not have materials that were written in other languages translated.

The Kodak was published between 1903 and 1904 and was authored completely by Iskander Makarius, a student likely enrolled in the Collegiate program but for whom there is no other information available. The journal is striking in the level of care with which it was created—it is clearly handmade: The front cover of two of the issues (three have been preserved) are collages of text and image overlaying each other. On the issue published in January 1904, images of opened books are pasted in the center of the page, with the title of the journal overlaid in large, black letters and the name of the journal and other information presented in red and black lettering on the edges of the book images. On the issue from March 1904, what looks to be a newspaper image of a camera and a faded red-and-white triangular banner are pasted. Arabic-English text with the title of the journal and its date of publication is laid over the center of the camera picture. This design illustrates the care with which the author approached this project. Additionally, readers are given a hint, from this cover, of the interweaving of multiple languages and modes within, which is part of what makes this publication so special.

The Kodak is completely handwritten, and many photos appear alongside the essays contained therein. As indicated by the Arabic and English text on the journal's covers, Makarius (1903–1904) presented most of the journal's essays in both languages, the Arabic and English versions of each essay laid out in columns side by side, with the Arabic in one column and the English in the other. The issues primarily consist of informative essays about local places, like "Bridge El-Kadi" and "Up the Beirout River," and short reports about events, such as the visit of the Beirut "Wali," or governor, and the college's field days. Additionally, each issue contains several short instructive essays or brief tips about the hobby of photography, such as "Dangers of Flashlight," "How to Make a Ground Glass which will serve for Focussing," "Sizes of English Plates," and "The Dark Room and its Fittings."

In the two later issues of *The Kodak*, Makarius (1903–1904) commented on his goals for the journal and also what he expected of his readers; in the preface to the January 1904 issue, he explained,

> It has been my intention since a short time to introduce into the collection of papers in our Library a new Photographic paper. After deciding its issue, I came to the formation of the following sketch which shows how the paper shall appear.
>
> Its name shall be the Kodak because its editor is a Kodak amateur and the Kodak is his favorite.
>
> The "Kodak" shall appear at the end of each month.

> The language to be used in the "Kodak" is simple, clear and to the point.
>
> Articles in the Kodak deal only with photography or with subjects the photos in the number may arise.
>
> A dozen photos, at least, shall appear in each number.
>
> Photos are going to be of four kinds: -
>
> I Landscape
>
> II Cities, villages, buildings
>
> III Athletic sports and games
>
> IV Groups & portraits

Beneath this explanation of how he envisioned *The Kodak*'s content, Makarius wrote the following in red pen:

> I most respectfully, present this Review to Dr. H. Porter Ph.D. who will lay it in exhibition to the students, in the Library of the Syrian Protestant College. And shall remain there as a souvenir to the College after the Editor's departure.

Here, Makarius provided a rare explicit reference to what must have been a somewhat standard practice in the college—he expected one of the faculty members to put the journal on display for students in the library to peruse. He also imagined that the journal would be kept and preserved, as it ultimately was.

At the end of the same January 1904 issue, Makarius (1903–1904) provided instruction for his readers about how they should approach the journal. First, he invited readers to "kindly excuse him for the mistakes and errors he has done." Further, in contrast to Salim Zein's (1902) invitation in *I.O.U.* for readers to correct mistakes on a "free page," Makarius (1903–1904) asked "that if any corrections are to be made or criticisms to be said they should all be directly sent to the Editor." He concluded this final page with an imploration in red pen: "Readers are very kindly requested to handle the 'delicate' 'Koda'" as Carefully and as gently as possible because it has cost . . . [periods in original; no monetary amount given] and work."

Finally, at the end of the last preserved issue of *The Kodak*, from March 1904, Makarius (1903–1904) commented on his readers' disinclination to read the content of the journal and instead focus on the photographs integrated throughout. He wrote, "Some people are discouraging me in not reading the articles. They ask to see the KODAK for the sake of the pictures only. If so, I shall feel that pictures in it should become less or even, should be left in my room." In other words, Makarius wanted his words to hold as much weight as his pictures—even as much as he loved photography.

From these excerpts we can see that Makarius (1903–1904) had a clear sense for what he imagined *The Kodak* to be and what his readers would gain from it. He hoped to connect with readers who were interested in photography, like him, and he apparently saw value in intertwining English, Arabic, and visual communication. His instruction to the college to keep and preserve his work beyond his time there demonstrates his conviction that the project was inherently valuable. Makarius saw himself through the journal as a pedagogue—someone and something that should be respected and valued—though he did not invite response and did not apparently receive any, beyond praise for his photographs.

Happy Days of SPC

Happy Days of SPC was published between 1903 and 1905. Eleven issues are preserved in the archives, and the contents are written in English, although some contributions were ostensibly—according to authors' notes—translated from other languages, including Italian, Armenian, French, and Arabic. Unlike the other two publications featured in this section, which were written by individual students only, *Happy Days* was edited by a "board" of student writers and editors; the board's membership changed between 1904 and 1905. The contents of the magazine are varied and include allegories, historical and informational essays, reports on student organizations, poems, and a selection of riddles and proverbs.

Many hand-drawn visuals appear in each issue, though the drawings are more frequent and colorful in the magazine's second year; the same artist, Armenag Terzian, is listed for each issue. Unlike the visuals contained in *The Kodak*, where photographs served to illustrate the Arabic and English essays, the drawings included throughout *Happy Days*—though intricate and engaging—are not generally related to the written content in terms of subject matter.

At the beginning of the first issue, in December 1903, the editors described their plans for the magazine, writing that it would "be published on the 1st and 15th day of each month. Occasionally small illustrations will appear, drawn by our Artist." Later, in the issue dated January 1905—the first issue published since May 1904—the editors, who were mostly new, updated their plans to say that *Happy Days* would be published "on the first day of each month" and each issue would "have at least two illustrations."

Figure 5.3. Happy Days of SPC (1905, Jan.). Permission
to publish granted by AUB Libraries.

Further, the editors invited contributions from readers and described the process of submission and review. In the first issue of December 1903, they wrote that:

> All students are eligible to contribute stories, puzzles, riddles, or any interesting information. All contributions to be addressed to the Editor or one of the Assistant Editors, who will revise them, and if necessary, they will be corrected by Mr. Nikula Tabit [Chief Editor]. They will then be copied by the Copyist into the Review.

In the January 1905 issue, it becomes clear that some students—"the special members of 'Happy Days'"—were "obliged to hand in at least an article of two small pages every month." In this later issue, no review process was specified. The editors explained in this issue how they envisioned the new version of the magazine to improve upon the first year, writing,

> Last year by writing simple articles our object was to make "Happy Days" a pleasant interesting paper, but this year as we have more members and as they are too eager to go on with articles about ethical, historical, religious, and, literary subjects we will try to make it better and give it a higher standing.
>
> Friends, we want to do something this year; and that thing is to go forward in mind and in spirit. Let us not say that we are weak, and that we are ashamed to write because of the fun which the others make of us. No! Let us not say that. Every one of us has some talent in a particular line, and he can do something useful, in his little sphere. I hope every one of our members according to his promise will begin this work with devotion and enthusiasm.

The encouragement to readers and potential contributors found in the January 1905 issue of *Happy Days* is reminiscent of the encouragement found in Zein's (1902) *I.O.U. 5 Minutes*. However, the difference is that Zein's publication was authored only by him, whereas *Happy Days* required collaboration to be successful, making this encouragement all the more significant for intended readers.

What's more, just as Iskander Makarius (1903–1904) warned students against making corrections directly in the pages of *The Kodak*, so too were "Readers" of *Happy Days* "requested, if they should notice any mistake, to report the same to the publishers, and not to make the corrections themselves" (December 1903). In a much later issue, dated March 1, 1905, the *Happy Days* secretary addressed contributors, noting, "We can not publish any article, which is not corrected by Greiner, and which is not written in clear penmanship." Here, we have some evidence that the magazine may have been published by and for an English class, as—at least in later issues—students were "obliged" to contribute, and Otto Greiner, an English instructor, was referenced as a person outside of the editorial board who reviewed all content. It is difficult to say whether or not the magazine was initially formed as a class project, but it seems that, at least in its later instantiations, it may have been a part of a class. While features such as requests for polite corrections may suggest that *The Kodak*, *I.O.U. 5 Minutes*, and *Happy Days* were all written in similar contexts, *The Kodak* stands out as the publication among the three that seems markedly independent of the classroom, in that it does not make reference to the English-language classroom or a teacher creating the impetus for its publication.

The details about *Happy Days'* regular publication schedule, submission process, and instructions about corrections are not presented in every issue. The most regular feature is the magazine's "Editorial," one of which was published in nearly every issue. These editorials were directed toward readers and were pedagogical in nature, providing advice or encouragement on a central (usually abstract) idea or issue, such as happiness, with the description, "the feeling that comes in the successful use of our energies for the best ends" (December 15, 1903); the passage of time and seasons of life, with the advice, "Regret not the past with its faded hopes, its dismal failures. . . . Build for the future on the failures and success of the past" (March 1, 1904); and conscience, with the observation, "Any free voice of conscience will push the man forward and onward. Generals, Statesmen, bishops and priests have left their names in History, simply because they have done things, which they have thought was right" (March 1, 1905).

In *Happy Days of S.P.C.*, we see a publication produced by many hands. While the magazine may have been mandated by a teacher or teachers, its production appears to have been led by motivated students who were intent on developing their English-language education. They also hoped to engage their peers and solicited submissions from classmates. In spite of the collaboration of peers, the magazine's contents, including visuals, do not cohere according to a single theme or overall message. The contents, on the whole, appear to serve dual purposes—they provide instruction or advice and also provide entertainment for readers. *Happy Days* also provides a sense of what students were expected to *do* with the publication—although they were not invited to provide corrections or respond to the magazine's contents directly, it is clear the editors hoped that students would be inspired to contribute their own writing to the publication.

Taken together, these three publications—*I.O.U. 5 Minutes*, *The Kodak*, and *Happy Days*—can help us understand, more broadly, the beliefs that SPC students held about what writing might do and how they might use writing, in multiple languages, to construct and convey their identities. In each of these examples, students positioned themselves as learners as well as facilitators of learning, and their publications operated as sponsors of literacy for their peers. The authors and editors of these publications were aware of the role they might play in the development of their peers, and they also seem to have been cognizant of the other possible audiences their work could attract.

Student Writing, Language, and Identity

The student magazines and newspapers at SPC appear to have served multiple purposes, including the promotion of Arabic, practice in English, celebration of the promise of science and literature, and cultural or social critique. What's more, student writers imagined engaged and responsive audiences that included their peers and instructors, and possibly a world outside the college. This broader understanding of the range of student publications circulating between 1899 and 1920 at SPC helps frame this section's introduction to representative examples that show how student writing was connected to language ideology and identity. On the whole, these publications exemplify a geopolitics of writing, in which translingual writing practices are tied to the political and cultural realities of the region, including the fall of the Ottoman Empire, the emergence of Arab nationalism, and the West's growing influence. The analysis presented here helps illustrate what is gained when we push beyond some of the discipline's "structuring tenets" (Cushman, 2016, p. 239) that presume the history of rhetoric and writing studies is a monolingual and Americentric one. Here, I explore the pluriversal possibilities that emerge through a transnational and translingual examination of this history.

In the introduction to النهضة الإصلاحية (*al-Nahda al-Islahiya*), or *The Reformist Movement* (published 1909–1910), the unnamed writer(s) articulated a desire to use the journal—whose title refers to the larger *al-Nahda* movement—as a way to encourage the use of the Arabic language even as they saw it declining at SPC:

قد جئنا بهم جديدة نطلب الاصلاح و نعمل ما في وسعنا لترقية اللغة
العربية التي صار من شأنها و شأن تعليمها ما صار في الكلية. فالنهضة
صوت صارخ في الكلية انهضوا اللغة العربية و اجعلوا سبل تعليمها
مستقيمة. و انها تقبل مساعدة كل من اراد ان يتحفها بشائن[sic]

افكاره و دُرر نظمه و نثره فهي باب مفتوح لكل من اراد الولوج فيه
لتدوين خير ما عنَّ على الفكر من مقالات علمية او مباحث ادبية او
ملاحظات لغوية بل من كل العجالات الاصلاحية ميدانٌ يتجارون فيه و
يشحذون [القرائح] و يقدحون زناد الافكار

Now reform has come again, and we are working with determination to elevate the Arabic language that deteriorated in status and its teaching at the college. This reform is a piercing voice in the college that screams "elevate the Arabic language and make way for proper methods of teaching it; give power to it!" Arabic language accepts the help of anyone willing to use it to share his thoughts and write poetry and narration; it is an open door for whoever wishes to step in and nourish it with intellectual thoughts in the form of scientific articles, literary research or language observations. In fact, all reformist movements open up space to compete for ideas, steer the mind towards deeper awareness, and let go of marginal thoughts. (مقدمة [Introduction], 1910)

The editors of this publication presented the practice of the Arabic language as a step toward necessary social and cultural improvement.

At the same time, English-language publications were often seen as means through which students could practice English, the language most privileged at SPC. For example, another student publication, *The Business Man* (published 1911) emerged as an extension of the English language classroom; the editors described the magazine's origination as follows:

> Every member of the sophomore class has been contributing articles to an imaginary magazine in the English Class. Why not start a real magazine ourselves? This idea struck some of the students of the Sophomore Class and in a class meeting this matter was presented and carried by a majority vote. A committee of five was appointed to look after the magazine and in its first meeting the committee decided to run the magazine by the name of "The Business Man." ("Introduction," 1911)

The editors of the magazine were members of the School of Commerce and wrote about regional and global politics, government, and business issues. That students wrote about these topics in English suggests that they saw English as integral to their professional futures and acknowledged the growing influence of the West in local and regional contexts.

Some writers articulated a desire to share their understanding of literature, history, philosophy, and science and to share their observations, opinions, expertise, and news with peers. This desire manifested itself in both Arabic- and English-language publications, and centralizing the role of language in deploying the intended message is necessary to understand exactly how language politics played out in the SPC and larger Syrian context. Those writing in Arabic, however, may have been explicitly working against the dominance of English at SPC. Evidence from the Arabic-language publications—such as students' discussions of Western history and politics—suggests that students hoped to present all of their knowledge in the Arabic language so as to revitalize its use at the college.[5] For example, Isaac Attieh (1901), the author of الحظ (*al-Haz*), or *Luck*, wrote,

> أما انا ليس لي مقصد و غاية سوى نشر معارفكم في هذه المجلة التي أوقفت نفسها على خدمتكم و خدمة الأدب و العلم. و إني مستعد ان أنشر ما يعرفه فردكم ليقرأه جمعكم و بهذا أخدم الآداب و الإنسانية «طوبى لمن يخدمون العلم و الادب» راجياً ان تساعدوا العاجز الساعي الى خير الجميع بنفثات أقلامكم الدرية و لطيف عباراتكم الجوهرية فأكون واسطة لإيصال معرفة شخص الى عدة اشخاص و إني أستعين بمن تستمد منه المعونة إنه لقدير.

> I have no reason or purpose to expand your knowledge about this magazine you are reading, which is only made to serve your preferences as well as varied literary and scientific needs. I am ready to write what one individual of you knows for all of you to read; in this sense, I would be serving literature and humanity. Praise to those who spend their whole lives serving science and literature. I beg of you to help those in need by writing valuable truths and meanings with your pens and minds. I am but a messenger who wants to transmit knowledge to people, with the help of others who can write as well.

In addition to personally promoting literary and scientific knowledge, Attieh (1901) praised scholars and implored readers to share their knowledge as well. He and the other authors who created these Arabic-language publications did so in part because they opposed the dominance of the West as evidenced on SPC's campus, and writing in Arabic was one way to reclaim some of the space they perceived as lost. This practice is similar to the ways in which the

---

5   See, for example, one anonymous student's article in Arabic that discussed another student's speech on the topics of William Gladstone, Napoleon, and the Transvalian War in الحظ (*al-Haz*) or *Luck* (تنبيه الضمير [*Warning to the Conscience*], 1901).

student protestors discussed in Chapter 4 strategically used their linguistic resources to engage with a variety of audiences.

While the influence of these publications cannot ultimately be known, the vast majority of editors and authors recognized that their primary audience would be comprised of SPC students, even if at times they had aspirations that their words would go beyond the college. Some authors and editors, such as those who published the English-language journal *Al-Kulliyah*, or *The College* (published 1910–1914), idealistically imagined that their work could spread beyond SPC campus itself. They explained, "To keep those who are still interested in their Alma Mater informed in regard to the life and growth of the College, and to stimulate all phases of wholesome College life, is the aim of *Al-Kulliyah*" "(With this opening number . . .," 1910). More commonly, however, student writers spoke directly to their peers, demonstrating that this was the primary audience they imagined, as seen in this excerpt taken from the introductory article of المنتهون (*al-Muntahoun*), or *The Terminators*:

> ها مجلتنا ننشرها أمامكم فتصفحوها و انتقدوها املاؤها مما يفيض من غزارة فضكم و مكنون أربكم و يكفينا جزاءً أن تكونوا مسرورين بمشروعنا مرتاحين إلى عملنا.

This is our newspaper. We publish it in your presence. Scroll through its pages and criticize it. Fill it with an overflow of your abundant thoughts and hidden ambitions. It would be enough reward if you are content with our project and satisfied with our work. (مقدمة [*Introduction*], 1905)

Students also composed social and cultural critique, and this critique was launched primarily—though not exclusively—in Arabic. The focus of the critique varied (both the East and the West were subject to criticism), but it nearly always served the purpose of promoting national and cultural identity. Compare, for example, the ways in which two magazines, published 15 years apart, highlighted the role of education in order to critique how national and cultural identity was promoted or dismantled in and through schooling: In غادة الفكر (*Ghada al-Fakr*), or *Graceful Thought* (published 1899–1901), the editor blamed Syrians for the dearth of schools administered by locals:

> هذه بيروت أهم مدينة في سوريا و مع ذلك فمعظم مدارسها أجنبية و هي تكاد تخلو من مدرسة كلية وطنية تسد بحاجة أبناء الوطن. و هل ننتظر من الأجانب أن يربوا أولادنا و يغرسوا في قلوبهم حب الوطن.

> This is Beirut, the most important city in Syria! And yet, most schools in Beirut are foreign, and the city no longer has many national schools for its country's youth. Do we wait for foreigners to come raise our children and plant patriotism in their hearts? (Fouad, 1900b)

In الثمرة (*al-Thamra*), or *The Fruit* (published 1914–1916), author Bahaa Al-Din Al-Sabbah (1915) praised the high quality of education in the region during the Abbasid Caliphate of Baghdad (750–1517 CE), in order to underline the role of schools in spreading nationalism, writing:

فالمدارس التي كانت العامل الوحيد لنشر آداب العرب و مدنيتهم و حفظ الملك و المملكة فإذا أردنا النجاح فلا سبيل إلا بالمدارس حيث تنقلب عقول الناشئة الجديدة و تجعلهم أبناء أولئك الأبطال الذين خلد و سيخلد اسمهم التاريخ اسماً خالداً لا يفنى ما دام في الأمة رجال أعمال فإلى المدارس إلى المدارس [sic] أيها الناشئة وإلى العلم إلى العلم [sic] أيتها الأمة فبهذا تنجح.

> Indeed, the schools were the only factor to spread the morals of Arabs and their civilization and preserve the power of the king and his kingdom. There is no means to success except in schools that transform the minds of its youth and raises them to become the sons of the immortal heroes whose names will forever be ingrained in history and never fade away. The nation will succeed as long as there are educated men. Oh rising youth, to the schools, to the schools you must go. Oh nation, seek knowledge, seek all the knowledge, for that is how you succeed.

Both excerpts seem to implicate contemporary society and culture for failing to promote Arab identity generally and Syrian identity specifically. Although similar critiques were also offered in English-language student publications, most of this kind of critique was levied through the Arabic language. By writing about these topics primarily in Arabic, student authors seem to have been intent on excluding readers unfamiliar with Arabic, which would have included many SPC administrators and faculty. Importantly, local instructors and staff at SPC, who were excluded from faculty status or rights before 1920, would have had access to the arguments made by students in these publications and would perhaps have been more sympathetic to the students' critiques. These examples demonstrate that students were deeply engaged in local and regional politics and that they were highly aware of the colonial epistemology brought to the region through the West and represented in and through Western education. Students understood how to deploy their linguistic resources to position themselves in relation to the coloniality that threatened a growing sense of Arab identity.

A Geopolitics of Student Writing—A Case Study

We can see more vividly translingual exchange at work in, through, and—in this case—*on* student writing by focusing on a single page of one student-authored publication, which attracted the attention of several SPC students. The May 1904 issue of the *SPC Commercial Paper* covered a variety of topics loosely related to world events and other news relevant to students in the School of Commerce, including "Exports of Egypt during the Month of March for the Year 1904," the "Treatment of Jewish Travellers in Russia," and "How Can Agriculture Make Syria Famous." This issue, with a front cover designed by hand but with the rest of the contents typed, is the only one preserved in the archives; however, the authors, who wrote in English, made reference to previous issues, suggesting that this was one of a series.

The *SPC Commercial Paper* does not stand out as a particularly provocative publication—the largely informative essays were written by several different students and like many of the student publications preserved in the archives, it is unclear how the publication circulated among SPC students, staff, and faculty. At the same time, the publication's typed contents—unusual when compared to other student magazines and newspapers published at around the same time, which were handwritten—suggest that the authors wanted the publication to be understood as "final," not open to revision. The *SPC Commercial Paper* did not issue any explicit invitation for a response from its readers. In other newspapers and magazines published at around the same time, only a few responses by students are found—usually very brief comments or minor grammar corrections, handwritten in pencil.

However, readers *did* respond to the *SPC Commercial Paper*, and they scrawled their responses across a page toward the end of the May 1904 issue containing two poems authored by student Michael Risgalla. The poem that elicited response is titled "My Dearest Japan" and addresses the Russo-Japanese War, which had begun just a few months earlier, in February 1904. Comprised of six stanzas, each four lines with rhyming couplets, the poem expresses support for Japan, characterizing the nation and its people as brave in the face of "a jealous nation [that] wants [Japan's] decay." Most assumed that Russia would win the war because it was a major European power, and the Japanese would have been seen as victims in the conflict. However, the Japanese eventually prevailed, maintaining their independence at a time of widespread colonization; at the time, it was the first Asian victory against a European power.

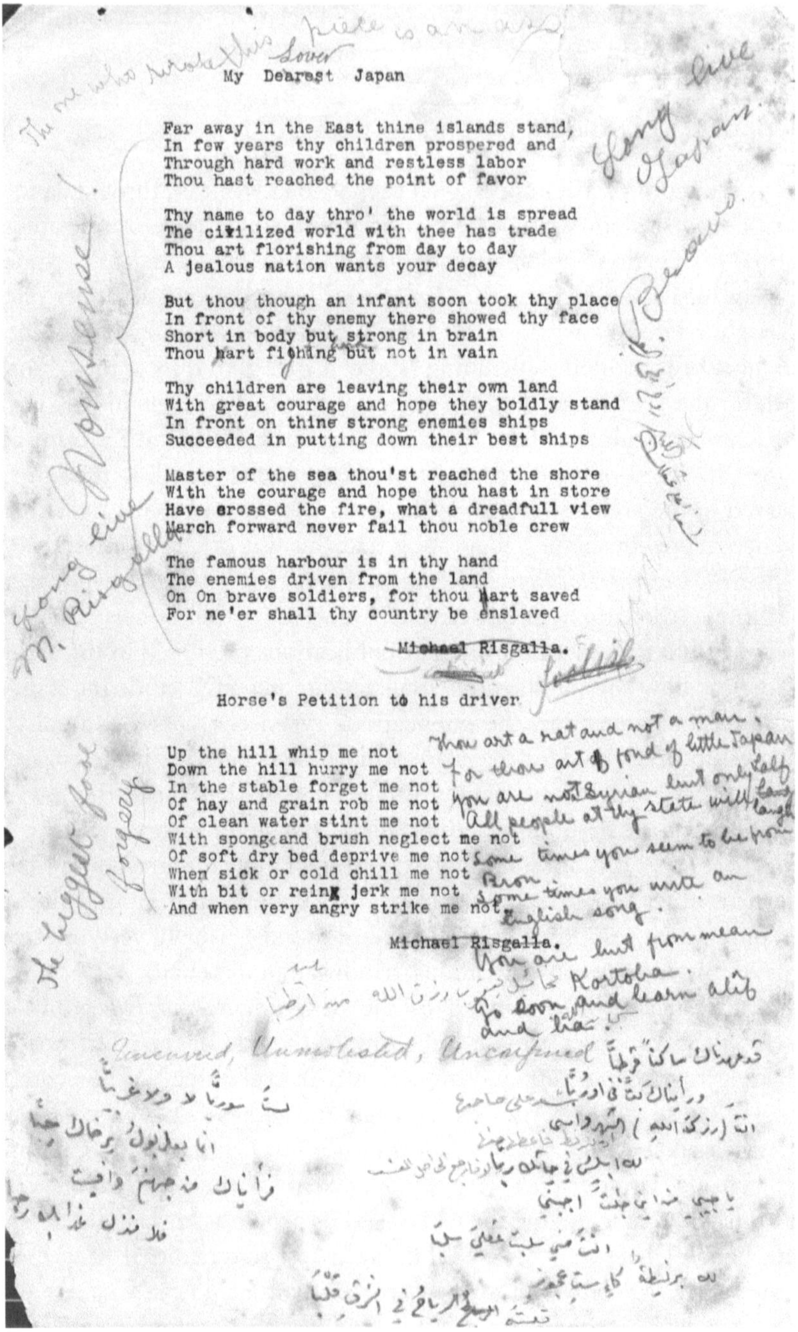

My Dearest Japan

Far away in the East thine islands stand,
In few years thy children prospered and
Through hard work and restless labor
Thou hast reached the point of favor

Thy name to day thro' the world is spread
The civilized world with thee has trade
Thou art florishing from day to day
A jealous nation wants your decay

But thou though an infant soon took thy place
In front of thy enemy there showed thy face
Short in body but strong in brain
Thou hart fighing but not in vain

Thy children are leaving their own land
With great courage and hope they boldly stand
In front on thine strong enemies ships
Succeeded in putting down their best ships

Master of the sea thou'st reached the shore
With the courage and hope thou hast in store
Have crossed the fire, what a dreadfull view
March forward never fail thou noble crew

The famous harbour is in thy hand
The enemies driven from the land
On On brave soldiers, for thou hart saved
For ne'er shall thy country be enslaved

                    Michael Risgalla.

Horse's Petition to his driver

Up the hill whip me not
Down the hill hurry me not
In the stable forget me not
Of hay and grain rob me not
Of clean water stint me not
With sponge and brush neglect me not
Of soft dry bed deprive me not
When sick or cold chill me not
With bit or reing jerk me not
And when very angry strike me not

                    Michael Risgalla.

Figure 5.4. SPC Commercial Paper (1904, May).
Permission to published granted by AUB Libraries.

The sentiment expressed in the poem—support for the underdog Japan in the face of Russia—would not have been unusual in the local or regional context; Russia's long-standing antagonism toward the Ottoman Empire would have bred deep-seated contempt for Russia and much sympathy for a country like Japan in Greater Syria (Sharabi, 1970).[6] In the same issue of the *SPC Commercial Paper*, in fact, a different student who went by the name of A. D. Karlvas (1904), wrote an essay titled "Current Events Throughout the World," in which he used two anecdotes about the war to present Japanese people as sympathetic characters.[7] So, it is surprising to see the hostility expressed by some students in response to the poem and to Risgalla himself.

Around and across this poem, an unidentifiable number of students (perhaps two or four students) composed marginalia—handwritten comments and poems, some in English and some in Arabic, in all margins and even laid over the poem itself. A few of the responses appear to be positive (though, given their seeming hyperbole, they could be interpreted as facetious), such as "Long live M. Risgalla" (below the poem), "Long live Japan" (to the right of the poem), and "Bravo" (also in the right margin). However, the majority of the responses are explicitly negative; for example, next to "Bravo," there is a negative response written in Arabic:

آسف على عقلك و الله، روح ارعى البقر

This phrase, written in colloquial Arabic, translates to, "For the love of God, I feel sorry for your futile brain, go away and feed the cows," and suggests that Risgalla's peers viewed him as someone from a poor background, an outsider. The word "Nonsense!" is written to the left of the poem, as well as below it. At the top of the page, someone scribbled, "The one who wrote this piece is an ass." Someone crossed out the word "Dearest" in the poem's title, writing the word "Lover" above, so the poem's title became "My Lover Japan."

Also, to the left of the second poem, which is more mundane, someone wrote "Forgery," and another wrote "The bigger fool" next to it, perhaps in an attempt to refute the person who wrote the word "Forgery." The author's name at the end of both poems is crossed out. The word "foolish" is

---

6   Sharabi (1970) provided evidence that Arabs generally supported Japan in 1905 when they defeated Russia: "When Japan defeated Russia in 1905 its triumph was joyously hailed throughout the Arab world. It was the first defeat of a western power at the hands of an eastern nation. It was not merely a Japanese victory, but in a psychological sense an Arab, Muslim victory as well" (p. 129).

7   The name A. D. Karlvas is not an Arab name and suggests that the writer was using a pseudonym, was born outside of Syria, or had family connections outside of the region. At the time, there were some SPC students who attended the school from outside of the region, though not many.

penciled underneath the author's name for the first poem—but this word is also crossed out, presumably by someone else. Underneath Michael Risgalla's crossed-out name below the first poem is yet another a crossed-out word, this one in Arabic, that is not fully legible but may be كلب, or dog. And below the author's name under the second poem is a phrase in Arabic that reads:

مخائل يعقوب رزق الله من أرطبا[8]

سبحان الله

This phrase translates, in colloquial Lebanese Arabic, to "Michael Yaakoub Risgalla from Qartaba, *Subhan Allah* [a common Arabic expression that is similar to saying 'Praise God']." Although a literal reading of the phrase may suggest that it is positive or neutral, it in fact was probably meant to mock Risgalla, calling attention to his village of Qartaba (قرطبا), which is in the Lebanon mountains in Syria but has deep ties to France through the silk trade and also because of the Maronite Catholic identity of the villagers, which France protected during the 19th century.[9] Because of these ties to France, most villagers would have spoken French and valued French traditions, making a student like Risgalla seem like an outsider within Syria, even at a school like SPC.

Below both poems, toward the bottom of the page, someone wrote lightly, "Unenvied, Unmolested, Unconfined"—a line from Oliver Goldsmith's epic poem, "The Deserted Village," published in 1770 (2025). For context, this line in Goldsmith's poem comes in the middle of the poem, in which the author

---

8   In Syrian or Lebanese Arabic, the ق is often dropped from words and not pronounced. Although the word as written on the page reads ارطبا (pronounced *Artaba*), it is reasonable to deduce that the writer was transliterating the name of the village of قرطبا (pronounced *Qartaba*), as it can be pronounced in the Syrian or Lebanese dialect without the ق. In the Arabic-language poem transcribed later in this section, a different writer refers to Risgalla as hailing from قرطبا, further substantiating the assumption that the writer here simply dropped the ق to transliterate the pronunciation of the village's name in Syrian or Lebanese Arabic. An alternative reading could consider the place referenced to be Córdoba, Spain, but the context in this line and the later Arabic-language poem simply does not support such an interpretation.

9   Qartaba (قرطبا), Syria (present-day Lebanon) is tied to France in part for two reasons: First, until the mid-20th century, the village was home to seven silk factories that exported primarily to Lyon, France. Second, the vast majority of the village's residents were Maronite Catholic (and they still are—the most recent census recorded the village's population as 99% Maronite) (Qartaba, 2025). France had intervened to protect the Maronites during the 1860 war between the Druze and Maronites in Mount Lebanon, and when the French brought in its army (alongside other European powers) to reestablish order in the region, they gave power over the Mount Lebanon district to the Maronites. See Makdisi (2000) and Masters (2013), as well as my discussion of these relationships in Chapter 2 for a larger historical context.

reflects on the "spontaneous joys" (1770/2025, Line 254) of innocent rural village life and contrasts this with the impending and unwelcome changes brought on by the growing agricultural industry. For Goldsmith, these "spontaneous joys" are "unenvied, unmolested, unconfined" (Line 257). Perhaps this line was scribbled underneath Risgalla's work to suggest a certain naivety in his poetry as well as his upbringing in a relatively isolated mountain village, and perhaps it was written to mock the "joy" he derived in publishing these poems, which are not, ultimately, all that good.

An overview of these initial pencil wars tells us that students, for whatever reasons, were *deeply* engaged with Michael Risgalla's writing—as well as with each other as readers. While it is difficult to know how this publication was circulated among students, it was probably the only copy and may have been left for readers to peruse in a public space like an open area of the library. One can imagine the students returning to this page of the *SPC Commercial Paper* to read the accumulating marginalia, perhaps adding their own or at least telling their friends to read it themselves.

But even this description does not do justice to the full extent of the marginalia found on Michael Risgalla's page of poetry. Two additional critical poetic responses to Risgalla's poems are written on the right-hand margin of the page. These two poems, one in English and the other in Arabic, were written with a darker, more forceful stroke, which parallels the deep critique contained in each. The poem in English reads:

> Thou art a rat and not a man
>
> For thou art fond of little Japan
>
> You are not Syrian but only half
>
> All people at thy state will laugh
>
> Sometimes you seem to be from Bron
>
> Sometimes you write an English song
>
> You are but from mean Kortoba
>
> Go soon and learn alif and ba

Here, the writer suggested that Risgalla could not fully claim a Syrian identity. According to this poem, Risgalla was "only half" Syrian—he was "from Bron" (a suburb of Lyon, France, to which the seven silk factories in Risgalla's home village exported their silk) and later "from mean Kortoba" (Kortoba is another way to transliterate Qartaba [قرطبا]). In other words, the writer here clearly demarcated Risgalla not only as an outsider to Syria but also as someone who had a provincial, "mean" (poor) background. What's more, according to this writer, Risgalla wrote "an English song" and ostensibly did not even know ألف و باء, *alif* and *ba*, the first two letters of the Arabic alphabet. Although this poem suggests that Risgalla spoke English and French, these skills were seemingly not valued by the writer of this critique. The devaluing of these languages in the poem seem also to have been a resistance to or rejection of the West and its influence in the region. Risgalla's "fond[ness]" for "little Japan"—coupled with his loose claims to Syrian identity and lack of proficiency in Arabic—marked him, for this writer at least, as an outsider to the college and the surrounding cultural and linguistic context.

The other poem, written originally in Arabic (with an English translation to the left), seems to directly address the author and reads:

We always knew that you lived in Qartaba	قد عهدناك ساكناً قرطبًا
And we saw your arrival in Europe	و رأيناك بثَّ في أورُبًّا [sic]
You, Risgalla, who announced and denied	أنتَ (رزكَ اللهِ) أشهرَ و أبى
Chose the devil to be your God in this life	لك ابليس في حياتك ربّا
My dear, when did you come back, answer me	يا حبيبي منذ متى جئت أجبني
You robbed my mind and drove me insane	أنتَ مني سلبت عقلي سلباَ
You have a fedora [hat] like an old lady does	ستِ عجوز[sic]لك برنيطة- كاءِ
The winds of the East perished you completely	تبّته الرياحُ في الشرق قلبًا
You are not a Syrian nay, nor a Westerner	لست سوريًّاً لا و لا غربيًّاً
They torture you with your consent	إنما بعض يرضاك حِبًّا [sic]
So, we saw you arrive from hell	فرأيناك من جهنَم وافيت
And tomorrow you shall find no home to welcome you [in the East]	فلا منزل غدا بك رحبا

This poem appears to have been written by the same hand as the other critical poem, in that the size and style of the handwriting and force of the stroke appear similar on the page. Just as the critical poem originally written in English criticizes Risgalla for not being fully Syrian, this poem, too, suggests that Risgalla was somehow in between, not truly Syrian *or* Western. Additionally, the line "You have a fedora [hat] like an old lady does," seems to suggest that Risgalla was a phony bad writer who pretended to be European and did not write well in English; this interpretation is further supported by the same writer's critical poem in English. The writer of this poem may have seen Risgalla as promoting the West's views while on Syrian soil, as he implied that these views may corrupt, or "rob," the Eastern mind. The writer of this poem was apparently so offended that he concluded the poem by explicitly saying that Risgalla was not welcome in Syria.

The most important component of this second critical poem, perhaps, is the fact that it is written in Arabic. At the time of the *SPC Commercial Paper*'s publication, the study of Arabic was required of all Arabic-speaking students at SPC, and studying at least two languages other than English were required for all students; these additional languages were selected from Arabic, Turkish, or French (Syrian Protestant College, *Minutes of Faculty*, 1904–1905; Syrian Protestant College, *Catalogue*, 1905–06). Given this context, it is possible that Risgalla truly lacked proficiency in Arabic and was unable to read the poem in Arabic (tongue in cheek, the writer even instructed Risgalla—in Arabic—to find an Arabic teacher). If Risgalla were proficient in Arabic, then he would certainly feel attacked on a personal level. However, if Risgalla could not actually read Arabic—which the writer suggested was the case— then the writer must have been imagining a different audience, most likely Arabic-speaking peers. In this case, the writer's criticism of Risgalla may have stood for more than Risgalla himself. Instead, we can imagine that Risgalla stood for what some may have perceived as outside threats to Syrian culture and identity, particularly as they manifested themselves in specific languages and ways of knowing.

This example of subversive marginalia in the *SPC Commercial Paper* highlights the ways in which students negotiated the politics of language and what it meant to "belong" to the educational, linguistic, and cultural context at SPC. The example of poems written in multiple languages in the margins of the publication also suggests that not all SPC students fully embraced the America presented to them through the English-language literacy education offered at the college. Indeed, Arabic remained a signifier for who truly belonged in Syria, suggesting that as much as SPC's American faculty and administrators may have presented English as a signifier of cultural citizenship and belonging to a distant, imagined America, students may have been skeptical of its value in their specific geopolitical location. Student writing, in other words, reveals tensions between the value, or "weight," of both English and Arabic. These tensions arose out of the inherently transnational context of SPC, in which foreign exchange—of ideas, epistemologies, and language—was the norm and required constant negotiation. The example of *SPC Commercial Paper*'s marginalia makes these tensions visible. The remainder of this chapter explores these tensions as they emerge in and through SPC's many student newspapers and magazines.

Language, Identity, and Imagining America

The following sections present a closer analysis of the ways in which students negotiated their identities and leveraged agency in and through their writing. In particular, the remainder of this chapter demonstrates that the tensions that emerged in response to Michael Risgalla's (1904) poem in the *SPC Commercial Paper* were not uncommon—the student publications, it seems, worked as rhetorical spaces in which students could explore and express their identities as Arabs attending an American institution of higher education in a specific sociopolitical moment, at the end of the Ottoman Empire and the height of the *al-Nahda* movement.

Throughout the student publications, whether in Arabic, English, or other languages, students took up contemporary and historical issues, exploring them in both creative and mundane ways. As I explain in the following sections, SPC students drew on rhetorics of nationalism, resistance, and Occidentalism, revealing conflicting beliefs about language, identity, "the West," and America. I define these rhetorics as follows: A *rhetoric of nationalism* expressed praise for Arab identity, the Arabic language, Arab history, loyalty to Syria, or a related theme. A *rhetoric of resistance* presented a more skeptical or critical version of nationalism. While a rhetoric of resistance may appear to have critiqued nationalist views, it in fact used critique rhetorically to promote nationalism and Arab identity. Finally, a *rhetoric of Occidentalism* praised the "West" in order to highlight the current shortfalls of the "East" and/or Arab identity, while at the same time nodding toward the potential for a better future, one that could match or be superior to the "West."

Students' use of these rhetorics teaches us how they perceived their agency in relation to faculty and administrators, as well as how they made sense of—and sometimes resisted—their positioning at SPC, Syria, and the Ottoman Empire in and through writing. In turn, students' choice of language—Arabic versus English—in these publications corresponded in part, with the positions they took in their writing. The analysis presented in the following sections highlights the geopolitics of language and knowledge-making as central to the history of rhetoric and writing studies.

Language(s) and Nationalism

The earliest student-authored publications were composed in Arabic. Because most of the faculty and administrators at the time were not literate in Arabic, these early publications would have been read only by fellow students and local instructors, who did not have the same privileges or rank as foreign faculty at the college. Perhaps because they knew that those in power at the college would not have access to what they had to say, students promoted the study of Arabic in these early publications. What's more, students often promoted the study of and writing in Arabic in opposition to writing in English, which was presented as an activity that would detach students from their home culture and identity. These discussions of the value of language(s) relied on a rhetoric of nationalism, in which Arabic—both as a language and as the vehicle for student voices—operated as a signifier for Syria or the East more generally.

In 1899, for example, in المبدأ الصحيح (*al-Mabda al-Saheeh*), or *The Right Principle* (published 1899–1900), a student named Najib Boulous argued for the importance of the Arabic language in schools, writing that the study of foreign languages served as propaganda to make students dislike their home country and culture:

> كيف ترجون النجاح من ولدٍ تدخلونه المدرسة لتبعدونه [sic]عن لغته الوطنية و تعبّدوه للغةٍ أجنبية و غاية ما تزرعون فيه من الأفكار. إن ذلك يفيده إذا تغرب إلى بعض الأقطار و يؤهله أن يكون ترجماناً للسياح في هذا الديار فلا يسمع حي العائلة و لا الوطن و لا سيستعد امهنة من المهن فيخرج طائش الآمال غير ميّال إلى شيء من الأعمال و آنيه إذا تكلم أن [يتأسف] و يتأفّف على بلاده التي لا يُصرف فيها قدر ما تعلّم و ما يقع وراء ذلك في طباع الشبان و لا يحتاج إلى بيان.

How do you expect your child to be successful if you enroll him in school only to keep him away from his native language and make him worship a foreign one and plant its ideology in his head? He might use the foreign language if he emigrates to some countries, and it will qualify him to be a translator for tourists visiting his home country. However, this language will not serve his family or country, nor prepare him for a future career. Instead, he will graduate with reckless hopes and disinterest in pursuing a profession. Still, you hear him regret and complain about his country. He believes he cannot make the same amount of money he spent on his education, among other juvenile thoughts. To him, there is no need for evidence to prove that he is right.

In making an argument for the importance of the Arabic language to cultural identity, Boulous (1899) also argued for the formation of public schools, which would يوسوسونها على حب الدولة و الوطن [replicate patriotism in the heart of its students]. In other words, Boulous located the nexus between cultural and national identity at the (public) school where Arabic was taught. By composing his argument in Arabic, Boulous imagined an educated local audience who held—or would hold—the power to make change along these lines.

In a different publication, a student named Fouad (no last name given; 1900a) introduced an article about the problematic "titles" (or honorifics) used in local newspapers by first reflecting on the value of reading Arabic-language newspapers:

لي رغبة شديدة في مطالعة الجرائد لأظنها إلاّ و توجد في كل طالب علم و فائده و إقبالي على قراءة العربية منها أشد منه على الأجنبية و ذلك لأمور شتى منها الوقوف على آراء أهل الوطن و مشربهم و ذوقهم و كيفية تقدمهم أو تأخرهم. كل ذلك يعرف على ما أعرف من الجرائد لأنها لسان حال الأمة و الباعث الأكبر على ترقيتها في مراقي الإقبال و الكمال و من أقدس واجباتها سلوك مسلكٍ تنتفع به قراؤها و يقتبسون منه عوائد و أساليب تبثُّ فيهم روح النشاط و التمدن و حب التقدم.

As any student who seeks knowledge and its benefits, I possess a deep desire to read newspapers. Personally, I am inclined to read newspapers written in the Arabic language more than I would for those written in other languages. There are many reasons for my preference, including the need to learn about people's opinions, tastes, and ways of advancement and regress in my country. I would gain more knowledge because the country's newspapers in Arabic speak the truth about the nation's situation and paves the road to reach better and more notable positions. Also, these newspapers' most sacred duty is to choose the path that most benefits its readers and inspires them to acquire habits and practices that transmit productivity, styles of civilized living, and love for progress.

For Fouad, reading local Arabic-language newspapers kept him tied to his nation and culture; he implied that reading English-language newspapers may have had the opposite effect of distancing him from the same. He characterized Arabic-language newspapers as offering a kind of education that foreign newspapers could not—to him, local newspapers offered solutions to local problems and suggested ways in which the nation as a whole could improve. What's more, Arabic-language newspapers, according to Fouad, presented "styles of civilized living" appropriate for the local context and culture. Although the focus of the whole article did not remain on these points, in this introductory paragraph he further articulated the ideologies that SPC students at the time associated with the Arabic language—the language was tied, as both Fouad and Boulous demonstrated, to cultural and national identity. Fouad's assertion, articulated in Arabic, underlined his own cultural and national ties, which would be difficult to communicate so strongly in a language other than Arabic. Further, readers without ties to the language or culture would have been unlikely to be drawn to Fouad's argument, making Fouad's choice of writing in Arabic especially important.

Another student, Najib Nassar (1903), admonished contemporary students for neglecting their study of Arabic in حسناء الكلية (*Hasnaa' al-Kulliyeh*), or *Beauty of the College*. He urged his peers to pursue the study of Arabic because ما كان لها من العلو و رفعة الشأن و المنزلة or "it is surely of high status, importance, and prestige." To make his point, Nassar held up Western teaching practices as ideal, in that أن يدرس لغة والديه و يتقنها جيداً ثم يزاول درس اللغات الأخرى or "firstly, they learn the mother tongue, and then all the other languages follow." In contrast, according to Nassar, Arab students:

> إنهم يندّدون بوجوب اهمالها و تركها في زوايا النسيان فيترفعون عن درسها و الانصباب على مزاولتها صارفين معظم اوقاتهم في أحكام اللغات الاجنبية و الميل الى طرسها و اتقانها دارسين تحت أقدامهم معالم أوضاع لغتهم و حقِّرين رجالها العظام.

> are intentionally neglecting their language, calling for languages and learning their rules, all whilst stepping on the landmarks of their mother tongue and despising its great men.

In composing this argument, Nassar (1903) appealed to readers' ostensible desire for an elevation in status, which seemed to be associated (at least implicitly) with Western practices and values, including the use of English. Like Fouad (1900a) and Boulous (1899), Nassar's (1903) decision to write in Arabic seems particularly important to making an argument favoring the study of Arabic. His writing embodied the very practice he sought to promote in Syria. As such, we can identify a kind of linguistic economy within educational institutions such as SPC, in which certain arguments could be deployed to specific audiences through specific language choices. The choice of language, as in the example cases explored in this chapter, was combined with a rhetoric of nationalism through which these student authors insisted on, and demonstrated, the way in which their local language could be used to promote Arab identity and values.

Nationalism, Resistance, and Identity

As the previous section demonstrates, student publications allowed students to work with language, particularly the Arabic language, in order to articulate arguments about education that may have been unavailable to them otherwise. Students' discussions of education, the act of writing, and the interplay of language drew on rhetorics of nationalism to explore identity. Indeed, the SPC students' Arabic-language newspapers and magazines at the turn of the 20th century repeatedly took up questions of nationalism and identity in a way that the English-language publications generally did not. Further, many student writers in these publications used rhetorics of resistance to implicitly or explicitly critique their homeland, while at the same time expressing deep love for Syria and Arab culture more generally, as well as hope for the future of the country.[10] In this way, these student writers drew from and contributed to the *al-Nahda* movement, in which progress and enlightenment was positioned dichotomously against the past. What's more, the rhetorics expressed in these Arabic-language publications paralleled the debates surrounding the 1909 SPC student protest, detailed in Chapter 4.

Student writers often coupled praise for Syria with implicit or explicit critique, as can be seen in an article titled حب الوطن, or "Patriotism," in غادة الفكر (*Ghada al-Fikr*), or *Graceful Thought*, by Fouad (the same student mentioned in the previous section). Fouad (1900b) exclaimed, هذه بيروت أهم مدينة في سوريا [This is Beirut, the most important city in Syria!] Then, he argued that تخلو من مدرسة كلية وطنية تسد بحاجة أبناء الوطن [devoid of a national collegiate school that will fulfill the needs of its country's youth], Syrian citizens no longer had patriotism because the schools were run by foreigners (Fouad, 1900b). Fouad (1900b) suggested that Syrians had placed responsibility for their children's education in the hands of foreigners; he posed a rhetorical question:

هل ننتظر من الأجانب أن يربوا أولادنا و يغرسوا في قلوبهم حب الوطن

> Do we wait for foreigners to raise our children and plant patriotism in their hearts?

Student writers like Fouad (1900b) repeatedly placed local education on a pedestal because of the link they saw between schools and national identity

---

10 Students use the word "country" or "nation" repeatedly to refer to Syria, even though it was a territory of the Ottoman Empire at the time. Syria and Beirut were both "vilayets" within the Ottoman Empire, which enjoyed a great deal of autonomy at the turn of the 20th century (see Chapter 2). We might best understand these students' use of "country" as an informal reference to Syria's history and comparatively relative independence in the present context.

or loyalty. Noting that هذه الشيمة العربية, or "the character of an Arab," still resided in the people, an unnamed speech writer in الحديقة (*al-Hadiqa*), or *The Garden* (published 1902–1903) argued that التعليم و التهذيب أنوار ربوعنا في, or "the fires of civility and education ignited in our homes." For this writer, فها قد افتتحت المدارس و نهجت المناهج القويمة في سبيل احيآء الوطن or "The utmost proof of Arabs' determination is opening schools and adopting strong curriculum to revive the country" (ارتقاء التهذيب في سورية [*Elevating Civility in Syria*], 1903). In other words, according to this writer, Arabs could reclaim their identity in and through the development of local schools.

Similar strains tying education to the growth or progress of Syria, and Arab culture more generally, continued in other publications, including in *Syria*, a bilingual publication published in 1906. In an English-language article titled "Patriotism vs. Syria," the editor of the publication, Amin Butrus Hilal (1906), wrote, in English,

> Let every educated Syrian—the educated, I say, on whom hangs the future development—let him stay in Syria and be a factor in its enlightenment. Let him apply the knowledge and principles that he has gained to the end of bettering the conditions of the community into which he is thrown. Let him work in his own limited sphere and in his own way, putting before his eyes the high ideal of service in the widest sense of the term.

Here, Hilal argued that educated Syrians who stayed in their native country had the ability to forward the country's development—the implication being that staying was a gesture of patriotism. This argument was premised on the assumption that the state of Syria required improvement and suggested that many Syrians left the country after they had received an education, and perhaps they left *because* they had been educated.

Along similar lines, student Elias Attieh (1906), writing in the Arabic-language publication المنتهون (*al-Muntahoun*), or *The Terminators*, used a rhetoric of resistance to denounce writers who urged others to stay in Syria or speak Arabic but who themselves were ready to leave or to adopt the languages of the West:

> يا أيها الكاتب التحرير الذي تدعونا الى البقاء في سوريا لماذا [نرا]
> [sic] عندما تصير قادراً على تحصيل المعش [sic] تركب متن البحار
> تاركاً لنا صدى كتاباتك يرنُّ في الآذان و أنت أيها الشاعرُ المطبوع يا
> من إذا نثرت علينا درر أقوالك تهجينا في تلك الساعة الى حب الوطن
> لماذا عندما تخرج لما نرى عليك غباراً ما كنت تدعونا إليه و أنت يا

أديبنا العزيز الذي تدعونا الى درس اللغة العربية و التكلم بها لماذا لا
نسمع منك إلا بونجور بونسوار يا مونشار good morning و غيرها من
المقتبسات الأجنبية كأن لغتك ضيقة بمثل هذه المصطلحات

To the newspaper editor, who encourages us to stay in Syria, you will be the first to sail away when you have the money for it, leaving us the echo of your writings to resonate in the ear. To the famous poet, who enchanted us with abundant words about patriotism in that hour, why is it that when you go out, we never see the dust of what you say on you? And you, our dear writer, who invites us to study the Arabic language and speak it, why do we only hear "bonjour", "bonsoir," and "good morning" among other foreign borrowings; it is as though your language is constricted to these terms.

In other words, he distrusted writers who romanticized Arabic but in fact were eager to leave it behind for the West. Elias Attieh's (1906) refusal to be swayed by these writers appears, on the surface, to have critiqued nationalism, but in fact the critique worked rhetorically to spur readers to act on their beliefs:

تصرفون الوقت في الافتكار و الكتابة فقط فيما يؤول الى خير البلاد و
تنشرونه على رؤوس الإشهاد ظناً منكم أنه يكفي لإصلاحها و لكن لماذا
لا نرى نتيجة لتلك الجمل البليغة و الأشعار النفسية.

You spend your time thinking and writing about the richness of this country and publish your declarations, believing your words are enough to bring reform, but we do not see the influence of all these eloquent words and sentimental poetry you give us.

Habib Khalil Sayegh (1902), an SPC student writing for صدى الاستعدادية (*Sada al-Isti'dadiyah*), or *Elementary Echo,* used a more forceful rhetoric of resistance to persuade his audience to improve Syria. In an article titled وفاة الشرق or *Death of the East*, Sayegh asked readers hyperbolically,

ما لي أرى لوائح الأسف تلوح على مجالكم؟ و لماذا لا أراكم تلوون
سوى على البكاء و الخيب [sic]؟ كيف لا و قد فقد هذا الشرق العظيم؟
فهل لا يحق لنا أن نرثيه و ننوح على هذا الخطب الجسيم مدى الدهر و
الآوان؟ فُقد الشرق!!!.... نعني بالشرق بحد سوريا القديم بحد ناطح
السماء بعزه. قوة كانت ترتجف منها المكونة بأسرها. علم أنار العالم
اجمع. و لكنه قد رحل و غادرنا نندب بعده مدى العهود. فو أسفي عليك
أيها الشيخ الجليل.

> Why don't I see grief on your faces? Why are you not crying and mourning? How can you not feel that when the great East is lost forever? Is the East not worthy of lament at its unfortunate fate and death? The East is lost!!! . . . By East, I mean ancient Syria, this glorious heaven and powerful force that the cosmos used to fear. It is the same Syria that lit up the whole world [with knowledge]. However, it left us, and we have no one but ourselves to blame. Oh, wise leader, we grieve your loss.

Sayegh proceeded to lament the departure of Syrian writers and thinkers to Egypt, as well as what he perceived as an empty rhetoric of change in contemporary Syrian publications and speeches. Additionally, Sayegh noted the corrupting influence of the West, represented by a French woman who opened a liquor store near the SPC campus that employed and catered to "the East's youth." In spite of his lengthy critique, Sayegh reassured readers in the conclusion of the article that, الشرق و لا أغار على الوطنية فهو في ضلال مبين و لرب قائل يقول انني رجل من أعداء, or while "some readers may think [he is] an enemy of the East," he was "just frustrated at the darkness that our East"—by which he meant Syria—"is trapped in." He urged his readers toآم. فلنترك الشرق , بعيداً عنا و لنطلي ارض الحرية و العدل و المساواة و or "leave the East"—by which he meant the version of the East he had criticized—and "step into the land of freedom, justice, equality, and peace," which is how he imagined a reformed Syria.

Sayegh (1902) and the other writers highlighted in this section used a rhetoric of resistance to explicitly denounce the perceived failures of their homeland while expressing a belief that Syria could be redeemed. Importantly, students chose Arabic most often as the language through which to deploy this rhetoric of resistance—and this aligns with the rhetoric of nationalism described in the previous section. For both rhetorics, Arabic operated as the language that could best support students' messages, as well as their ability to appeal to their readers, with whom they constructed a shared Arab identity through language.

Imagining the West, Imagining America

As the evidence from the previous sections attests, SPC student writers did not hesitate to critique their homeland—their rhetorics of nationalism and resistance served the purpose of engaging with and improving Syria and its future. At the same time, some student writers adopted a rhetoric of Occidentalism in leveling critique, in which the "West" was presented as an ideal against which the "East" and/or Arab culture or identity was contrasted negatively. This rhetoric shared a similar purpose to the rhetorics of nationalism or resistance previously discussed, in that the critique was intended to motivate Syrians to improve their social and economic situation. As we see in the rhetoric of resistance, the rhetoric of Occidentalism similarly suggested that Syria, and Arab culture more generally, could save itself. However, this salvation, it was implied, could only occur by turning to the "West"—not necessarily because Western practices were what would save the "East," but because they served as educative examples from which Syrians could learn. As I explain in Chapter 1, this rhetoric is similar to what Conceison (2004) called a "discourse of Occidentalism," and it can be understood as a response to the "domineering presence" of the West. As Stephen Sheehi (2004) pointed out, leading Arab intellectuals of the *al-Nahda* movement could not "have rejected European hegemony and formulated a sense of self that was separate from" this Western presence (p. 10). Similarly, SPC students were at once defined by, and defined themselves against, the West and an imagined America that was represented in the very college they had committed themselves to attending. This push-pull tension resulted in the rhetoric of Occidentalism that emerged in student writing at SPC. Analysis of this rhetoric shows how SPC students drew from their own agency to speak back to the West. In other words, Western colonial epistemology was not hegemonic, even as it demanded those who were in its shadow to engage with it.

Importantly, SPC as an institution represented the "West," but not the European West, which was where most students focused their attention in critiquing Syria. Some student writing adopted a rhetoric of Occidentalism that praised America; this strand, which was most often presented in English, reveals how students imagined America and what it meant to *be* American, in and through their education in English at an American-style college. The rhetoric of Occidentalism found in some of the student writing ultimately reveals tensions and contradictions within discourses of Arab nationalism. What's more, this rhetoric highlights students' own perceptions of themselves as an "Other" in the discourse of the West, and likely also in the discourse of the college.

Some students, writing in Arabic and English, held up the (European) West as a standard by which Syria, or Arab culture more generally, fell short. For example, in an article titled مفاخر الرجال or "The Pride of Men" (1900), an unnamed author criticized the "East" for being more interested in reputation and influence than in taking action to help others, pointing out, in Arabic that:

... نرى أهل الغرب يعملون أعمالاً كثيرة خيرية ... فمن تلك الأشياء المدارس و التأسيسات الخيرية حتى في بلاد الأجانب كبلادنا مثلاً و عدا عن ذلك تراهم متحدين قلباً و قالباً كل واحد منهم يريد خير الآخر

و بالعكس نحن الشرقيين فإننا لم نعمل بعد شيئاً يستحق الذكر بل انما افتخارنا في ما سلفنا من الجدود العظام وكل ذلك تهامل و من عدم اتفاق. فلنهب و نفوق من غفلتنا هذه و لنشمر عن ساعد الاجتهاد و لنتفق قلباً و قالباً فإننا قادرون على إجراء أعمال تفوق تلك التي يعملها الغربيون بشرط أن نجتهد و نتفق كما قدمنا

… We see the people of the West committing to many humanitarian contributions, including building schools and charitable institutions, even in our Eastern communities. Besides that, you see them united in mind and body; each of them wishing the best for others. On the other hand, as Easterners, we have done nothing worth mentioning. We only take pride in what our great ancestors left us. This is all because of our negligence and disagreement. We must wake up from our slumber, roll up our sleeves and get to work. We must unite because we are capable of excelling in works that exceed what Westerners are doing. We can do this if we work hard and agree like we used to.

This writer pointed to the growth of foreign schools and other "charitable institutions," including by implication SPC, as an indicator that Western practices and culture were superior to that of the East. At the same time, the writer maintained a belief that the East had the potential to match and even exceed what was seen in the West.

Similarly, Elias Afansar Abeed (1902) traced the evolution—or "deterioration"—of the East in a lengthy Arabic-language article titled حالتنا الحاضرة or "Our Current State," in which he recalled the successes of the ancient Phoenicians but noted that

و ما فتئوا سائرين في سبيل التقدم و الفلاح راقين طرافي العلاء و النجاح حتى اخذتهم الفتن على غرة و داهمتهم العداوات.

They did not yearn to become the most successful and never asked for excellence because they became divided and quarreled among themselves.

He urged readers to strive toward higher achievements, writing:

فهذه يا قوم حالنا شاهدة بما نفعل فقد بلينا بمصائب وويلات تثور لها عواطف الاحزان و الأكادر من أعماق القلب و الفؤاد. مصائب تدك الجبال و تذيب الجماد. فإلى متى نحن الشرقيون ناعمي طرف الفكرة غير مبالين بما يحدث و يقع علينا من الافساد و حقوقنا من الاهتضام و أموالنا من الانتهاب و لا بما يتهدد بلادنا من الخراب لابتزاز الغربي

أموالها و استنزاف دمها و استخراج كنوز ثروتها و خسف بدر رونقها
كأنه لم يكن شيء ممّا هو كائن حولنا بل نحن في غفلة الغافل و رقدة
الكسول لا نبدي حراكاً لدرء شرٍ او جلب منفعة غير اننا صابرون على
ما هو احرُّ من الجمر قد سبقنا الغربيون في مضمار هذه الحياة مراحل
كثيرة و نحن غافلون ذاهلون عن السير في سبيلهم حتى أصبح ذلك
متعذراً إلّا بعد اجهاد النفس زمناً طويلا للوصول الى ما وصلوا إليه الان
من ذروة المجد و النعمة.

This is our current state of deterioration, a matter that evokes feelings of sadness in the heart and mind. We have been cursed with hardships higher than mountains and tougher than stones. Till when will the Easterners remain indifferent to the corruption happening around them? When will we realize that our rights are crushed, our money is robbed, and our country is threatened and destroyed because of the West? The Westerner took the East's money, sucked its blood, took its resources, and dimmed its light. Still, we act as though nothing has happened around us. We are in our deepest slumber and laziness. We do not take action when there is trouble, nor do we benefit ourselves. We stand by patiently and watch as the Westerners beat us in every track of life and on every level. We have become unaware and distracted from following their path, to the point where it will take immense hard work for a long time to reach what they now possess: a state of glory and bliss.

In this passage, Abeed referenced the West's appropriation and theft of the East's assets and culture—he seems to have blamed the West for the East's decline. However, he also argued that the West had succeeded where the East had not, and his rhetoric therefore positioned the East as subordinate to the West, but having the possibility to eventually reach "a state of glory and bliss."

Many students took on the topic of education in their articles, comparing the state of education in Syria or the Middle East more generally against European or American models. For example, a student named Kamal Haddad (1906), writing six years later in the English-language publication *Zion*, urged his classmates to complete their degrees in order to meet the standards (and progress) of the West: "Indeed, if the Syrian young men want to race with the young men of Europe in science, art, etc., they must be well educated like them, and to be so they must at least have the B.A. degree." For Haddad, in other words, Syrians needed to follow the example of Westerners by emulating their pursuit of higher education.

Student writers' discussions about education at SPC compared it to what they imagined occurred elsewhere, particularly in the United States. Importantly, this discussion took place most often in English and not in Arabic, and it drew upon a rhetoric of Occidentalism. Writing about SPC occurred most often in English likely because English was the language of instruction, making it logical to discuss the college in the same language. Additionally, students may have chosen to write about the college in English because they knew that their audience could then include English-speaking faculty, and they wanted to persuade them to take up their causes. Or, perhaps, in those instances in which they weren't criticizing SPC, students may have wanted to show American faculty that they belonged to the imagined America represented by the college and its teachers. The following examples help us understand how students conceived of American education, and America more generally, through their own educational experiences at SPC.

Some students compared the situation at SPC negatively against what they imagined happened at American colleges. For example, one of the editors of the English-language publication *Light*, Mohammed Abdus Sattar El-Khairi (1906), urged students to form a "Union Club," a debating club like those found in other universities throughout the world, and outlined the benefits of such a club, noting that having one would have prepared students to "stand up and thank Mr. [William Jennings] Bryan, on behalf of the students and show their appreciation of his memorable speech," upon Bryans' recent visit to SPC from America. In contemplating this missed opportunity, El-Khairi wrote, "We wonder, why such an institution [of a Union Club], which is the life and soul of college days, has been ignored up to this time. We cannot for a moment think that an institution of this sort does not exist in the big colleges of the United States." However, he suggested that SPC students had difficulty sustaining extracurricular activities after they began. Drawing on a rhetoric of Occidentalism by way of explanation, El-Khairi wrote,

> We are very much ashamed, when we read or hear an American or a European say, among many ill-striking expressions, that an Oriental mind is incapable to keep a work go on well [*sic*]. It can start any work on a grand style and with great zeal and earnestness, but long before it loses all enthusiasm, and leaves the work take care of itself [*sic*].

Here, El-Khairi reproduced a rhetoric that "othered" himself, along with his fellow Arab peers. He suggested that the rhetoric of Occidentalism may have been true, based on his experience at SPC: "Are we like this?" El-Khairi asked rhetorically, and he answered affirmatively, exclaiming "Shame! Shame!! Shame!!!"

Other students compared local teachers negatively against their foreign counterparts, particularly American teachers. In one issue of the English-language magazine *Pioneers of SPC* (published 1905–1906), an anonymous student writer who called himself simply "A Syrian" (1905) noted that:

> Not few of the Preparatory students complain that the Syrian teachers do not treat them fairly, speak harsh words to them, and consequently have no sympathy with them. Indeed, the Syrian teachers are not half as popular as the Americans because the majority lack the qualities which characterize nearly all our foreign teachers. I mean gentleness and sympathy. This, besides all others, is the chief ground for discontent on the part of the student ["s" is added in pencil].

This excerpt, which creates a stark, generalized division between Syrian and American approaches toward education, suggests that students imagined that the Syrian culture itself produced bad pedagogy (and, by implication, that American culture produced good pedagogy). This kind of discourse positioned local students as at odds with their own culture; they imagined a superior culture represented in and through the Americans who happened to teach at their college.

As we can see in the foregoing excerpts of student writing, the rhetoric of Occidentalism, like the rhetorics of nationalism and resistance, critiqued students' home region and culture, but this critique was delivered differently, as student writers used representations of the "West" and Western culture to construct their arguments. In this rhetoric, students drew upon their imagining of the "West" (which included, but was not exclusive to, America) in order to argue for improvements to Syrian culture and, in particular, education. The "West," therefore, acted as a mirror through which the flaws of the region could be exposed—while also, in most cases, revealing paths toward improvement or salvation. And, as seen in the excerpt written by El-Khairi (1906) in his reference to "an Oriental mind," as well as the anonymous *Pioneers* writer's description of "Syrian teachers" (A Syrian, 1905), this rhetoric also adopted problematic representations of Syrians as the "Other" within Western discourse. Collectively, these examples also show that language(s) matter to the history of rhetoric and writing studies, as language(s) can produce different forms of knowledge: Paying attention to the role of language(s) in these discussions shows how important it is to resist taking English for granted in representations of what the discipline has been, is, and can be.

Conclusion

This analysis of almost 50 English- and Arabic-language student newspapers and magazines helps further establish the transnational, translingual history of rhetoric and writing studies. The proliferation and semi-public circulation of SPC student publications at the turn of the 20th century, and the rhetorics contained therein, teaches us that local literacy practices and instruction were grounded in the local population's diverse linguistic resources and specific geopolitical context. Further, evaluating the evidence presented here through a decolonial frame challenges key premises of rhetoric and writing studies, including assumptions that the discipline's history is primarily monolingual; that English, and America, are central to the discipline; and that writing instruction in the late 19th century was dominated by "current-traditional" approaches.

Journals such as *I.O.U. 5 Minutes*, *The Kodak*, and *Happy Days at SPC* illustrate that students were deeply engaged with writing; they anticipated and received engagement from their peers and teachers; and they believed their writing would make a difference on campus and beyond. Although there is no complete picture of how these publications circulated, it is clear that at least some student writing was publicly on display. And through references to students' teachers and classmates in the publications themselves, it can be inferred that instructors encouraged students to engage in writing for public consumption and for professional purposes. In other words, rhetorical education was alive and well at the turn of the 20th century in Beirut, disrupting historical narratives that assume "current-traditional" rhetoric and pedagogy overtook more robust writing instruction in the late 19th century (see Chapter 4 for a more extensive problematization of these historical accounts).

Further, this analysis adds to a larger understanding, developed throughout the chapters of this book, of SPC's role as an important site of writing instruction, a sponsor of literacy in the region, and a manifestation of an imagined America that was constructed for students in and through the college's curriculum, faculty, and administrators. For SPC students, writing across languages meant engaging across regional, political, linguistic, and cultural borders. As we see in the marginalia found in the *SPC Commercial Paper*, students' writing reflected the geopolitical realities that surrounded them, including the decline of the Ottoman Empire, the rise of Arab nationalism through *al-Nahda*, and the growing influence of the West.

Translation also proves to be an important yet seemingly mundane activity in many of the examples of SPC student writing discussed in this chapter. Whether translations were presented side by side, as in *The Kodak*, mentioned in passing, as in *Happy Days*, or expected to be done by readers, as in the *SPC Commercial Paper's* marginalia, it is clear that cross-language work was central to SPC student literacy. Notably, student writers did not comment explicitly on the labor of translation, suggesting that the activity was such a normal and expected part of communicating that it did not need to be mentioned.

Student writing operated at SPC as an exploration and expression of students' identities as Arabs attending an American college in the Ottoman Empire at the turn of the 20th century. Particularly in Arabic-language publications, students drew upon rhetorics of nationalism and resistance to signify their Arab identities and loyalty to their homeland. And students used English to measure their region and culture against the apparent success of the West and an imagined America. These publications offered students an important opportunity to negotiate competing epistemologies and develop identity through writing. At the same time, there was a marked difference between what students wrote in English compared to Arabic, suggesting that their ability to negotiate and express identity may have been facilitated by language itself.

As we have come to see through the evidence presented here and in earlier chapters, the literacy offered by SPC was complicated for students: Their writing in English and in Arabic demonstrates that they both drew upon and resisted what this literacy promised and promoted. Students' use of different languages reveals competing epistemologies at work, highlighting conflicts that can also be seen in the decision to change the language of instruction at SPC discussed in Chapter 3, as well as in the SPC student protests discussed in Chapter 4.

This analysis pushes us to consider the implications of this history for contemporary research, program administration, and pedagogy in rhetoric and writing studies: Examination of SPC student writing challenges the "tacit language policy of unidirectional English monolingualism" that Horner and Trimbur (2002, p. 594) argued is problematically foundational to the contemporary discipline and that they traced to the decline of classical rhetoric and promotion of English rather than the study of multiple languages at late-19th century Harvard. However, as I argue in Chapter 3, Horner and Trimbur did not go far enough in examining the much longer history of colonialism and nationalism that drove Harvard and other institutions of higher education, in the US and elsewhere, to elevate English and tie it to the global production, circulation, and over-valuing of Western knowledge. Scholars, program administrators, and practitioners in rhetoric and writing studies have taken English for granted in part because of this longer history, as well as our own failure to recognize translingual practices and transnational perspectives even in seemingly monolingual contexts such as the United States.[11] As this chapter attests, there is much to discover about how writing across languages has been and continues to be used to negotiate competing epistemologies and the conflicts that arise out of them. Monolingual ideology, as well as writing scholars' and teachers' own monolingualism, has worked and continues to work within the discipline to mask and devalue the rich and resourceful translingual practices that are exemplified in this chapter.

In order to uncover and place value on translingual practices that disrupt the centrality of English in the contemporary discipline, scholars, program leaders, and educators should consider the role of translation in both research and pedagogy. Cushman (2021) proposed decolonial translation as a methodology through which we might see "the gaps in knowing that were created by the colonial difference . . . [and that] reveal[] the boundaries created by the imperial difference in an effort to include again the knowledges which have been lost or erased" (p. 203). In the context of archival research in rhetoric and writing studies, decolonial translation makes visible those discourses that have historically been suppressed through a prioritization of English-language literacy. This in turn shifts our understanding of the discipline's history as fundamentally translingual. As scholars, we should consider how to build up our own linguistic resources, including multilingual and intercultural knowledge, to more effectively account for literacy practices that cross languages, cultures, and epistemologies. In particular, when publishing about writing produced in languages other than English, we should present this writing in the language of the original whenever possible, as I have done throughout this chapter. Enoch and Ramírez's (2019) anthology of Spanish-language women's journalistic writing around the turn of the 20th century is a good example of writing studies scholarship that effectively *decentralizes* English in presenting the texts in their original Spanish, but which makes the work accessible to those of us without fluency in the language.[12] We must also be cognizant of the absences in the historical record that occur because of a prioritization of English: For example, much of my interpretation of the 1909 student protests

---

11   See Chapter 1 for a fuller discussion of historiography that has accounted for, or elided, evidence of translingual practices and transnational perspectives.

12   It is important to recognize that this kind of translation work requires a great deal of labor, collaboration, and money. I could not have written this chapter without the assistance of two Arabic-language specialists, Ghada Seifeddine and Yasmine Abou Taha, who transcribed and translated the student writing in the archives for me, nor without grants provided by the American University of Beirut that paid them for this work. Enoch and Ramírez (2019) also discussed these components of the work explicitly in the acknowledgements and introduction to their book.

in Chapter 4 relies on English-language translations of newspaper articles that were originally written in Arabic; however, the original articles were not preserved, perhaps because they had been translated into English at the time and it was determined that English-language records were all that was needed for an assumed English-speaking audience. Additionally, we must consider how we fail to recognize translingual literacy practice(s) in the past or the present simply because we are not aware of language practices that we do not understand or use ourselves. In our classrooms, we can highlight the multiple linguistic resources that our students hold by engaging students in translation and critical language awareness activities such as those recommended by Laura Aull and Shawna Shapiro (2024), Nancy Bou Ayash (2021), Lu (2006), Julia Kiernan et al. (2016), S. Shapiro (2022), Xiqiao Wang (2020), and others.

Finally, this chapter's study of SPC student writing disrupts explicit or implicit assumptions that locate the history, present, and future of rhetoric and writing studies in the United States. Instead, this historical account highlights the deeply transnational nature of the discipline. SPC student writing exposes how representations of the West infiltrated local discourses and rhetorics in Syria, as well as in American higher education. Additionally, SPC student writing highlights how representations of "the East" entered local discourses and rhetorics and interacted with ideas about the West and the America imagined in and through the college. Flows of knowledge and exchange, in other words, are not unidirectional or hegemonic—transnational exchange itself shapes our identities and the literacy practices and possibilities available to us. When we as writing scholars, program leaders, and teachers reorient ourselves to a discipline that is fundamentally transnational, we can better recognize in our scholarship, programs, and pedagogy the multiple epistemologies and rhetorics that circulate, explicitly or implicitly, within literacy practices. What's more, recognizing transnational exchange allows for us to identify the unique challenges and opportunities afforded in contemporary English-language literacy instruction for multilingual and monolingual students alike. When we recognize the work of the discipline as transnational, we can identify the ways in which language and literacy education may determine the arguments and rhetorical positions actually available to students.

6 Imagining a Transnational and Translingual Past, Present, and Future

In this final chapter, I synthesize the historical accounts illuminated in the previous chapters in order to argue that a careful examination of the writing practices and policies at Syrian Protestant College (SPC) moves the discipline of rhetoric and writing studies from a primarily Anglocentric and monolingual view of the history of literacy education to one that is fundamentally transnational and translingual. The decolonial frame through which I have analyzed the historical evidence allows for rhetoric and writing studies to be refracted through a new lens, offering members of the discipline opportunities to understand their work and scope more expansively. Studying non-Anglophone cases of literacy education such as SPC presents opportunities for teachers, administrators, and scholars in Anglophone contexts to apply what they learn to their own writing pedagogy, programs, and research going forward.

Additionally, the history investigated in the foregoing chapters points to the high stakes experienced by students, teachers, program administrators, and communities involved in the transnational knowledge economy of higher education. These stakes have been produced as a result of colonial epistemology and its historical hold on English-language literacy education. This history holds implications for students today, particularly their ability to occupy specific national, religious, linguistic, and cultural identities while pursuing literacy development that complements, rather than corrupts, those identities. Ultimately, I argue, understanding the colonial epistemology underlying an imagined America in relation to the development of literacy education around the turn of the 20th century can lead to a more nuanced understanding of contemporary processes and power relations of globalization and transnational exchange, particularly as flows of knowledge—in this case, American-style literacy education—intersect and move across national, linguistic, religious, and cultural borders. The case of SPC equips us with a new historical understanding of the stakes and complications of contemporary literacy education, leaving six key takeaways, which I elaborate below.

Power, Language, and Literacy Education

First, the history discussed in this book throws the relationship among power, language, and literacy education into high relief. Chapter 3 discusses SPC's decision to shift from Arabic to English as the primary language of instruction less than 20 years after its founding. The justifications provided by administrators suggested that this shift was meant to benefit students, to give them direct access to Western knowledge. Upon further examination, however, the justifications offered for teaching in Arabic when the college was founded, and in English later, were grounded on maintaining the needs and power of the college's American administrators and faculty. The college's founders, who were previously missionaries, initially followed the American Board of Commissioners for Foreign Missions' (ABCFM's) approach toward proselytization in the region by choosing Arabic as the language of instruction: Arabic was believed to be the more powerful means through which students might be converted to Protestant Christianity (see Chapter 2 for a fuller discussion of the ABCFM's approach). Additionally, focusing on Arabic would mean that new graduates (potentially new converts) of the college were more likely to stay in the region and even work for the college. As the college grew and new faculty were needed, SPC administrators sought to hire American and European faculty rather than looking to their own Arabic-speaking graduates. Faced with the choice of providing years of Arabic-language training to new faculty or shifting to English as the language of instruction, SPC administrators chose the latter, with justifications that differed from those offered previously but which ultimately upheld the centrality of Western or American identity and knowledge.

As discussed in Chapter 4, SPC students' protests against college decisions show that students held a keen understanding of how to rhetorically navigate the politics of language and literacy education, even as they aspired to perform the American "cultural citizenship"—citizenship through behavior rather than by law—valued at SPC. Specifically, when students protested the administration's decision in 1882 to force the resignation of Edwin Lewis, a professor in the medical school, they drew from their understanding of SPC's American educational context to make their case: In their petitions for Lewis' reinstatement, the students specifically appealed to the college administrators' sense of Christian morality and values, and, relying upon a Western definition of justice, the students argued that they had the right to a specific kind of (American) education, a right that the college had taken away. Later, in 1909, students protested the college's insistence that they attend Christian religious services at the college. During this protest, which lasted for several months, students communicated with SPC administration in English while debating the conflict with local and regional community members in Arabic-language magazines and newspapers. Student writers, while holding various perspectives about the conflict, ultimately relied on their literacy education at SPC to construct an imagined America through their writing, which contained both positive and negative references to American laws and Christianity, as well as contrasts between the "West" and the "East." Of course, in spite of students' best efforts to appeal to American faculty and administrators at the college and to demonstrate their ability to belong to the college as cultural citizens, in the end neither of the protest movements succeeded. While students felt empowered to protest because they believed that they belonged to the college and implicitly to the America it represented, college administrators made it clear that they could never be American enough to negotiate their power.

We can also see the workings of power in relation to language and literacy education by analyzing the publications produced by SPC students around the turn of the 20th century, as described in Chapter 5. The writing contained within these publications, in Arabic and English as well as in other languages, shows how SPC students understood and navigated the power associated with specific languages and how they used their literacy education to work with(in) those languages. In English, SPC students occupied a learner identity and understood that their writing would be on public display, easily accessible to the predominantly English-speaking faculty. Perhaps it was for this reason that the English-language publications tended to contain expository essays as well as stories or essays praising the West. In Arabic, SPC students seemed more comfortable composing analyses and arguments; these publications contained articles that were less informational and instead more critical of their peers or (Western or Eastern) society. Students were well aware that their Arabic-language publications, while available to the public, were unlikely to be read or understood by their American professors, and their rhetorical approaches reflected that reality. This awareness demonstrates students' ability to negotiate conflicting and sometimes contradictory epistemologies, resulting in the articulation of their own (Arab) identity or the performance of (American) cultural citizenship in an effort to belong both to the college as well as to greater Syria.

The Weight of English

Second, this historical account illustrates the different "weight" or value that English can carry depending on the context, and it highlights the consequences of this weight for literacy education (see Arnold, 2021; Vieira, 2019). The weight of English, this history reveals, depends on one's past, location, identity—and perhaps one's future too. As discussed in Chapter 3, the opportunity to learn and use English within the Ottoman Empire around the turn of the 20th century meant, for students, having the chance to communicate and work across cultural and national boundaries at a time of great geopolitical change. At the same time, English presented risks for students, in that the language could signal a psychological or physical move away from their home culture and identity. SPC administrators and faculty were aware of this, and the question of whether students should have access to the language, and to what extent, was key to the decisions made about the college's language of instruction.

The historical accounts of student protests conveyed in Chapter 4 illustrate English's weight. Although Edwin Lewis' dismissal, which sparked student protests in 1882, was justified by SPC administrators on the grounds that he discussed Darwin during a commencement address, the dismissal can also be understood as an attempt to force the departures of most of the medical school faculty, who were also the last holdouts at the college teaching in Arabic in the early 1880s. SPC had already made the decision to transition fully to English as the medium of instruction, but medical school faculty continued teaching and writing in Arabic. In fact, Lewis' address was later published in an Arabic-language journal, meaning that the Western scientific knowledge represented in and through Darwin would have been transmitted directly to the local population. This connection to the local population likely bolstered the medical faculty's insistence on maintaining its curriculum in Arabic. Dismissing Lewis, which resulted in the resignations of four out of the remaining five medical faculty, meant a complete shift to English as the medium of instruction throughout the college and maintenance of the institutional and ideological hierarchy that privileged English and the Anglo-centric knowledge carried with it. This privileging manifested itself again in the 1909 "Muslim Controversy," during which students and administrators negotiated in English over the college's requirement that all students attend Protestant chapel services. While the protesting students temporarily managed to disrupt the college's status quo, the balance of power always tipped in favor of SPC's American leaders. In order to make their case effectively, the protesting students had to cross into linguistically foreign territory to be heard. Forced to use the foreign language of English to persuade American faculty and administrators, and facing impossible odds, they must have found relief debating the merits of their case—and finding affirmation of their concerns—in Arabic-language journals and newspapers.

The weight of English is also tangible when exploring student-authored publications, as highlighted in Chapter 5. I have already mentioned the ways in which students' writing identities and purposes seemed to change depending on the language in which they composed. The weight of English can be further understood by considering the example presented in Chapter 5 of handwritten marginalia surrounding one student's poetry published in an English-language publication called *SPC Commercial Paper*. While the marginalia surrounding the poems can be understood on the surface as immature bullying by the writer's peers, looking more closely reveals a politics of language: The writer's peers questioned and ridiculed the writer's identity because, ostensibly, he could only write in English and probably French but not in Arabic, and because he was born in a rural area in Syria with deep connections to France. English in this case marked the student writer as an outsider, even within the American college—he could not be Western, nor could he be Arab. English separated him from his peers, many of whom would have come from socially privileged Arab families. At the same time, as his peers pointed out, his Arab and lower-class positionality meant he would never fully belong to the West or to the America represented by the college. Thus, English was both a burden and a barrier for this student, and he would never truly belong to the American or Arab world because of it.

Colonialism and English Literacy Education

Third, this historical account provides further evidence of Phillipson's (1992) and Pennycook's (1998) arguments that English literacy education outside of Anglophone contexts is deeply, perhaps inextricably, tied to colonialism. While Syria at the turn of the 20th century was not yet colonized by a European nation, SPC's curricular decisions, as described in Chapter 3, foreshadowed the geopolitical shifts that would soon propel Europe into the region and through which American influence would also grow. I have already summarized the colonial logics that provided the grounds for the college to shift to English as the medium of instruction. Beyond this macro shift, however, micro decisions about the language curriculum also reflected the larger geopolitical and colonial contexts in which the college operated. Until the mid-1880s, Greek and Latin were offered as electives; these languages would have allowed students direct access to key Western rhetorical texts, supplementing their study of English. After the shift to English, other languages never left the curriculum. Students continued studying Arabic and French intensively, alongside English, until the end of the 19th century. Turkish was later offered as an elective to substitute for French, reflecting larger geopolitical developments. Extracurricular activities such as literary societies and student-run journals engaged students as they developed fluency in multiple languages. Together, this evidence suggests that multilingualism was well understood by students and faculty alike to be necessary for professional success in the region. This reality is another marker of colonial ideology at work, exemplifying Benedict Anderson's (2006) point that multilingual brokers served key roles in the functioning of colonies. At the same time, English remained a priority at SPC, justified in part because it served as a signifier of American or "civilized" society. As Phillipson (1992) pointed out, colonial discourses linking English with "civility" have more recently transformed into discourses linking English to progress and social mobility.

Colonialism's ties to English literacy education can also be seen in relation to the 1882 and 1909 student protests at SPC that constitute the focus of Chapter 4. In 1882, Edwin Lewis' dismissal was instigated as a result of his reference to Darwin during a commencement address. The address, which also discussed the work of Western scientists Charles Lyell and Louis Pasteur, was later published in an Arabic-language journal. At the time, Darwin was controversial in the Christian Protestant world because the theory of evolution he advanced challenged the Christian story of creation. Although Lewis described Darwin's work in neutral terms,[1] his reference to evolution was enough to produce the grounds upon which he was forced to resign. Another dimension of the controversy becomes apparent through the lens of colonialism when considering that Lewis' address was published and disseminated through Arabic: In this case, Lewis transmitted a controversial theory—one that called the Christian mission into question—directly to the local population in and through Arabic. As a result, English was not required for the local population to gain access to contemporary Western knowledge, nor could English be used to mediate how it would be understood. SPC students and other locals were given the tools to work with Western ideas and knowledge in their own language. They could use these tools, potentially, to subvert the authority of the college and the value of English literacy education. We can imagine how Lewis' Christian counterparts may have viewed this unsanctioned transmission as a betrayal of sorts, an effort to weaken their power—a view manifested out of colonial epistemology.

Colonial epistemology also triggered the 1909 student protest that is also discussed in Chapter 4. The protest occurred when a visiting missionary characterized Muslims as "enemies . . . await[ing] the opportunity to devour [Christians]" (Nickoley, 1909). Students relied on their SPC education to guide their conduct throughout the protest. Their writing shows that they were well aware of the colonial mentality that gave the speaker the freedom to denigrate the local Muslim population so openly in front of an audience that contained Muslim SPC students. As faculty scrambled to contain the

---

1   Ironically, Darwin's work eventually formed the foundation for the eugenics movement and scientific racism, ideas grounded upon colonial epistemology (Helfand, 2020).

crisis, records show that they never put any blame on the visitor himself, with one faculty member describing the students' interpretation of the speech as grounded on the "wildest rumors" (Hall, 1909). While some of the faculty seemed to sympathize with the protesting students, this sympathy always came with a caveat that relied on seeing the Muslim students at SPC as different than the surrounding local Muslim community; faculty saw the surrounding community as a threat (just as did the visiting speaker) that could push the students toward "mob violence" (Moore, 1909a). In order to escape criticism that they were not "civilized," the striking students comported themselves professionally throughout the protest, attending every class and meeting except religious services. Their understanding of the behavior that was expected of a cultural citizen of the college was learned in and through their American-style literacy education at SPC.

Student writing at SPC also highlights the connection between colonialism and English literacy education. As discussed in Chapter 4, students wrote about the 1909 crisis in various Arabic-language publications and made explicit reference in their writing to SPC's position as a foreign college funded and founded by missionaries. They criticized the ways in which the college's religious teachings and Western curriculum conflicted with the local Muslim population. These writers understood that "The Occidentals . . . erected schools to educate the young not for our benefit but for theirs, and not to augment thereby our power but their own" (*The Mohammedan Nation*, 1909). Likewise, student-authored publications at SPC reveal similar connections, as Chapter 5 attests. Students used both English and Arabic to offer social and cultural critiques of both the Arab and Western worlds. However, this criticism was more severe in the Arabic-language publications, suggesting that students understood English to be a medium through which such criticism would not be as welcome, or through which they struggled to find language that would fully convey the nuances of their critique. Students' deployment of different language(s) for specific purposes illustrates how they negotiated colonial epistemology as it entered their social and intellectual worlds through Western education and the English language.

Language Constructs Place, Identity, Nationhood, and Belonging

Fourth, this historical account demonstrates the ways in which language constructs place, identity, nationhood, and belonging. As Chapter 3 explicates, when SPC was founded, it was decided that Arabic should be the medium of instruction in part to emphasize the "place" of students in relation to the college and to Western knowledge. The college's founders thought English would "corrupt" the minds of students because knowing the language would draw students away from Syria and toward opportunities outside of their homeland. When English became the medium of instruction, students were expected to aspire to American culture, values, and beliefs—in and through the language of English. At the same time, the college's structure and hierarchies proved time and again that its students could never actually *be* American; they would always be foreigners inside of the college's American walls, no matter how well they acquired the English language or mimicked American behavior (see also Chapter 4).

While English held a great deal of power within the college, its power was not ubiquitous (nor is it today at the American University of Beirut). Students and faculty alike negotiated multiple languages inside the college's hallways, classrooms, and on the hills leading from the college grounds to the seaside—a linguistic reality that continues to this day. Multiple languages held prominence in the curriculum, too, and they have never disappeared. The complicated linguistic situation at SPC then, and at AUB today, reflects the larger geopolitical context, in which multiple languages construct the space and where translingual practice is an everyday, almost mundane activity. Multiple languages were (and are) necessary for navigation through everyday life. This history shows how language can both construct and expose the geopolitics of a place. Both today and in the past, when someone on campus speaks in Arabic, they signal their belonging to a locally diverse Arab community and culture; when they use English, they signal an economic and intellectual agility valued in the West; when they use French, they signal a religious and cultural identity that is both distinct from and an integral part of the local culture—and connected to the French who colonized Syria after World War I. Turkish too, at the time, signaled a connection to the Ottoman colonizers who ultimately controlled the region until the Great War. As such, language serves not only as a marker, but also as a builder, of the spaces people occupy as well as those they imagine. Viewing the college's curriculum in relation to the larger geopolitical context highlights how language constructs identity and nationality, serving as a tool for inclusion and exclusion.

The work of language and writing in constructing place and identity can also be seen in Chapter 4, where I discuss SPC students' efforts to perform a kind of American cultural citizenship while also protesting SPC decisions and policies that they felt violated implicit promises the college had extended to them through its education. In the 1882 protests against Edwin Lewis' dismissal, students pled their case to the administration in Arabic, the language they were most comfortable using even as the college shifted the language of instruction to English. In their arguments, they signified their belonging to the institution rhetorically, appealing to their American audience through "rational" argumentative strategies that would have been promoted in the college's rhetoric curriculum. Their writing in the petitions suggests that the students believed they possessed a kind of American identity, one in which they had agency and deserved to be heard. In the 1909 protest, students appealed, in English, to what they knew to be American values—liberty and freedom—in order to argue for their own religious freedom. In Arabic, some students constructed an identity that was Arab and specifically Muslim; others also identified themselves as members of the Ottoman Empire, a state that supported Islamic values and beliefs. Still others defended the college or suggested that Christianity would never hold any sway over Muslims, who were unified in their beliefs. In all of these examples, students constructed their own identities and an imagined America in and through their writing. For these students, "this [was] the meaning of the American College": To be American, or to truly belong in the American college, was to be Christian and to adopt Christian views of morality and behavior, and to learn in English (Abu Raad, 1909). In both of these protest movements, even as students complained about the college, their good behavior exemplified their desire to be seen as cultural citizens, to remain a part of the college community, and to belong to a distant and foreign America that was constructed, in part, through language and literacy education at SPC.

Similarly, the student publications at SPC analyzed in Chapter 5 show how language was used to construct identity and a sense of belonging. Using the Arabic language, students spoke directly to their peers and their Syrian instructors. In this language, students articulated their identities as Arab and emphasized their belonging to the region. This is exemplified particularly in the liberty they took to critique their homeland and their culture. Positioned between their home culture and the American culture represented in and through the college curriculum, students brought a new perspective about their geopolitical positioning to their readers. Students writing in English, on the other hand, knew their audience would include college faculty and administrators, and they used the language sometimes to praise Western culture and to critique Arabs or Arab culture. English was a tool through which students could construct an identity that they believed would belong to their imagined America, in which they knew Arabs and Arab culture were often contrasted negatively with the West. In the various examples presented in Chapter 5, we can see how writing and language were used to communicate cross-culturally, to demonstrate transnational engagement and "worldliness," and to establish identity and a sense of belonging to different, sometimes competing, communities and the epistemologies attached to them.

The Implied Promises of Literacy Education

Fifth, this historical account reveals the high stakes and implicit promises constructed in and through literacy education, which are particularly well highlighted in transnational and translingual contexts of education such as SPC. For example, the shift to English as SPC's language of instruction, discussed in Chapter 3, further underlined the Western knowledge and values that were already tied to the Protestant Christianity of the faculty. The shift to English implied that students would be successful only if they became proficient in the language and adopted the values and behaviors that the language represented. It was further implied that students would have access to opportunities through their education in English, such as being able to teach and work at the college after graduation. While some graduates did eventually teach at the college, they did not gain equal status to their foreign counterparts as faculty until 1920, when the institution changed its name and shifted to a new, secular identity. The college, in other words, failed to live up to the promises implied by its English-language literacy education.

Examination of the documents surrounding the SPC student protests in Chapter 4 makes clear that students took up the democratic ideals of freedom and liberty espoused in their American education and held them to be true, leading to their efforts to behave as cultural citizens of the college. The students referred to specific elements of American culture and law that they understood from a distance, including freedom of religion and the separation of church and state, and then attempted to apply these principles to the problems at the college. The students' literacy education suggested a version of American education—and America itself—in which they had rights and agency within the college. These assumptions empowered them to protest. Unfortunately, students found that their attempts to belong to an imagined America remained a promise that could not be fulfilled.

The implied promises of English literacy education are similarly on display in the English-language student-authored publications analyzed in Chapter 5. These publications reveal who students thought they were supposed to be and how they thought they were supposed to behave *in English*—in their writing, students positioned themselves as learners of the language, and the publications featured informational and expository writing on topics such as business, world events, and hobbies. In marked contrast to their writing in Arabic, in English, students apologized for mistakes in advance and invited readers to correct anything that they found problematic. This suggests that the students assumed themselves to be inferior users of English with much to learn. While students at SPC were indeed relatively new users of the language, the explicit positioning found in their writing underlines assumptions about their capabilities learned in and through their literacy education in English at the college. These publications reveal that students had internalized a belief that they were always-already English language *learners* rather than agentive *users* of the language. Even as they were promised opportunity through the language, they were reminded that they would never be enough. Students were keenly aware of their English-speaking audience, and their writing reflects the colonial beliefs that this audience likely had about them.

Agency in Literacy Practices

Finally, this historical account reveals that despite the powerful colonial epistemology underlying English literacy education in Syria, this set of beliefs was neither homogenous nor totalizing. As I describe in Chapter 3, multiple languages remained a key part of the curriculum even after English became the language of instruction at SPC. While the logics underlying this shift to English were certainly colonial, translingual practices were a necessary part of students' and faculty members' daily lived experience. In a richly multilingual environment such as SPC, other language practices could not be erased.

There are parallels between SPC students' use of English and Spack's (2002) study of Native American writers who were educated in English in U.S. government schools during the second half of the 19th century—for Spack, these writers "used English to speak for themselves and represent their own lives . . . [they] manipulated the English language for their own purposes and played with it" (p. 112). Similarly, SPC students used their literacy education, as evidenced in Chapter 4, to speak out against the college's decisions and to appeal to administrators' values and beliefs. In the student-authored publications at SPC described in Chapter 5, students manipulated language to reflect the values and beliefs of their audience. Students ultimately drew on their own knowledge and identity to engage and negotiate with(in) the imagined America represented by the American college and through the English language.

Reconceptualizing the Past, Present, and Future of Rhetoric and Writing Studies

On its face, the account in this book most obviously complicates traditional narratives about the history of rhetoric and writing studies, narratives that tend to assume that the discipline's history is based primarily in the United States and is primarily monolingual. Such Americentric and monolingual views can be traced to the colonial foundations of English-language literacy education. The complications offered in this book reveal how these histori-cal narratives have limited what we as rhetoric and writing studies scholars, program administrators, and teachers conceive of as the scope of the disci-pline. Examining its history through a decolonial lens encourages us to locate transnational and translingual writing practices and pedagogies even within seemingly monolingual and homogenous contexts. This lens suggests we need to confront the deep ties between colonialism and the English language that inextricably bind us—and our work—to this legacy.

The history of literacy education at SPC underlines the ways in which language ideology is deeply intertwined with literacy education, particularly literacy education in English—a phenomenon that Phillipson (1992) called linguistic imperialism and which I describe more thoroughly in Chapter 1. Throughout this historical account, SPC students and faculty are seen nav-igating colonial epistemology and problematic monolingual and nationalist ideologies that emerged out of it. As a result of colonial epistemology under-lying the American-style education offered by SPC, students and faculty car-ried markedly different assumptions and values about literacy and education into their classrooms. They repeatedly tried and failed to co-construct an imagined America that could never materialize and to which students could never fully belong. So, too, do students and faculty today meet in classrooms with competing ideas about what literacy education can or should do and what literacy in English means or represents.

In the United States, where rhetoric and writing studies as a discipline was born, students arrive to classrooms carrying invisible, but weighty, legacies of colonialism and slavery on their backs. These legacies impact how students—particularly but not only international, domestic multilingual, and students of color—understand, receive, and accept what is offered, and as Milu (2021) pointed out, many educators do not interrogate how these legacies alter stu-dents' experiences. Just as SPC students navigated the misaligned visions and false promises of literacy education offered at the college, so too do students today navigate histories and futures that weigh down their relationship to literacy in English (see Lagman, 2018; Lorimer Leonard, 2013; MacDonald, 2015; Pederson, 2010). Students may have no reason to trust the promises made by writing curriculum or their instructors, implicitly or explicitly, about literacy education, and this lack of trust can help explain why students so often resist taking up the risks asked of them in writing classes.

In short, as educators and program administrators, we must critically con-sider the epistemologies that we promote in and through literacy education and the consequences thereof: What do we assume about what English and/or literacy represent or can do for students? How can we better account for these assumptions and ensure we are making these assumptions explicit in our daily practice? What do we explicitly or implicitly promise to students about what literacy can or should do? In what ways can we recognize and rectify the factors that may disrupt or impede these promises?

Willinsky (1998) argued that imperialism's "will to know became an integral part of [its] economic and administrative apparatus . . . dedicated to defining and extending the privileges of the West" (p. 27). This "will to know" included a "conquering, civilizing, collecting, and classifying" approach to the world that was marked through the constant identification and highlighting of difference (p. 13). This marking out of difference operated to *master* the world through the production of a supposedly universal knowledge that inevitably favored the West. Today, that marking out of difference can be seen in programmatic and pedagogical approaches that promote final products rather than processes of writing; that prioritize Standard American English without interrogating the monolingualism supporting its prioritization; or that decontextualize writing practices, such as through generic five-paragraph essay or research paper assignments that assume there is such a thing as a universal reader (or writer). And that marking out of difference can be seen in research practices that rely on so-called foundational scholars without identifying how their work is grounded in Western colonial epistemology or that fail to seek out and engage with scholarship produced by transnational and/or multilingual scholars, and/or scholars from historically minoritized backgrounds.

Decolonial and Indigenous scholars in rhetoric and writing studies have proposed a number of alternative pedagogical approaches that work to delink literacy education from its colonial underpinnings. Canagarajah (2023) defined decolonial pedagogy as one that "focuses on developing the ethical, relational, and critical dispositions that will help students negotiate very diverse and unpredictable communicative contexts for meaningful and inclusive communication, drawing from the semiotic resources in the environment" (p. 283). There are a number of strategies that have been proposed by scholars to support such a pedagogical approach, some of which I have outlined at the end of Chapters 3, 4, and 5. Most importantly, we as writing instructors and program administrators need to educate ourselves about language ideology and literacy education in the context of colonial history. Program leaders and literacy educators should be able to articulate ways in which colonial epistemology has influenced their own thinking about what writing is, what it can do, why it matters to students, and how it should be assessed (see Poe, 2022). Administrators can provide professional development to promote this learning, to complicate curriculum, and to provide practical tools that will help instructors support student writers' specific identities, needs, and goals. In the writing classroom, teachers can provide instruction about language ideology and coloniality, followed by opportunities for students to explore how these ways of thinking have and continue to influence their own writing practices and rhetorical choices (see Arnold, 2018; Jackson, 2021; Milu, 2021; R. Shapiro & Watson, 2022; Zhang-Wu, 2021, 2023).

Additionally, program leaders and writing instructors can update curriculum and pedagogical practices to better account for the contextual, embodied, semiotic, and relational nature of all writing practices (see E. Lee, 2024). This can problematize existing curriculum and individual classroom discussions about developing authorial voice and integrating research by framing these practices as communal rather than individual (see Arola, 2018). Multimodal composition should also be considered as a potential site of decolonial and translingual meaning-making, especially as such practices integrate and place value on non-alphabetic forms of communication (see Jiang, 2024; E. Lee, 2022; Rivera, 2020). Program administrators and individual instructors can promote curriculum that engages students in experimentation with translingual and translation practices, placing explicit value on multiple modes of communication and risk-taking. This curriculum can include investigation into how these practices are connected to colonial history, nationality, and race (see Cushman, 2021; Do, 2022; Milu, 2021; R. Shapiro & Watson, 2022; Wang, 2020; Zhang-Wu, 2021).

The decolonial historiography implemented throughout this book is one step along the path to delinking from the colonial "structuring tenets" (Cushman, 2016, p. 239) that lie at the heart of the discipline of rhetoric and writing studies, particularly those tenets that place America and the language of English at the center of focus. As we in the discipline expand our scope and reframe our history, we can better understand the value of program curriculum and pedagogical practices that centralize the politics of language and promote transnational exchange, rather than ignoring them in favor of seemingly more efficient and practical approaches toward writing instruction. Indeed, decolonizing the discipline's past as translingual and transnational provides a pathway to more effectively build a decolonial, transnational, and translingual present and future.

§ References

Primary Archival Sources

A. of the Syrian College (1909, Jan. 24). *The Beirut college and Islam* [Previously translated article in *Lewa* (اللواء or *The Major-General*)]. Students 1900s (AA: 4.3.2, Box 1, File 15). Archives and Special Collections, American University of Beirut, Beirut, Lebanon.

Abeed, E. A. (1902, June 5). حالتنا الحاضرة [*Our current state*] (G. Seifeddine, Trans.) [Article published in الحظ (*al-Haz* or *Luck*)]. AUB Students' Magazine Collection 1899–1934 (AA: 4.2.1, Series I, Box 4). Archives and Special Collections, American University of Beirut, Beirut, Lebanon.

Abu Fadhil, W. (1909, February 4). *The American college: Criticism of its course* [Previously translated article in *Mukattam* (المقدم or *The Presenter*)]. Students 1900s (AA: 4.3.2, Box 1, File 15). Archives and Special Collections, American University of Beirut, Beirut, Lebanon.

Abu Raad, T. (1909, February 23). *Do not toil in vain* [Previously translated article in *Ahwal* (الأحوال or *The Circumstances*[1])]. Students 1900s (AA: 4.3.2, Box 1, File 15). Archives and Special Collections, American University of Beirut, Beirut, Lebanon.

Al-Sabbah, B. A. (1915, April 4). لنفذ هنا السبيل [*We used up all possible means*] (G. Seifeddine, Trans.) [Article published in الثمرة (*al-Thamra* or *The Fruit*)]. AUB Students' Magazine Collection 1899–1934 (AA: 4.2.1, Series II). Archives and Special Collections, American University of Beirut, Beirut, Lebanon.

The American college. (1909, January 15). [Previously translated article in *Ittehad* (الاتحاد or *The Union*]. Students 1900s (AA: 4.3.2, Box 1, File 15). Archives and Special Collections, American University of Beirut, Beirut, Lebanon.

Annual reports by the presidents to the Board of Managers and trustees, Syrian Protestant College. (1866-1921). Archives and Special Collections, American University of Beirut, Beirut, Lebanon.

'Asmet, M. (1909). *Extract from the "Nazam" (Egypt)* [Previously translated article in *Nazam*[2] (نظام or *Order*)]. Students 1900s (AA: 4.3.2, Box 1, File 15). Archives and Special Collections, American University of Beirut, Beirut, Lebanon.

Attieh, E. (1906, February 8). *Why? Why? Why?* لماذا[*Why? Why? Why?*] (G. Seifeddine, Trans.) [Article published in المنتهون (*al-Muntahoun* or *The Terminators*)]. AUB Students' Magazine Collection 1899–1934. (AA: 4.2.1, Series I, Box 8). Archives and Special Collections, American University of Beirut, Beirut, Lebanon.

---

[1]   This word could also be translated as "the conditions." It is difficult to know what is most accurate without the original.

[2]   The transliteration of this title is probably incorrect—a better transliteration would be *Nizam* to reflect a kasra, not fatha, over the noon. The translation of this title could also be "method, "regulation," or "arrangement." It is difficult to know the most accurate translation since the original copies of these journals/articles were not preserved.

Attieh, I. (1901, November 14). المقدمة[*Introduction*] (G. Seifeddine, Trans.) [Article published in الحظ (*al-Haz* or *Luck*)]. AUB Students' Magazine Collection 1899–1934. (AA: 4.2.1, Series I, Box 4). Archives and Special Collections, American University of Beirut, Beirut, Lebanon.

Awad, J.-U. (1919, March). *Editorial: This is our class gazette* [Article published in *Cedar*]. AUB Students' Magazine Collection 1899–1934 (AA: 4.2.1, Series II). American U of Beirut/Library Archives, Beirut, Lebanon.

Bliss, D. (1866–1902). *Correspondence from David Stuart Dodge to Daniel Bliss (34 letters)*. Daniel Bliss Collection (AA: 2.3.1, Series 2, Box 3, File 2). Archives and Special Collections, American University of Beirut, Beirut, Lebanon.

Bliss, D. (1989). Reminiscences: The founding of the Syrian Protestant College, 1861–1866. In C. S. Coon, Jr. (Ed.), *Daniel Bliss and the founding of the American University of Beirut* (pp. 65–72). Middle East Institute. (Original work published 1920)

Bliss, H. (1909a, April). *The recent difficulty in connection with the religious instruction and worship in the Syrian Protestant College, Beirut, Syria* [Posted policy on religious instruction on the bulletin board in the library]. Students 1900s (AA: 4.3.2, Box 1). Archives and Special Collections, American University of Beirut, Beirut, Lebanon.

Bliss, H. (1909b, April 8). *To the members of the Board of Trustees* [Letter summarizing the 1909 crisis for the SPC Board of Trustees]. Students 1900s (AA: 4.3.2, Box 1). Archives and Special Collections, American University of Beirut, Beirut, Lebanon.

Boulous, N. (1899, June 15). مقالة في العلم والعمل [*An article on science and progress*] (G. Seifeddine, Trans.) [Article published in المبدأ الصحيح (*al-Mabda al-Saheeh* or *The Right Principle*)]. AUB Students' Magazine Collection 1899–1934 (AA: 4.2.1, Series I, Box 2). Archives and Special Collections, American University of Beirut, Beirut, Lebanon.15 June 1899.

The college and the Moslem students. (1909, February 23). [Previously translated article in *Ittehad* (الاتحاد or *The Union*)]. Students 1900s (AA: 4.3.2, Box 1, File 15). Archives and Special Collections, American University of Beirut, Beirut, Lebanon.

The college in Beirut and Islam. (1909, January 28). [Previously translated article in *Lewa* (اللواء or *The Major-General*)]. Students 1900s (AA: 4.3.2, Box 1, File 15). Archives and Special Collections, American University of Beirut, Beirut, Lebanon.

The Committee of the Moslem Students in the Syrian Christian College. (1909, July 20). *Complaint from the Moslem student body to the Ottomans* [Previously translated article in *Mufid* (المفيد or *The Useful*[3]]. Students 1900x (AA: 4.3.2, Box 1, File 15). Archives and Special Collections, American University of Beirut, Beirut, Lebanon.

The Committee on Discipline. (1909). [Handwritten report and recommendations to the faculty]. Students 1900s (AA: 4.3.2, Box 1). Archives and Special Collections, American University of Beirut, Beirut, Lebanon.

---

3   This word could also mean "beneficiary" or "profitable."

Dodge, D. S. (1909, February 4). *Letter to the Secretary of State from Dr. Dodge*. Students 1900s (AA: 4.3.2, Box 1, File 10). Archives and Special Collections, American University of Beirut, Beirut, Lebanon.

Editorial. (1903, May 26). [Article in *Miltonian*]. AUB Students' Magazine Collection 1899–1934 (AA: 4.2.1, Series I, Box 6). Archives and Special Collections, American University of Beirut, Beirut, Lebanon.

Editorial. (1907, April 27). [Article in *Life of Service*]. AUB Students' Magazine Collection 1899–1934 (AA: 4.2.1, Series I, Box 11). Archives and Special Collections, American University of Beirut, Beirut, Lebanon.

ارتقاء التهذيب في سورية [*Elevating civility in Syria*]. (1903, April 28). (G. Seifeddine, Trans.) [Speech published in الحديقة (*al-Hadiqa* or *The Garden*)]. Students' Magazine Collection 1899–1934 (AA: 4.2.1, Series I, Box 4). Archives and Special Collections, American University of Beirut, Beirut, Lebanon.

El-Ghalieni. (1909, January 22). *Foreign schools in the Ottoman Empire* [Previously translated article in *Ittehad* (الاتحاد or *The Union*)]. Students 1900s (AA: 4.3.2, Box 1, File 15). Archives and Special Collections, American University of Beirut, Beirut, Lebanon.

El-Khairi, M. A. S. (1906, April). *Union club . . .* [Article in *Light*]. AUB Students' Magazine Collection 1899–1934 (AA: 4.2.1, Series I, Box 4). Archives and Special Collections, American University of Beirut, Beirut, Lebanon.

A former student of SPC. (1909, August 19). *Knowledge rather than ignorance* [Previously translated article in *Mukattam*[4] (المقدم or *The Presenter*)]. Students 1900s (AA: 4.3.2, Box 1, File 15). Archives and Special Collections, American University of Beirut, Beirut, Lebanon.

Fouad. (1900a, January 8). الألقاب [*Titles*] (G. Seifeddine, Trans.) [Article published in غادة الفكر (*Ghada al-Fakr* or *Graceful Thought*)]. AUB Students' Magazines Collection, 1899–1934 (AA: 4.2.1, Series I, Box 3). Archives and Special Collections, American University of Beirut, Beirut, Lebanon.

Fouad. (1900b, March 1). حب الوطن [*Patriotism*] (G. Seifeddine, Trans.) [Article published in غادة الفكر (*Ghada al-Fakr* or *Graceful Thought*)]. AUB Students' Magazine Collection 1899–1934 (AA: 4.2.1, Series I, Box 3). Archives and Special Collections, American University of Beirut, Beirut, Lebanon.

The founding of the college, 1862–1866. (n.d.). History of Syrian Protestant College/American University of Beirut: General (AA: 1.6.1, Box 1, File 4). Archives and Special Collections, American University of Beirut, Beirut, Lebanon.

A Friend of the College. (1909, May). *The crisis in the Syrian Protestant College at Beirut* [News article in *Missionary Review of the World*]. Students 1900s (AA: 4.3.2, Box 1, File 15). Archives and Special Collections, American University of Beirut, Beirut, Lebanon.

---

4   Although the transliteration indicates a ت, this is probably inaccurate based on the context. A better transliteration to reflect a word that would make sense as a magazine/newspaper title would be *Mukadam*. The translation is based on the assumption that this is probably the word reflected in the original.

Haddad, K. (1906). *The B.A. degree* [Article in *Zion*]. AUB Students' Magazine Collection 1899–1934 (AA: 4.2.1, Series I, Box 9). Archives and Special Collections, American University of Beirut, Beirut, Lebanon.

Hall, W. (presumed). (1909, Febuary 5). *Report of the "strike" from the students' point*. Students 1900s. (AA: 4.3.1, Box 1, File 12). Archives and Special Collections, American University of Beirut, Beirut, Lebanon.

Hantes, F. (1909, July 31). *The vigor of the new youth (Maybe: The New Flourishing, Al Nubt al Jadeed).* [Previously translated article in *Al Mufid*[5] (المفيد or *The Useful*)]. Students 1900s (AA: 4.3.2, Box 1, File 15). Archives and Special Collections, American University of Beirut, Beirut, Lebanon.

Happy Days of SPC. (1903–1905). AUB Students' Magazine Collection 1899–1934 (AA: 4.2.1, Series I, Box 7). Archives and Special Collections, American University of Beirut, Beirut, Lebanon.

Hilal, A. B. (1906, Feb. 6). *Patriotism vs. Syria* [Article in *Syria*]. AUB Students' Magazine Collection 1899–1934 (AA: 4.2.1, Series I, Box 8). Archives and Special Collections, American University of Beirut, Beirut, Lebanon.

Himmet. (1909a). *Is this journalism?* [Previously translated article in *Ittehad* (الاتحاد or *The Union*)]. Students 1900s (AA: 4.3.2, Box 1, File 15). Archives and Special Collections, American University of Beirut, Beirut, Lebanon.

Himmet. (1909b, February 25). *What they say about the Moslem students* [Previously translated article in *Ittehad* (الاتحاد or *The Union*)]. Students 1900s (AA: 4.3.2, Box 1, File 15). Archives and Special Collections, American University of Beirut, Beirut, Lebanon.

In lighter vein. (1909, January 19). [Previously translated article in *Ittehad* (الاتحاد or *The Union*)]. Students 1900s (AA: 4.3.2, Box 1, File 15). Archives and Special Collections, American University of Beirut, Beirut, Lebanon.

الفاتحة [*Introduction*]. (1905, November 24). (G. Seifeddine, Trans.) [Article in المنتهون (*al-Muntahoun* or *The Terminators*)]. AUB Students' Magazine Collection 1899–1934 (AA: 4.2.1, Series I, Box 8). Archives and Special Collections, American University of Beirut, Beirut, Lebanon.

Introduction. (1906, January 17). [Article in *The Business Amanuensis*]. AUB Students' Magazine Collection 1899–1934. (AA: 4.2.1, Series I, Box 10). Archives and Special Collections, American University of Beirut, Beirut, Lebanon.

مقدمة [*Introduction*]. (1910, March). (G. Seifeddine, Trans.) [Article in النهضة الإصلاحية (*al-Nahda al-Islahiya* or *The Reformist Movement*)]. AUB Students' Magazine Collection 1899–1934 (AA: 4.2.1, Series I, Box 11). Archives and Special Collections, American University of Beirut, Beirut, Lebanon.

Introduction. (1911, February). [Article in *The Business Man*]. AUB Students' Magazine Collection 1899–1934 (AA: 4.2.1, Series II). Archives and Special Collections, American University of Beirut, Beirut, Lebanon.

---

5   The title of this journal is inconsistently transliterated, sometimes with "Al" (indicating the definite article الـ) and sometimes without. The translation reflects the assumption that the original title probably included the definite article.

Karlvas, A.D. [likely pseudonym]. (1904, May). *Current events throughout the world*. [Article in *SPC Commercial Paper*]. AUB Students' Magazine Collection 1899–1934 (AA: 4.2.1, Series I, Box 7). Archives and Special Collections, American University of Beirut, Beirut, Lebanon.

Laurie, T. (1862). *Historical sketch of the Syria mission*. American Board of Commissioners for Foreign Missions. https://hdl.handle.net/2027/njp.32101033550722.

الجرائد [Magazines]. (1903, February 2). (G. Seifeddine, Trans.) [Article in حسناء الكلية (*Hasnaa' al-Kulliyah* or *Beauty of the College*)]. AUB Students' Magazine Collection 1899–1934 (AA: 4.2.1, box 6). Archives and Special Collections, American University of Beirut, Beirut, Lebanon.

Makarius, I. (1903–1904). *The Kodak*. AUB Students' Magazine Collection 1899–1934. (AA: 4.2.1, Series I, Box 7). Archives and Special Collections, American University of Beirut, Beirut, Lebanon.

The Mohammedan nation. (ca. 1909). Students 1900s (AA: 4.3.2, Box 1). Archives and Special Collections, American University of Beirut, Beirut, Lebanon.

Moore, F. (1909a, January 25). [Speech to faculty.] Students 1900s. (AA: 4.3.2, Box 1, File 11), Archives and Special Collections, American University of Beirut, Beirut, Lebanon.

Moore, F. (1909b, February 5). [Letter to Howard Bliss]. Students 1900s. (AA: 4.3.2, Box 1, File 13). Archives and Special Collections, American University of Beirut, Beirut, Lebanon.

The Moslems in the American college, Beirut. (1909, January 21). [Previously translated article in *Moweyid* (المؤيد or *The Advocate*)]. Students 1900 (AA: 4.3.2, Box 1, File 15). Archives and Special Collections, American University of Beirut, Beirut, Lebanon.

Nassar, N. (1903, February 22). كلمة لأبناء العربية [*A Word to the children of the Arabic language*] (G. Seifeddine, Trans.) [Article in حسناء الكلية (*Hasnaa' al-Kulliyah* or *Beauty of the College*)]. AUB Students' Magazine Collection 1899–1934 (AA: 4.2.1, Series I, Box 6). Archives and Special Collections, American University of Beirut, Beirut, Lebanon.

Nickoley, E. (1909, January 20). [Letter to Howard Bliss]. Students 1900s (AA: 4.3.2, Box 1, File 9). Archives and Special Collections, American University of Beirut, Beirut, Lebanon.

مفاخر الرجال [*The pride of men*]. (1900, March 26). (G. Seifeddine, Trans.) [Article in زهرة الكلية (*Zahra al-Kulliyah* or *Flower of the College*)]. AUB Students' Magazine Collection 1899–1934 (AA: 4.2.1, Series I, Box 3). Archives and Special Collections, American University of Beirut, Beirut, Lebanon.

سؤال نوجهه للأساتذة [*Question directed to the teachers*]. (1905, November 24). (G. Seifeddine, Trans.) [Article in المنتهون (*al-Muntahoon* or *The Terminators*)]. AUB Students' Magazine Collection 1899–1934 (AA: 4.2.1, Series I, Box 8). Archives and Special Collections, American University of Beirut, Beirut, Lebanon.

Risgalla, M. (1904, May). *My dearest Japan* [Poem in *SPC Commercial Paper*]. AUB Students' Magazine Collection 1899–1934 (AA: 4.2.1, Series I, Box 7). Archives and Special Collections, American University of Beirut, Beirut, Lebanon.

Salim. (1908, September 27). [Previously translated letter to President Howard Bliss in *Ittehad* (الاتحاد or *The Union*)]. Students 1900s (AA: 4.3.2, Box 1, File 15). Archives and Special Collections, American University of Beirut, Beirut, Lebanon.

Sayegh, H. K. (1902, Feb. 3). وفاة الشرق [*Death of the East*] (G. Seifeddine, Trans.) [Article in الاستعدادية (*Sada al-Isti'dadiyah* or *Elementary Echo*)]. AUB Students' Magazine Collection 1899–1934 (AA: 4.2.1, Series I, Box 5). Archives and Special Collections, American University of Beirut, Beirut, Lebanon.

Sherwood, J. M. & Pierson, A. T. (1887). Prospectus of the review for 1888. *Missionary Review of the World*, *1*(1), pp. 1–3. https://cafis.org/files/MRW-1888-1.pdf.

The strike of the Moslem students, in the American college. (1909, January 26). [Previously translated article in *Moweyid* (المؤيد or *The Advocate*)]. Students 1900s (AA: 4.3.2, Box 1, File 15). Archives and Special Collections, American University of Beirut, Beirut, Lebanon.

A Student in the College. (1909, July 30). *The American college and foreign schools*. [Previously translated handwritten letter in *Ittehad* (الاتحاد or *The Union*)]. Students 1900s (AA: 4.3.2, Box 1, File 15). Archives and Special Collections, American University of Beirut, Beirut, Lebanon.

[Student reply to faculty]. (ca. 1909, March). Students 1900s (AA: 4.3.2, Box 1). Archives and Special Collections, American University of Beirut, Beirut, Lebanon.

A Syrian. (1905, December). *An open Letter to the Syrian teachers* [Article in *Pioneers of SPC: A Monthly Review*]. AUB Students' Magazine Collection 1899–1934 (AA: 4.2.1, Series I, Box 8). Archives and Special Collections, American University of Beirut, Beirut, Lebanon.

كتاب (1871). [Syrian Protestant College (Beirut)]. المدرسة السورية السورية الإنجيلية (بيروت). *Catalogue* المدرسة الكلية السورية الإنجيلية، بيروت / المدرسة الكلية السورية الإنجيلية السنوي. *of the Syrian Protestant College*] (CA:PA:AUB 378:K461kA:1871: c. 1). Archives and Special Collections, American University of Beirut, Beirut, Lebanon.

[Syrian Protestant College (Beirut)]. المدرسة الكلية السورية الإنجيلية (بيروت). (1872–1873). كتاب المدرسة الكلية السورية الإنجيلية السنوي / المدرسة الكلية السورية. *Catalogue of the Syrian Protestant College*] الإنجيلية، بيروت. (CA:PA:AUB 378:K461kA:1872-1873: c. 1–2). Archives and Special Collections, American University of Beirut, Beirut, Lebanon.

Syrian Protestant College. (1880–1920). *Catalogue of the Syrian Protestant College*. (CA:P:AUB v. 1–6). Archives and Special Collections, American University of Beirut, Beirut, Lebanon.

Syrian Protestant College. (1867–1920). *Minutes of faculty meetings of the Syrian Protestant College & the American University of Beirut*. (AA: 3.4.2, Series I). Archives and Special Collections, American University of Beirut, Beirut, Lebanon.

Thabit, A. (ca. 1909). [Previously translated summary of 1909 student movement in *Al-Ahwal*, (الأحوال or *The Circumstances*)]. Students 1900s (AA: 4.3.2, Box 1, File 15. Archives and Special Collections, American University of Beirut, Beirut, Lebanon.

[*To the dean managing the college's school in Beirut*]الى عمدة إدارة المدرسة الكلّية في بيروت. (1882, December 4). (Y. Hamade, Trans.) [Handwritten student petition].

Edwin Lewis Affair Collection (AA6.1, Series IV, Box 1, File 3), Archives and Special Collections, American University of Beirut, Beirut, Lebanon.

Towfik, S. (1909, January 23). *Bigotry in the American college*. [Previously translated article in *Ittehad* (الاتحاد or *The Union*)]. Students 1900s (AA: 4.3.2, Box 1, File 15). Archives and Special Collections, American University of Beirut, Beirut, Lebanon.

The triumvirate will be glad. . . . (1906, January 29). [Article in *The Commercial Triumvirate: A Tri-Weekly Review of Commercial, Social, and Economical Discussion*]. AUB Students' Magazine Collection 1899–1934 (AA: 4.2.1, Series I, Box 8). Archives and Special Collections, American University of Beirut, Beirut, Lebanon.

تنبيه الضمير [*Warning to the conscience*]. (1901, December 5). (G. Seifeddine, Trans.) [Article published in الحظ (*al-Haz* or *Luck*)]. AUB Students' Magazine Collection 1899–1934. (AA: 4.2.1, Series I, Box 4). Archives and Special Collections, American University of Beirut, Beirut, Lebanon.

With this opening number . . . (1910, February). *Al-Kulliyah*. AUB Students' Magazine Collection 1899–1934 (AA: 4.2.1, Series I). Archives and Special Collections, American University of Beirut, Beirut, Lebanon.

A Witness. (1909, September 17). *The American college and the freedom of religion and instruction* [Previously translated article in Al-Watan (الوطن, or *The Homeland*)]. Students 1900s (AA: 4.3.2, Box 1, File 15). Archives and Special Collections, American University of Beirut, Beirut, Lebanon.

Zahlan, A. B. (1962). *The American University of Beirut: An essay* [Typescript]. Archives and Special Collections (AUB 378.5692:Z19a:c.1), American University of Beirut, Beirut, Lebanon.

Zakhariya, M. (1909, February 3). *No danger to Islam* [Previously translated article in *Moweyid* (المؤيد or *The Advocate*)]. Students 1900s (AA: 4.3.2, Box 1, File 15). Archives and Special Collections, American University of Beirut, Beirut, Lebanon.

Zeidan, J. (1924–1925). وفيها تاريخ أول ثورة مدرسية في العالم العربي : تذكارات المدرسة [*School mementos: The history of the first school rebellion in the Arab world*] (C. Hodroj, Trans.) [Published in *Al-Hilal* v. 33]. Archives and Special Collections, American University of Beirut, Beirut, Lebanon.

Zein, S. M. (1902, June). *I. O. U. 5 minutes: A monthly review of "criticism" closing with a "French supplement" and an "Arabic" one.* AUB Students' Magazine Collection 1899–1934 (AA: 4.2.1, Series I, Box 4). Archives and Special Collections, American University of Beirut, Beirut, Lebanon.

Zeki, M. (1909, Feb. 3). *The Beirut college and Islam* [Previously translated article in *Lewa* (اللواء or *The Major-General*)]. Students 1900s (AA: 4.3.2, Box 1, File 15). Archives and Special Collections, American University of Beirut, Beirut, Lebanon.

Secondary Sources

1860 civil conflict in Mount Lebanon and Damascus. (2025, May 25). In *Wikipedia*. https://en.wikipedia.org/w/index.php?title=1860_civil_conflict_in_Mount _Lebanon_and_Damascus&oldid=1292121353.

Ahmadi, M. (2023). Semicolonial viscerality: *Gharbzadegi* and the geopolitics of sensing. In R. García, E. Cushman & D. Baca (Eds.), *Pluriversal literacies: Tools for perseverance and livable futures* (pp. 196–208). University of Pittsburgh Press.

American University of Beirut. (n.d.). *Accreditation and quality assurance*. Retrieved May 20, 2025, from https://www.aub.edu.lb/accreditation/Pages/default.aspx.

American University of Beirut Libraries. (2025, April 4). *Al-Nahda (Arabic Renaissance)* النهضة العربية: *Societies*. https://aub.edu.lb.libguides.com/Al-Nahda/Societies.

American University of Beirut Libraries. (2023). *Founding of the Syrian Protestant College (SPC) later known as the American University of Beirut (AUB)*. https://online-exhibit.aub.edu.lb/exhibits/show/founders--legacy---honoring-th/----founding-of-the-syrian-pro.

Anderson, B. (2006). *Imagined communities: Reflections on the origin and spread of nationalism*. Verso.

Anderson, B. S. (2011). *The American University of Beirut: Arab nationalism and liberal education*. University of Texas Press.

Arneil, B. (2023). Colonialism versus imperialism. *Political Theory, 52*(1), 146–176. https://doi.org/10.1177/00905917231193107.

Arnold, L. R. (2014). "The worst part of the dead past": Language attitudes, policies, and pedagogies at Syrian Protestant College, 1866–1902. *College Composition and Communication, 66*(2), 276–300. https://doi.org/10.58680/ccc201426225.

Arnold, L. (2016). An imagined America: Rhetoric and identity during the "first student rebellion in the Arab world". *College English, 78*(6), 578–601. https://doi.org/10.58680/ce201628628.

Arnold, L. R. (2018). "Today the need arises" اليوم موق دق مسّت الحاجة: Arabic student writing at the turn of the 20th century. In You, X. (Ed.), *Transnational writing education: Theory, history, practice* (pp. 95–111). Routledge.

Arnold, L. R. (2021). Weighing English: Accounting for power in translingual writing. In T. Silva & Z. Wang (Eds.), *Reconciling translingualism and second language writing* (pp. 189–198). Routledge.

Arola, K. L. (2018). Composing as culturing: An American Indian approach to digital ethics. In K. A. Mills, A. Stornaiuolo, A. Smith & J. Z. Pandya (Eds.), *Handbook of writing, literacies, and education in digital cultures* (pp. 275–284). Routledge.

Aull, L. & Shapiro, S. (2023). *FAQs about language and linguistics in writing*. The WAC Clearinghouse. https://wac.colostate.edu/repository/articles/faqs-about-language-and-linguistics-in-writing/.

Baca, D. (2009). The Chicano codex: Writing against historical and pedagogical colonization. *College English, 71*(6), 564–583. https://doi.org/10.58680/ce20097168.

Bailey, E. (2020). *Separation of church and state: Overview*. EBSCO. https://www.ebsco.com/research-starters/law/separation-church-and-state-overview.

Baktiaya, A. (2008). The Ottoman-French domination struggle over the Syrian-Lebanon territory: The case of St. Joseph Medical School. *International Journal of Turcologia, 3*(6), 69–94.

Bazerman, C., Dean, C., Early, J., Lunsford, K., Null, S., Rogers, P. & Stansell, A. (2012). *International advances in writing research: Cultures, places, measures.* The WAC Clearinghouse; Parlor Press. https://doi.org/10.37514/PER-B.2012.0452.

Berlin, J. A. (1980). Richard Whately and current-traditional rhetoric. *College English, 42*(1), 10–17. https://doi.org/10.58680/ce198013871.

Berlin, J. A. (1984). *Writing instruction in nineteenth-century American colleges.* Conference on College Composition and Communication; Southern Illinois University Press.

Berlin, J. A. (1987). *Rhetoric and reality: Writing instruction in American colleges, 1900–1985.* Conference on College Composition and Communication; Southern Illinois University Press.

Bhatia, A., Cabreros, I., Elkeurti, A. & Singer, E. (2025, May 22). Trump has cut science funding to its lowest level in decades. *The New York Times.* https://www.nytimes.com/interactive/2025/05/22/upshot/nsf-grants-trump-cuts.html?unlocked_article_code=1.VE8.KXKi.OWrv2kQLVS6d&smid=url-share.

Bizzaro, R. C. & Bizzaro, P. (2023). The language of imitation: A pedagogy of representations. In R. García, E. Cushman & D. Baca (Eds.), *Pluriversal literacies: Tools for perseverance and livable futures* (pp. 135–155). University of Pittsburgh Press.

Bloom, T. (2018). Citizenship and colonialism: Liberal concepts of citizenship are not adequate for understanding contemporary individual-state relationships. *Soundings: A journal of politics and culture, 67,* 114-127. https://muse.jhu.edu/article/685603.

Bonnett, A. (2004). *The idea of the West: Culture, politics and history.* Palgrave Macmillan.

Bou Ayash, N. (2016). Conditions of (im)possibility: Postmonolingual language representations in academic literacies. *College English, 78*(6), 555–577. https://doi.org/10.58680/cc201628627.

Bou Ayash, N. (2019). *Toward translingual realities in composition: (Re)working local language representations and practices.* Utah State University Press.

Bou Ayash, N. (2021). Beyond disciplinary divides: Coming to terms with the centrality of translation. In T. Silva & Z. Wang (Eds.), *Reconciling translingualism and second language writing* (pp. 199–209). Routledge.

Brereton, J. C. (Ed.). (1995). *The origins of composition studies in the American college, 1875-1925: A documentary history.* University of Pittsburgh Press.

Campbell, J. (1992a). Controlling voices: The legacy of English A at Radcliffe College 1883–1917. *College Composition and Communication, 43*(4), 472–485. https://doi.org/10.58680/ccc19928853.

Campbell, J. (1992b). Women's work, worthy work: Composition instruction at Vassar College, 1897–1922. In M. Secor & D. Charney (Eds.), *Constructing rhetorical education* (pp. 26–42). Southern Illinois University Press.

Canagarajah, A. S. (2006). *Geopolitics of academic writing.* University of Pittsburgh Press, 2002.

Canagarajah, A. S. (2013). Negotiating translingual literacy: An enactment. *Research in the Teaching of English, 48*(1), 40–67. https://doi.org/10.58680/rte201324158.

Canagarajah, S. (2018). Transnationalism and translingualism: How they are connected. In X. You (Ed.), *Transnational writing education: Theory, history, and practice* (pp. 41–60). Routledge.

Canagarajah, S. (2019). Weaving the text: Changing literacy practices and orientations. *College English, 82*(1), 7–28. https://doi.org/10.58680/ce201930302.

Canagarajah, S. (2023). Decolonization as pedagogy: A praxis of 'becoming' in ELT. *ELT Journal, 77*(3), 283–293. https://doi.org/10.1093/elt/ccad017.

Canagarajah, S. (2024). Decolonizing academic writing pedagogies for multilingual students. *TESOL Quarterly, 58*(1), 280–306. https://doi.org/10.1002/tesq.3231.

Carr, J. F., Carr, S. L. & Schultz, L. (2005). *Archives of instruction: Nineteenth-century rhetorics, readers, and composition books in the United States.* Southern Illinois University Press.

Case, J. (2024, March 20). *Push for terminology change: Middle East.* Arabizi Translations. https://www.arabizitranslations.com/blog/push-for-terminology-change-middle-east.

Christian Archives for Islamic Studies. (n.d.). *Missionary Review of the World.* Retrieved June 9, 2025, from https://cafis.org/periodicals/missionary-review.html.

Clark, G. & Halloran, S. M. (1993). Introduction: Transformations of public discourse in nineteenth-century America. In G. Clark & S. M. Halloran (Eds.), *Oratorical culture in nineteenth-century America: Transformations in the theory and practice of rhetoric.* Southern Illinois University Press.

Conceison, C. (2004). *Significant other: Staging the American in China.* University of Hawai'i Press.

Conference on College Composition and Communication. (n.d.). *CCCC Richard Braddock award.* Retrieved May 26, 2025, from https://cccc.ncte.org/cccc/awards/braddock.

Conference on College Composition and Communication. (2017, November). *CCCC statement on globalization in writing studies pedagogy and research.* https://cccc.ncte.org/cccc/resources/positions/globalization.

Connell, R. (2020). *Southern theory: The global dynamics of knowledge in social science.* Routledge. https://doi.org/10.4324/9781003117346.

Connors, R. J. (1981). Current-traditional rhetoric: Thirty years of *Writing with a Purpose. Rhetoric Society Quarterly, 11*(4), 208–221. https://doi.org/10.1080/02773948109390614.

Connors, R. J. (1986). The rhetoric of mechanical correctness. In T. Newkirk (Ed.), *Only connect: Uniting reading and writing* (pp. 27–58). Boynton/Cook.

Connors, R. J. (1997). *Composition-Rhetoric: Backgrounds, theory, and pedagogy.* University of Pittsburgh Press.

Crowley, S. (1986). The current-traditional theory of style: An informal history. *Rhetoric Society Quarterly, 16*(4), 233–250. https://doi.org/10.1080/02773948609390752.

Crowley, S. (1990). *The methodical memory: Invention in current-traditional rhetoric.* Southern Illinois University Press.

Crowley, S. (1998). *Composition in the university.* University of Pittsburgh Press.

Cushman, E. (2016). Translingual and decolonial approaches to meaning making. *College English, 78(3)*, 234–242. https://doi.org/10.58680/ce201627654.

Cushman, E. (2021). Decolonial translation as methodology for learning to unlearn. In K. Blewett, T. Donahue & C. Moore, C. (Eds.), *The expanding universe of writing studies: Higher education writing research* (pp. 199–212). Peter Lang. https://www.peterlang.com/document/1062242.

Cushman, E., Baca, D. & García, R. (2021). Delinking: Toward pluriversal rhetorics. *College English, 84(1)*, 7–32. https://doi.org/10.58680/ce202131450.

Cushman, E. & Juzwik, M. (Eds.). (2014). [Special issue]. *Research in the Teaching of English, 49(1)*. https://publicationsncte.org/content/journals/rte/49/1.

Cushman, E. W., Juzwik, M., Macaluso, K. & Milu, E. (2015). Editors' introduction: Decolonizing research in the teaching of English(es). *Research in the Teaching of English, 49(4)*, 333–339. https://doi.org/10.58680/rte201527346.

Dajani, N. H. (1992). *Disoriented media in a fragmented society: The Lebanese experience.* American University of Beirut Press.

Dawn, C. E. (1991). The origins of Arab nationalism. In R. Khalidi, L. Anderson, M. Muslih & R. S. Simon (Eds.), *The origins of Arab nationalism* (pp. 3–30). Columbia University Press.

Dayton-Wood, A. (2012). "What the college has done for me": Anzia Yezierska and the problem of progressive education. *College English, 74(3)*, 215–233. https://doi.org/10.58680/ce201218408.

deTar, M. (2022). Decolonizing rhetorical history. In Turner, K. J. & Black, J. E. (Eds.), *Reframing rhetorical history: Cases, theories, and methodologies* (pp. 192–211). University of Alabama Press.

Diab, R. (2024). Holding memory, reclaiming time: Women's biographies and archives in the Arab(ic)-Islamic world. In J. Rhodes & S. N. Cooley (Eds.), *The Routledge handbook of contemporary feminist rhetoric* (pp. 34–43). Routledge.

Diab, R. (2025). (Vernacular) rhetorics for women's rights. In B. N. Larson & E. C. Britt (Eds.), *Rhetorical traditions and contemporary law* (pp. 181–204). Cambridge University Press. https://doi.org/10.1017/9781009524087.013.

Dingo, R. (2012). *Networking arguments: Rhetoric, transnational feminism, and public policy writing.* University of Pittsburgh Press.

Do, T. H. (2022). Knowing with our bodies: An embodied and racialized approach to translingualism. *College English, 84(5)*, 447–466. https://doi.org/10.58680/ce202231906.

Do, T. & Rowan, K. (Eds.). (2022). *Racing translingualism in composition: Toward a race-conscious translingualism.* Utah State University Press.

Donahue, C. (2009). "Internationalization" and composition studies: Reorienting the discourse. *College Composition and Communication, 61(2)*, 212–243. https://doi.org/10.58680/ccc20099470.

Donahue, P. (2007). Disciplinary histories: A meditation on beginnings. In P. Donahue & G. F. Moon (Eds.), *Local histories: Reading the archives of composition* (pp. 220–236). University of Pittsburgh Press.

Donahue, P. & Moon, G. F. (Eds.). (2007). *Local histories: Reading the archives of composition.* University of Pittsburgh Press.

References

Elshakry, M. (2010). When science became Western: Historiographical reflections. *Isis, 101*(1), 98–109. https://doi.org/10.1086/652691.

Elshakry, M. (2011). The gospel of science and American evangelism in late Ottoman Beirut. In M. A. Doğan & H. J. Sharkey (Eds.), *American missionaries and the Middle East: Foundational encounters* (pp. 167–210). University of Utah Press.

Engelson, A. (2014). The "hands of God" at work: Negotiating between Western and religious sponsorship in Indonesia. *College English, 76*(4), 292–314. https://doi.org/10.58680/ce201424596.

Engelson, A. (2024). *The hands of God at work: Islamic gender justice through translingual praxis*. National Council of Teachers of English.

Enoch, J. (2008). *Refiguring rhetorical education: Women teaching African American, Native American, and Chicano/a students, 1865–1911*. Southern Illinois University Press.

Enoch, J. & Ramírez, C. D. (2019). *Mestiza rhetorics: An anthology of Mexicana activism in the Spanish-language press, 1887–1922*. Southern Illinois University Press.

Epps-Robertson, C. (2018). *Resisting Brown: Race, literacy, and citizenship in the heart of Virginia*. University of Pittsburgh Press.

Espina, T. (2023). *I* is for *Isla*: (Pre/ap)positioning the decolonial rhetorics of Filipinos on Guåhan. In R. García, E. Cushman & D. Baca (Eds.), *Pluriversal literacies: Tools for perseverance and livable futures* (pp. 209–226). University of Pittsburgh Press.

Evans, S. (2002). Macaulay's Minute revisited: Colonial language policy in nineteenth-century India. *Journal of Multilingual and Multicultural Development, 23*(4), 260–281. https://doi.org/10.1080/01434630208666469.

Farag, N. (1972). The Lewis affair and the fortunes of al-Muqtataf. *Middle Eastern Studies, 8*(1), 73–83. https://doi.org/10.1080/00263207208700195.

Faroqhi, S. (2009). *The Ottoman Empire: A short history* (S. Frisch, Trans.). Markus Wiener Publishers. (Original work published 2004)

Ferguson, S. (2018). "A fever for an education": Pedagogical thought and social transformation in Beirut and Mount Lebanon, 1861–1914. *The Arab Studies Journal, 26*(1), 58–83. https://www.jstor.org/stable/26528991.

Fitzgerald, K. (2001). A rediscovered tradition: European pedagogy and composition in nineteenth-century midwestern normal schools. *College Composition and Communication, 53*(2), 224–250. https://doi.org/10.58680/ccc20011449.

Fogarty, D. (1959). *Roots for a new rhetoric*. Teacher's College, Columbia University.

Fortna, B. C. (2002). *Imperial classroom: Islam, the state, and education in the late Ottoman Empire*. Oxford University Press. https://doi.org/10.1093/oso/9780199248407.001.0001.

Fraiberg, S. (2017). Pretty bullets: Tracing transmedia/translingual literacies of an Israeli soldier across regimes of practice. *College Composition and Communication, 69*(1), 87–117. https://doi.org/10.58680/ccc201729297.

Fredlund, K. (2021). A feminist and antiracist history of composition and rhetoric at Oberlin College (1846–1851). *College Composition and Communication, 72*(3), 413–439. https://doi.org/10.58680/ccc202131161.

Galler, R. W., Jr. (2011). Indian missionaries. In D. J. Wishart (Ed.), *Encyclopedia of the Great Plains*. University of Nebraska-Lincoln. https://plainshumanities.unl.edu/encyclopedia/doc/egp.rel.027.html.

García, R. (2021). Decolonizing the rhetoric of church-settlers. *Across the Disciplines: A Journal of Language, Learning, and Academic Writing, 18*(1/2), 124-144. https://doi.org/10.37514/ATD-J.2021.18.1-2.11.

García, R., Cushman, E. & Baca, D. (Eds.). (2023). *Pluriversal literacies: Tools for perseverance and livable futures*. University of Pittsburgh Press.

Gilyard, K. (2016). The rhetoric of translingualism. *College English, 78*(3), 284–289. https://doi.org/10.58680/ce201627660.

Global Ministries. (2023). Timeline of global mission in the USA. *Global Ministries*. https://www.globalministries.org/resource/timeline_of_mission/.

Gold, D. (2008). *Rhetoric at the margins: Revising the history of writing instruction in American colleges, 1873–1947*. Southern Illinois University Press.

Goldsmith, O. (2025). *The deserted village*. Poetry Foundation. https://www.poetryfoundation.org/poems/44292/the-deserted-village (Original work published in 1770).

Green, N. (2020, December 8). The most influential magazine in Muslim history? *Los Angeles Review of Books*. https://lareviewofbooks.org/article/the-most-influential-magazine-in-muslim-history/.

Greer, J. (1999). "No smiling Madonna": Marian Wharton and the struggle to construct a critical pedagogy for the working class, 1914–1917. *College Composition and Communication, 51*(2), 248–271. https://doi.org/10.58680/ccc19991375.

Greer, J. (2015). Expanding working-class rhetorical traditions: The moonlight schools and alternative solidarities among Appalachian women, 1911 to 1920. *College English, 77*(3), 216–235. https://doi.org/10.58680/ce201526339.

Greer, J. (2023). *Unorganized women: Repetitive rhetorical labor and low-wage workers, 1834–1937*. University of Pittsburgh Press.

Haddad, M. (2002). Syrian Muslim attitudes toward foreign missionaries in the late nineteenth and twentieth centuries. In E. H. Tejirian & R. S. Simon (Eds.), *Altruism and imperialism: Western cultural and religious missions in the Middle East* (pp. 253–274). Middle East Institute.

Halloran, S. M. (1993). Rhetoric in the American college curriculum: The decline of public discourse. In V. J. Vitanza (Ed.), *Pre/Text: The first decade* (pp. 93–115). University of Pittsburgh Press. https://digital.library.pitt.edu/islandora/object/pitt%3A31735057897146 (Reprinted from "Rhetoric in the American college curriculum: The decline of public discourse," 1982, *Pre/Text, 3*(3), 245–269).

Harris, P. W. (1999). *Nothing but Christ: Rufus Anderson and the ideology of Protestant foreign missions*. Oxford University Press. https://doi.org/10.1093/oso/9780195131727.001.0001.

Haselby, S. (2015). *The origins of American religious nationalism*. Oxford University Press. https://doi.org/10.1093/acprof:oso/9780199329571.001.0001.

Hauser, J., Lindner, C. B. & Möller, E. (Eds.). (2016). *Entangled education: Foreign and local schools in Ottoman Syria and Mandate Lebanon (19th–20th centuries)*. Ergon Verlag.

Hawk, B. (2007). *A counter-history of composition: Toward methodologies of complexity*. University of Pittsburgh Press.

Helfand, J. (2020, August 3). Darwin, expression, and the lasting legacy of eugenics. *The MIT Press Reader*. https://thereader.mitpress.mit.edu/evolution-expression -and-the-lasting-legacy-of-eugenics/.

Herzstein, R. (2007). The foundation of the Saint-Joseph University of Beirut: The teaching of the Maronites by the second Jesuit mission in the Levant. *Middle Eastern Studies*, *43*(5), 749–759. https://doi.org/10.1080/00263200701422667.

Herzstein, R. (2008). Saint-Joseph University of Beirut: An enclave of the French-speaking communities in the Levant, 1875–1914. *Itinerario*, *32*(2), 67–82. https://doi.org/10.1017/S0165115300001996.

Herzstein, R. (2020). French colonial ambitions in the Levant: The creation of Saint Joseph University in Beirut (1875–1914). *Journal of Mediterranean Studies*, *29*(1), 19–33. https://muse.jhu.edu/article/779810.

Herzstein, R. (2024). St. Joseph's University in Beirut and its institutions: Places of knowledge of the Orient in the Christian East. *The Catholic Historical Review*, *110*(3), 514–534. https://doi.org/10.1353/cat.2024.a935512.

Hilberg, J. (2020). "The link between a rotting shack and a rotting America": Literacy education in the Mississippi Freedom Schools of 1964. *College English*, *82*(3), 281–300. https://doi.org/10.58680/ce202030478.

Holt, E. M. (2016). Narrating the *Nahda*: The Syrian Protestant College, *al-Muqtataf*, and the rise of Jurji Zaydan. In N. M. El-Cheikh, L. Choueiri & B. Orfali (Eds.), *One Hundred and Fifty* (pp. 273–279). American University of Beirut Press. https://doi.org/10.17613/2zbf-6z54.

Horner, B., Lu, M.-Z., Royster, J. J. & Trimbur, J. (2011). Language difference in writing: Toward a translingual approach. *College English*, *73*(3), 303–321. https://doi.org/10.58680/ce201113403.

Horner, B., NeCamp, S. & Donahue, C. (2011). Toward a multilingual composition scholarship: From English Only to a translingual norm. *College Composition and Communication*, *63*(2), 269–300. https://doi.org/10.58680/ccc201118392.

Horner, B. & Trimbur, J. (2002). English Only and U.S. college composition. *College Composition and Communication*, *53*(4), 594–630. https://doi.org/10.58680 /ccc20021465.

Hourani, A. (1983). *Arabic thought in the liberal age, 1798–1939*. Cambridge University Press. https://doi.org/10.1017/CBO9780511801990.

Hwang, I., Huang, J., Anthes, E., Migliozzi, B. & Mueller, B. (2025, June 4). The disappearing funds for global health, vaccine research, chronic diseases. *The New York Times*. https://www.nytimes.com/interactive/2025/06/04/health/trump -cuts-nih-grants-research.html?unlocked_article_code=1.VE8.BN77.qRjg3Slho Wxm&smid=url-share.

Indigenous Values Initiative. (2018, July 23). *Doctrine of Discovery project: Dum Diversas*. https://doctrineofdiscovery.org/dum-diversas/.

Issak, T. & Oweidat, L. (2023). Fulfilling Allah's trust: Rhetorics of *amanah* as a foundation for social change. In R. García, E. Cushman & D. Baca (Eds.),

Pluriversal literacies: Tools for perseverance and livable futures (pp. 185–195). University of Pittsburgh Press.

Istanbul University. (2025, 23 May). In *Wikipedia.* https://en.wikipedia.org/wiki/Istanbul_University.

Jackson, R. C. (2021). Red flags of dissent: Decoloniality, transrhetoricity, and local differences of race. *College English, 84*(1), 78–99. https://doi.org/10.58680/ce202131453.

Jackson, R. C. (2023). Decolonizing Black and Indigenous dispossession: Interculturality, transrhetoricity, and otherwise re-storying race. In R. García, E. Cushman & D. Baca (Eds.), *Pluriversal literacies: Tools for perseverance and livable futures* (pp. 71–92). University of Pittsburgh Press.

Jarratt, S. C. (2009). Classics and counterpublics in nineteenth-century historically Black colleges. *College English, 72*(2), 134–59. https://doi.org/10.58680/ce20098985.

Jeha, S. (2004). Darwin and the crisis of 1882 in the medical department and the first student protest in the Arab world, (S. Kaya, Trans.). American University of Beirut Press.

Jessup, H. H. (2002). *Fifty-three years in Syria* (Vol. 1). Garnet Publishing. (Original work published 1910)

Jeyaraj, J. (2009). Modernity and empire: A modest analysis of early colonial writing practices. *College Composition and Communication, 60*(3), 468–492. https://doi.org/10.58680/ccc20096967.

Jiang, J. (2024). Composing to enact affective agency: Engaging multimodal antiracist pedagogy in the first-year writing classroom. *College Composition and Communication, 75*(3), 534–557. https://doi.org/10.58680/ccc2024753534.

Jimenez, F. (2023). Beyond a native clearing: Translanguaging and decolonial potential at the American colonial schoolhouse. In R. García, E. Cushman & D. Baca (Eds.), *Pluriversal literacies: Tools for perseverance and livable futures* (pp. 107–120). University of Pittsburgh Press.

John, K. D. (2023). When I run, I'm not "half," I'm Diné: The pluriverse in connectedness of movement. In R. García, E. Cushman & D. Baca (Eds.), *Pluriversal literacies: Tools for perseverance and livable futures* (pp. 121–134). University of Pittsburgh Press.

Kassab, E. S. (2010). *Contemporary Arab thought: Cultural critique in comparative perspective.* Columbia University Press.

Kates, S. (2001). *Activist rhetorics and American higher education, 1885–1937.* Southern Illinois University Press.

Kendall Theado, C. (2013). Narrating a nation: Second wave immigration, literacy, and the framing of the American identity. *JAC, 33*(1–2), 711–738.

Khalaf, S. (2002). On doing much with little noise: Early encounters of Protestant missionaries in Lebanon. In E. H. Tejirian & R. S. Simon, (Eds.), *Altruism and imperialism: Western cultural and religious missions in the Middle East* (pp. 14–44). Middle East Institute.

Khalidi, R. (1991a). The origins of Arab nationalism: Introduction. In R. Khalidi, L. Anderson, M. Muslih & R. S. Simon (Eds.), *The origins of Arab nationalism* (pp. vii–xix). Columbia University Press.

Khalidi, R. (1991b). Ottomanism and Arabism in Syria before 1914: A reassessment. In R. Khalidi, L. Anderson, M. Muslih & R. S. Simon (Eds.), *The origins of Arab nationalism* (pp. 50–69). Columbia University Press.

Kiernan, J., Meier, J. & Wang, X. (2016). Negotiating languages and cultures: Enacting translingualism through a translation assignment. *Composition Studies, 44*(1), 89–107.

Kieser, H.-L. (2002). Some Remarks on Alevi responses to the missionaries in Eastern Anatolia (19th–20th Centuries). In E. H. Tejirian & R. S. Simon, (Eds.), *Altruism and imperialism: Western cultural and religious missions in the Middle East* (pp. 120–142). Middle East Institute.

Kimball, E. (2021). *Translingual inheritance: Language diversity in early national Philadelphia.* University of Pittsburgh Press.

Kitzhaber, A. R. (1990). *Rhetoric in American colleges, 1850–1900.* Southern Methodist University Press. (Original work published 1953)

Kynard, C. (2013). *Vernacular insurrections: Race, Black protest, and the new century in composition-literacies studies.* State University of New York Press.

Lagman, E. (2018). Literacy remains: Loss and affects in transnational literacies. *College English, 81*(1), 27–49. https://doi.org/10.58680/ce201829792.

Larsen, E. (1992). The progress of literacy: Edward Tyrrel Channing and the separation of the student writer from the world. *Rhetoric Review, 11*(1), 159–171. https://doi.org/10.1080/07350199209388994.

Leavitt, D. M. (1981). Darwinism in the Arab world: The Lewis Affair at the Syrian Protestant College. *The Muslim World, 71*(2), 85–98. https://doi.org/10.1111/j.1478-1913.1981.tb03430.x.

Lee, E. (2022). Writing toward a decolonial option: A bilingual student's multimodal composing as a site of translingual activism and justice. *Written Communication, 40*(1), 59–89. https://doi.org/10.1177/07410883221134640.

Lee, E. (2024). Knowing, feeling, and doing language with communities: Racialized multilingual students' critical raciolinguistic labor. *College English, 86*(3), 244–269. https://doi.org/10.58680/ce2024863244.

Lee, J. W. & Jenks, C. (2016). Doing translingual dispositions. *College Composition and Communication, 68*(2), 317–334. https://doi.org/10.58680/ccc201628883.

Legg, E. (2014). Daughters of the seminaries: Re-landscaping history through the composition courses at the Cherokee National Female Seminary. *College Composition and Communication, 66*(1), 67–90. https://doi.org/10.58680/ccc201426110.

Lindblom, K., Banks, W. & Quay, R. (2007). Mid-nineteenth-century writing instruction at Illinois State Normal University: Credentials, correctness, and the rise of a teaching class. In P. Donahue & G. F. Moon (Eds.), *Local histories: Reading the archives of composition* (pp. 94–114). University of Pittsburgh Press.

Lindner, C. B. (2013, July 9). American Mission Press: An American barn in Beirut. *NEST Digital Library.* http://nestlebanondigitallibrary.blogspot.com/2013/06/american-mission-press-american-barn-in.html.

Lindsay, R. H. (1965). *Nineteenth century American schools in the Levant: A study of purposes.* [Doctoral dissertation, University of Michigan]. University of Michigan School of Education, Comparative Education Dissertation Series.

Little, B. (2025, May 28). *Arab immigration to the United States: Timeline*. History. https://www.history.com/news/arab-american-immigration-timeline.

Lorimer Leonard, R. (2013). Traveling literacies: Multilingual writing on the move. *Research in the Teaching of English*, *48*(1), 13–39. https://doi.org/10.58680/rte201324157.

Lorimer Leonard, R. (2017). *Writing on the move: Migrant women and the value of literacy*. University of Pittsburgh Press.

Lu, M.-Z. (2006). Living-English work. *College English*, *68*(6), 605–618. https://doi.org/10.58680/ce20065040.

Lyons, S. R. (2009). The fine art of fencing: Nationalism, hybridity, and the search for a Native American writing pedagogy. *JAC*, *29*(1-2), 77–105.

MacDonald, M. T. (2015). Emissaries of literacy: Representations of sponsorship and refugee experience in the stories of the Lost Boys of Sudan. *College English*, *77*(5), 408–428. https://doi.org/10.58680/ce201527174.

Makdisi, U. (2000). *The culture of sectarianism: Community, history, and violence in nineteenth-century Ottoman Lebanon*. University of California Press. https://doi.org/10.1525/california/9780520218451.001.0001.

Makdisi, U. (2010). *Faith misplaced: The broken promise of U.S.-Arab relations, 1820–2001*. PublicAffairs.

Makdisi, U. (2011). *Artillery of heaven: American missionaries and the failed conversion of the Middle East*. Cornell University Press.

Martins, D. S. (2015). *Transnational writing program administration*. Utah State University Press.

Masters, B. (2001). *Christians and Jews in the Ottoman Arab world: The roots of sectarianism*. Cambridge University Press.

Masters, B. (2013). *The Arabs of the Ottoman Empire, 1516–1918: A social and cultural history*. Cambridge University Press. https://doi.org/10.1017/CBO9781139521970.

Matsuda, P. K. (2006). The myth of linguistic homogeneity in U.S. college composition. *College English*, *68*(6), 637–651. https://doi.org/10.58680/ce20065042.

Medina, C. (2019). Decolonial potential in a multilingual FYC. *Composition Studies*, *47*(1), 73–94. https://compstudiesjournal.com/wp-content/uploads/2019/04/medina.pdf.

Mendelsohn, S. (2017). "Raising Hell": Literacy instruction in Jim Crow America. *College English*, *80*(1), 35–62. https://doi.org/10.58680/ce201729260.

Meyer, J. (2025, March 22). Shackles, shock troops, windowless cells: How bad is Trump's favorite Salvadoran prison? *USA Today*. https://www.usatoday.com/story/news/politics/2025/03/22/cecot-trump-el-salvador-prison-deportation-video/82596983007/.

Mignolo, W. D. (2007). Delinking: The rhetoric of modernity, the logic of coloniality, and the grammar of de-coloniality. *Cultural Studies*, *21*(2–3), 449–514. https://doi.org/10.1080/09502380601162647.

Mihut, L. A. (2020). Enacting linguistic justice: Transnational scholars as advocates for pedagogical change. In A. Frost, J. Kiernan & S. B. Malley (Eds.), *Translingual dispositions: Globalized approaches to the teaching of writing* (pp. 269–294). The

WAC Clearinghouse; University Press of Colorado. https://doi.org/10.37514/INT-B.2020.0438.2.11.

Miller, S. (1991). *Textual carnivals: The politics of composition*. Southern Illinois University Press.

Miller, T. P. (1997). *The formation of college English: Rhetoric and belles lettres in the British cultural provinces*. University of Pittsburgh Press.

Milson-Whyte, V. (2015). *Academic writing instruction for Creole-influenced students*. University of the West Indies Press.

Milson-Whyte, V., Oenbring, R. & Jaquette, B. (Eds.) (2019). *Creole composition: Academic writing and rhetoric in the Anglophone Caribbean*. Parlor Press.

Milu, E. (2021). Diversity of raciolinguistic experiences in the writing classroom: An argument for a transnational Black language pedagogy. *College English, 83*(6), 415–441. https://doi.org/10.58680/ce202131357.

Morris, K. K. (1991) [Review of the book *Rhetoric in American Colleges, 1850–1900*, by A. R. Kitzhaber]. *Journal of Advanced Composition, 11*(2), 472–474.

Moulder, M. A. (2011). Cherokee practice, missionary intentions: Literacy learning among early nineteenth-century Cherokee women. *College Composition and Communication, 63*(1), 75–97. https://doi.org/10.58680/ccc201117248.

Muchiri, M. N., Mulamba, N. G., Myers, G. & Ndoloi, D. B. (1995). Importing composition: Teaching and researching academic writing beyond North America. *College Composition and Communication, 46*(2), 175–198. https://doi.org/10.58680/ccc19958742.

Murre-van den Berg, H. (2007). Introduction. In H. Murre-van den Berg (Ed.), *New faith in ancient lands: Western missions in the Middle East in the nineteenth and early twentieth centuries* (pp. 1–17). Brill. https://doi.org/10.1163/9789047411406.

Nahj al-balagha. (2024, July 11). In *Wikipedia*. https://en.wikipedia.org/w/index.php?title=Nahj_al-balagha&oldid=1233945795.

Navarro, F., Lillis, T., Donahue, T., Curry, M. J., Ávila Reyes, N., Gustafsson, M., Zavala, V., Lauría, D., Lukin, A., McKinney, C., Feng, H. & Motta-Roth, D. (2022). Rethinking English as a lingua franca in scientific-academic contexts: A position statement. *Journal of English for Research Publication Purposes, 3*(1), 143–153. https://doi.org/10.1075/jerpp.21012.nav.

Ndhlovu, F. & Makalela, L. (2021). *Decolonising multilingualism in Africa: Recentering silenced voices from the Global South*. Multilingual Matters. https://doi.org/10.21832/9781788923361.

NeCamp, S. (2014). *Adult literacy and American identity: The Moonlight schools and Americanization programs*. Southern Illinois University Press.

Nystrand, M., Greene, S. & Wiemelt, J. (1993). Where did composition studies come from? An intellectual history. *Written Communication, 10*(3), 267–333.

Ohmann, R. (1976). *English in America: A radical view of the profession*. Oxford University Press.

Ouahes, I. (2017). Catholic missionary education in early Mandate Syria and Lebanon. *Social Sciences and Missions, 30*(3–4), 225–253. https://doi.org/10.1163/18748945-03003005.

Paine, C. (1999). *The resistant writer: Rhetoric as immunity, 1850 to the present.* State University of New York Press.

Pandey, I. P. (2015). *South Asian in the mid-South: Migrations of literacies.* University of Pittsburgh Press.

Pashby, K. (2012). Questions for global citizenship education in the context of the 'new imperialism': For whom, by whom? In V. de Oliveira Andreotti & L. M. T. M. de Souza (Eds.), *Postcolonial perspectives on global citizenship education* (pp. 9–26). Routledge.

Pederson, A. M. (2010). Negotiating cultural identities through language: Academic English in Jordan. *College Composition and Communication, 62*(2), 283–310. https://doi.org/10.58680/ccc201013210.

Pennycook, A. (1998). *English and the discourses of colonialism: The politics of language.* Routledge. https://doi.org/10.4324/9780203006344.

Peters, J. (2013). "Speak White": Language policy, immigration discourse, and tactical authority in a French enclave in New England. *College English, 75*(6), 563–581. https://doi.org/10.58680/ce201323835.

Phillipson, R. (1992). *Linguistic imperialism.* Oxford University Press.

Poe, M. (2014). Diversity and international writing [Special issue]. *Research in the Teaching of English, 48*(3). https://publicationsncte.org/content/journals/rte/48/3.

Poe, M. (2022). Learning to unlearn the teaching and assessment of academic writing. *Discourse and Writing/Rédactologie, 32,* 161–190. https://doi.org/10.31468/dwr.977.

Porter, A. (2002). The missionary enterprise in the nineteenth century: An overview. In E. H. Tejirian & R. S. Simon, (Eds.), *Altruism and imperialism: Western cultural and religious missions in the Middle East* (pp. 1–13). Middle East Institute.

Qartaba. (2025, 19 May). In *Wikipedia.* https://en.wikipedia.org/w/index.php?title =Qartaba&oldid=1291131789.

Ramírez, C. D. (2015). *Occupying our space: The Mestiza rhetorics of Mexican women journalists and activists, 1875–1942.* University of Arizona Press.

Ribero, A. M. (2016). Citizenship. In I. D. Ruiz & R. Sánchez (Eds.), *Decolonizing rhetoric and composition studies: New Latinx keywords for theory and pedagogy* (pp. 31–45). Palgrave MacMillan. https://doi.org/10.1057/978-1-137-52724-0_3.

Rivera, N. K. (2020). Chicanx murals: Decolonizing place and (re)writing the terms of composition. *College Composition and Communication, 72*(1), 118–149. https://doi.org/10.58680/ccc202030893.

Romano, S. (2004). Tlaltelolco: The grammatical-rhetorical *Indios* of colonial Mexico. *College English, 66*(3), 257–277. https://doi.org/10.58680/ce20042834.

Roper, G. (1999). The beginnings of Arabic printing by the ABCFM, 1822–1841. *Harvard Library Bulletin, 9*(1), 50–68. https://nrs.harvard.edu/URN-3:HUL. INSTREPOS:37363517.

Rothermel, B. A. (2003). A sphere of noble action: Gender, rhetoric, and influence at a nineteenth-century Massachusetts state normal school. *Rhetoric Society Quarterly, 33*(1), 35–64. https://doi.org/10.1080/02773940309391245.

Rothermel, B. A. (2007). "Our life's work": Rhetorical preparation and teacher training at a Massachusetts state normal school, 1839–1929. In P. Donahue &

G. F. Moon (Eds.), *Local histories: Reading the archives of composition* (pp. 134–158). University of Pittsburgh Press.

Rounsaville, A. (2015). Taking hold of global Englishes: Intensive English programs as brokers of transnational literacy. *Literacy in Composition Studies, 3*(3), 67–85. https://doi.org/10.21623/1.3.3.5.

Rounsaville, A. (2017). Genre repertoires from below: How one writer built and moved a writing life across generations, borders, and communities. *Research in the Teaching of English, 51*(3), 317–340.

Royster, J. J. & Williams, J. C. (1999). History in the spaces left: African American presence and narratives of composition studies. *College Composition and Communication, 50*(4), 563–584. https://doi.org/10.58680/ccc19991348.

Ruiz, I. D. (2016). *Reclaiming Composition for Chicano/as and Other Ethnic Minorities: A Critical History and Pedagogy*. Palgrave MacMillan.

Ruiz, I. D. (2021). Critiquing the critical: The politics of race and coloniality in rhetoric, composition, and writing studies research traditions. In A. L. Lockett, I. D. Ruiz, J. C. Sanchez & C. Carter (Eds.), *Race, rhetorics, and research methods* (pp. 39–79). The WAC Clearinghouse; University Press of Colorado. https://doi.org/10.37514/PER-B.2021.1206.

Ruiz, I. D. & Baca, D. (2017). Decolonial options and writing studies. *Composition Studies, 45*(2), 226–229.

Said, E. W. (1979). *Orientalism*. Vintage Books.

Salameh, F. (2010). *Language, memory, and identity in the Middle East: The case for Lebanon*. Lexington Books.

Salibi, K. & Khoury, Y. K. (Eds.). (1995). *The Missionary Herald: Reports from Ottoman Syria 1819–1870* (Vol. 5, 1861–1870). Royal Institute for Inter-Faith Studies.

Serviss, T. C. (2013). *Femicide* and rhetorics of *Coadyuvante* in Ciudad Juárez: Valuing rhetorical traditions in the Americas. *College English, 75*(6), 608–628. https://doi.org/10.58680/ce201323837.

Shapiro, R. (2019). Transnational networks of literacy and materiality: Coltan, sexual violence, and digital literacy. *College English, 82*(2), 204–225. https://doi.org/10.58680/ce201930626.

Shapiro, R. & Watson, M. (2022). Translingual praxis: From theorizing language to antiracist and decolonial pedagogy. *College Composition and Communication, 74*(2), 292–321. https://doi.org/10.58680/ccc202232276.

Shapiro, S. (2022). *Cultivating critical language awareness in the writing classroom*. Routledge. https://doi.org/10.4324/9781003171751.

Sharabi, H. (1970). *Arab intellectuals and the West: The formative years: 1875–1914*. Johns Hopkins Press.

Sheehi, S. (2004). *Foundations of modern Arab identity*. University Press of Florida.

Shimabukuro, M. (2011). "Me inwardly, before I dared": Japanese Americans writing-to-gaman. *College English, 73*(6), 648–671. https://doi.org/10.58680/ce201116275.

Simmons, S. C. (1995). Radcliffe responses to Harvard rhetoric: "An absurdly stiff way of thinking." In C. Hobbs (Ed.), *Nineteenth-century women learn to write* (pp. 264–292). University Press of Virginia.

Simnowitz, A. (2022, March 7). The missionary review of the world: A journal worth rereading. *Journal of Biblical Missiology*. https://biblicalmissiology.org/blog/2022/03/07/the-missionary-review-of-the-world-a-journal-worth-rereading/.

Singer, E. (2025, Feb. 3). Thousands of U.S. government web pages have been taken down since Friday. *The New York Times*. https://www.nytimes.com/2025/02/02/upshot/trump-government-websites-missing-pages.html?unlocked_article_code=1.VE8.E3h9.gYSSPOJ1a91P&smid=url-share.

Smith, S. & Ellis, K. (Producers). (2017, September 4). Shackled legacy: History shows slavery helped build many U.S. colleges and universities [Audio podcast episode]. In *APM Reports*. American Public Media. https://www.apmreports.org/episode/2017/09/04/shackled-legacy.

Smitherman, G. (1999). CCCC's role in the struggle for language rights. *College Composition and Communication*, 50(3), 349–376. https://doi.org/10.58680/ccc19991335.

Spack, R. (2002). *America's second tongue: American Indian education and the ownership of English, 1860–1900*. University of Nebraska Press.

Stowe, D. M. (n.d.). *Anderson, Rufus (1796–1880): American Congregational administrator and theorist of foreign missions*. Boston University School of Theology. Retrieved June 2, 2025, from https://www.bu.edu/missiology/missionary-biography/a-c/anderson-rufus-1796-1880/ (Reprinted from Anderson, Rufus, in *Biographical dictionary of Christian missions*, p. 20, by G. H. Anderson, Ed., 1998, Macmillan Reference USA).

Stuckey, M. E. & Murphy, J. M. (2001). By any other name: Rhetorical colonialism in North America. *American Indian Culture and Research Journal*, 25(4), 73–98. https://escholarship.org/uc/item/4dt5v8bq.

Sullivan, P. (2012). Inspecting shadows of past classroom practices: A search for students' voices. *College Composition and Communication*, 63(3), 365–386. https://doi.org/10.58680/ccc201218443.

Sullivan, P., Zhang, Y. & Zheng, F. (2012). College writing in China and America: A modest and humble conversation, with writing samples. *College Composition and Communication*, 64(2), 306–331. https://doi.org/10.58680/ccc201222116.

Tejirian, E. H. & Simon, R. S. (2002). Introduction. In E. H. Tejirian & R. S. Simon, (Eds.), *Altruism and imperialism: Western cultural and religious missions in the Middle East* (pp. v–x). Middle East Institute.

Thaiss, C., Bräuer, G., Carlino, P., Ganobcsik-Williams, L. & Sinha, A. (2012). *Writing programs worldwide: Profiles of academic writing in many places*. The WAC Clearinghouse; Parlor Press. https://doi.org/10.37514/PER-B.2012.0346.

Thompson, E. (2002). Neither conspiracy nor hypocrisy: The Jesuits and the French Mandate in Syria and Lebanon. In E. H. Tejirian & R. S. Simon(Eds.), *Altruism and imperialism: Western cultural and religious missions in the Middle East* (pp. 66–87). Middle East Institute.

Tibawi, A. L. (1967). The genesis and early history of the Syrian Protestant College. In F. Sarruf & S. Tamim, (Eds.), *American University of Beirut festival book* (pp. 257–294). American University of Beirut Press.

Uranga, R., Mejia, B. & Buchanan, C. (2025, July 2). L.A. 'under siege': Brown-skinned people targeted, tackled, taken, and it must stop, federal suit says. *Los Angeles Times*. https://www.latimes.com/california/story/2025-07-02/federal-lawsuit-targets-trump-administration-immigration-raids.

U.S. National Archives and Records Administration. (n.d.). *Milestone documents: Morrill Act (1862)*. Retrieved June 16, 2025, from https://www.archives.gov/milestone-documents/morrill-act.

VanDeMark, B. (2012). *American sheikhs: Two families, four generations, and the story of America's influence in the Middle East*. Prometheus Books.

Varnum, R. (1996). *Fencing with words: A history of writing instruction at Amherst College during the era of Theodore Baird, 1938–1966* (ED393123). National Council of Teachers of English; ERIC. http://files.eric.ed.gov/fulltext/ED393123.pdf.

Ventura, L. (2014). History, religion and progress: The view of the 'modernity' of the American Protestant missionaries in late Ottoman Syria. *Middle Eastern Studies*, *50*(3), 442–456. https://doi.org/10.1080/00263206.2014.886572.

Ventura, L. (2018). The foreign universities in Syria: Competition among the "West." In L. Ventura, Ed., *Hegel in the Arab world: Modernity, colonialism, and freedom* (pp. 57–62). Palgrave Pivot Cham. https://doi.org/10.1007/978-3-319-78066-5_7.

Vieira, K. (2011). Undocumented in a documentary society: Textual borders and transnational religious literacies. *Written Communication*, *28*(4), 436–461. https://doi.org/10.1177/0741088311421468.

Vieira, K. (2017). *American by paper: How documents matter in immigrant literacy*. University of Minnesota Press. https://doi.org/10.5749/minnesota/9780816697519.001.0001.

Vieira, K. (2019). What happens when texts fly. *College English*, *82*(1), 77–95. https://doi.org/10.58680/ce201930306.

Vieira, K. (2024). Cross-border collaborations for peace: Writing from a common heart. In R. García, E. Cushman & D. Baca (Eds.), *Pluriversal literacies: Tools for perseverance and livable futures* (pp. 156–169). University of Pittsburgh Press.

Wan, A. J. (2011). In the name of citizenship: The writing classroom and the promise of citizenship. *College English*, *74*(1), 28–49. https://doi.org/10.58680/ce201117164.

Wang, X. (2020). Becoming multilingual writers through translation. *Research in the Teaching of English*, *54*(3), 206–230. https://doi.org/10.58680/rte202030519.

Weidner, H. Z. (2007). A chair "perpetually filled by a female professor": Rhetoric and composition instruction at nineteenth-century Butler University. In P. Donahue & G. F. Moon (Eds.), *Local histories: Reading the archives of composition* (pp. 58–76). University of Pittsburgh Press.

Welsch, K. A. (2007). Thinking like *that*: The ideal nineteenth-century student writer. In P. Donahue & G. F. Moon (Eds.), *Local histories: Reading the archives of composition* (pp. 14–37). University of Pittsburgh Press.

The White House. (2025a, March 1). Designating English as the official language of the United States. *The White House*. https://www.whitehouse.gov/presidential-actions/2025/03/designating-english-as-the-official-language-of-the-united-states/.

The White House. (2025b, January 20). Ending radical and wasteful government DEI programs and preferencing. *The White House.* https://www.whitehouse.gov /presidential-actions/2025/01/ending-radical-and-wasteful-government-dei -programs-and-preferencing/.

Willinsky, J. (1998). *Learning to divide the world: Education at empire's end.* University of Minnesota Press.

Wu, H. (2007). Writing and teaching behind barbed wire: An exiled composition class in a Japanese-American internment camp. *College Composition and Communication, 59*(2), 237–262. https://doi.org/10.58680/ccc20076393.

Yancey, K. B. (Ed.). (2014). Symposium on internationalization [Special section]. *College Composition and Communication, 65*(4). https://doi.org/10.58680/ccc2014 25450.

Yildiz, Y. (2012). *Beyond the mother tongue: The postmonolingual condition.* Fordham University Press. https://doi.org/10.5422/fordham/9780823241309.001.0001.

You, X. (2010). *Writing in the devil's tongue: A history of English composition in China.* Southern Illinois University Press.

You, X. (2016). *Cosmopolitan English and transliteracy.* Southern Illinois University Press.

You, X. (Ed.). (2018). *Transnational writing education: Theory, history, practice.* Routledge. https://doi.org/10.4324/9781351205955.

You, X. (2023). *Genre networks and empire: Rhetoric in early imperial China.* Southern Illinois University Press.

Young, R. E. (1978). Paradigms and problems: Needed research in rhetorical invention. In C. R. Cooper & L. Odell (Eds.), *Research on composing: Points of departure* (pp. 29–47). National Council of Teachers of English.

Zaleski, M. (2017). The word made secular: Religious rhetoric and the new university at the turn of the twentieth century. *College English, 80*(2), 159–183. https:// doi.org/10.58680/ce201729374.

Zaluda, S. (1998). Lost voices of the Harlem renaissance: Writing assigned at Howard University, 1919-31. *College Composition and Communication, 50*(2), 232–257.

Zhang-Wu, Q. (2021). (Re)imagining translingualism as a *verb* to tear down the English-only wall: "Monolingual" students as multilingual writers. *College English, 84*(1), 121–137. https://doi.org/10.58680/ce202131455.

Zhang-Wu, Q. (2023). Supporting superdiverse multilingual international students: Insights from an ethnographic exploration. *Research in the Teaching of English, 57*(4), 378–401. https://doi.org/10.58680/rte202332473.

Appendix A. Student Demographics, Syrian Protestant College, 1866–1920

Year		
1866–67	**Number of Students**	18
	Student Origin	Not reported
	Student Religions	Not reported
1871–72	**Number of Students**	66
	Student Origin	Not reported
	Student Religions	Not reported
1876–77	**Number of Students**	77
	Student Origin (reported)	Acre
		Alexandria
		Assuit
		Cairo
		Damascus
		Homs
		Jaffa
		Jerusalem
		Mosul
		Mt. Lebanon
		Sidon
		Tripoli
		Tyre
	Student Religions (reported)	Christian
		Coptic
		Druze
		Greek Armenian
		Greek Catholic
		Maronite
		Muslim

Year		
1876–77 continued	**Student Religions (reported)**	Protestant
		Roman Catholic
		Syriac
1881–82	**Number of Students**	160
	Student Origin	Not reported
	Student Religions	Not reported
1885–86	**Number of Students**	183
	Student Origin	Not reported
	Student Religions	Not reported
1890–91	**Number of Students**	228
	Student Origin (reported)	14–Egypt
		11–Cypros
		9–Damascus
		8–Asia Minor
		6–Leros
		1–Austria
		" . . . and the rest from Palestine and Syria, extending from Jerusalem to Aleppo; but the great majority are from Lebanon and the cities on the coast at the base of the mountains."
	Student Religions (reported)	8–Druze
		3–Jewish
		"various Christian sects of the East, including a large number of Protestants."
1896–97	**Number of Students**	309
	Student Origin	Not reported
	Student Religions (reported)	83–Greek Orthodox
		40–Protestants
		12–Greek Catholics
		11–Armenian
		7–Maronite
		7–Druze
		4–Jewish
		4–Muslim
		2–Roman Catholic
		1–Copt

Year		
1901–02	**Number of Students**	615
	Student Origin	Not reported
	Student Religions (reported)	252–Greek Orthodox
		153–Protestant
		45–Mohammedan
		35–Greek Catholic
		32–Armenian Gregorian
		30–Jewish
		24–Maronite
		19–Copt
		13–Roman Catholic
		9–Druze
		3–Armenian Catholic
1905–06	**Number of Students**	768
	Student Origin (reported)	439–Syria
		209–Beirut
		141–Egypt & Sudan
		80–Asia Minor
		45–Cairo
		43–Palestine
		41–Cyprus and Greek Islands
		40–Alexandria (Egypt)
		40–Damascus
		22–other locations, including US
		12–Aintab
		11–Jaffa
	Student Religions (reported)	600–Christians, including 130 Protestants; 300 Greek Orthodox; 100 Catholic
		100–Muslims
		40–Jewish
		20–Druze
1910–11	**Number of Students**	875
	Student Origin (reported)	Asia Minor
		Abyssinia
		Cyprus

Year			
1910–11 continued	**Student Origin (reported)**	Egypt
		Greece
		Haiti
		Macedonia
		Mesopotamia
		Persia
		Peru
		Poland
		Romania
		Russia
		Siberia
		Singapore
		Syria
	Student Religions (reported)	312–Greek Orthodox
		170–Protestant
		128–Muslim
		91–Jewish
		39–Greek Catholic
		32–Druze
		29–Maronite
		27–Gregorian
		14–Old Syrian or Syrian Jacobite
		6–Behais
		Unspecified number Roman Catholic, Armenian Catholic, Coptic Orthodox, and Coptic Catholic
1916–17	**Number of Students**	690
	Student Origin	Not reported
	Student Religions	Not reported
1920–21	**Number of Students**	1,001
	Student Origin (reported)	354–Beirut
		208–Lebanon
		125–Egypt
		113–Palestine
		67–Aleppo and North Syria
		59–Damascus

Year			
1876–77 continued	**Student Origin (reported)**	28–Asia Minor	
		14–Mesopotamia	
		9–Persia	
		8–US	
		3–Greece	
		3–South America	
		2–Cyprus	
		1–Albania	
		1–Algeria	
		1–Bulgaria	
		1–Eretria	
		1–Poland	
		1–Sweden	
		1–Turkey	
		1–Yugo-Slavia	
	Student Religions (reported)	382–Muslim	
		250–Greek Orthodox	
		130–Protestant	
		129–Other non-Christian	

Note. All data from Annual Reports by the Presidents to the Board of Managers and Trustees, Syrian Protestant College. (1866–1921). Archives and Special Collections, American University of Beirut, Beirut, Lebanon.

Appendix B. SPC Student-Authored Publications, 1899–1920

Year Begin	Year End	Publication Title	Lang. English	Lang. Arabic	Lang. French	Notes
1899	1900	الصحيح (The Right Principle)		Arabic		
1899	1900	الكلية (The College)		Arabic		
1899	1900	ثمرات الأذهان (Fruits of the Mind)		Arabic		
1899	1900	الاستعدادية (Preparatory/Elementary)		Arabic		Not preserved
1899	1900	زهرة الكلية (Flower of the College)		Arabic		
1899	1901	غادة الفكر (Graceful Thought)		Arabic		
1900	1900	العصر (The Times)		Arabic		
1900	1901	الكنانة (The Arrow Head)		Arabic		
1901	1903	الحظ (Luck)		Arabic		
1902	1902	IOU 5 Minutes	English	Arabic	French	
1902	1908	صدى الاستعدادية (Elementary Echo)	English	Arabic		
1902	1903	الحديقة (The Garden)		Arabic		
1902	1902	العلمية (The Scientific)		Arabic		Not preserved
1902	1902	الرقيب (The Sergeant/The Observer)		Arabic		
1902	1902	العفة (Chastity)		Arabic		
1902	1908	المنارة (The Lighthouse)		Arabic		
1903	1904	The Miltonian	English			
1903	1904	The Kodak	English	Arabic		

Year Begin	Year End	Publication Title	Lang. English	Lang. Arabic	Lang. French	Notes
1903	1904	حسناء الكلية (Beauty of the College)		Arabic		
1903	1903	الغادة (Grace)		Arabic		
1903	1904	الدائرة (The Circle)		Arabic		
1903	1905	Happy Days of SPC	English			
1904	1904	SPC Commercial Paper	English			
1905	1906	Pioneers of SPC	English			
1906	1906	Syria	English	Arabic		
1906	1906	The Commercial Triumvirate	English			
1906	1906	The Review Club Magazine	English	Arabic		Not preserved
1906	1906	The Commercial Review	English	Arabic		
1906	1906	Zion	English			
1906	1906	Seniors of the SPC	English			
1906	1906	Chemical and Industrial Gazette	English			
1906	1907	The Business Amanuensis	English			
1906	1906	Light	English			
1906	1906	The Alma Mater	English			Not preserved
1906	1907	The Commercial S.P.C. Editor	English			
1906	1906	المبتدئون (The Freshman/ Novice)		Arabic		
1905	1906	المنتهون (The Terminators)		Arabic		
1907	1908	The Life of Service	English			
1907	1908	الأرزة (The Cedar)		Arabic		Not preserved
1908	1908	SPC Missionary Review	English			
1908	1908	The University Times	English			
1909	1910	النهضة الإصلاحية (The Reformist Movement)		Arabic		

Year Begin	Year End	Publication Title	Lang. English	Lang. Arabic	Lang. French	Notes
1910	1914	Al-Kulliyeh: The Journal of Syrian Protestant College	English			
1911	1911	The Business Man	English			
1911	1911	Prep Progress	English			
1912	1932	Student Union Gazette	English			
1914	1916	الثمرة (The Fruit)		Arabic		
1919	1919	SPC Torch Gazette	English			
1919	1919	Cedar	English